Beyond Parochial Faith

Beyond Parochial Faith

A Catholic Confesses

JEANETTE BLONIGEN CLANCY

RESOURCE *Publications* • Eugene, Oregon

BEYOND PAROCHIAL FAITH
A Catholic Confesses

Resource Publications
An Imprint of Wipf and Stock Publishers
199 W. 8th Ave., Suite 3
Eugene, OR 97401

www.wipfandstock.com

PAPERBACK ISBN: 978-1-5326-7282-8
HARDCOVER ISBN: 978-1-5326-7283-5
EBOOK ISBN: 978-1-5326-7284-2

Manufactured in the U.S.A.   05/16/19

CONTENTS

Preface

THIS BOOK BEGAN WITH articles depicting life in a German-Catholic county of Minnesota. The Stearns County History Museum published them, and my writers group encouraged me to write more personal stories like them. Once started, I kept writing about my life without knowing where it was going. As my story unfolded, its trajectory and purposes revealed themselves. I could see how life experiences shaped my evolving spiritual consciousness from a parochial Catholic upbringing to growing awareness of an infinity beyond religious instruction.

Six years ago, a woman rang my doorbell and said she walked a mile to tell me that my book *God Is Not Three Guys in the Sky* had a profound effect on her. Its subversion of common Christian belief seemed undeniable but left her bereft. She asked me to write a sequel for people like herself who wonder, "If not Christianity, then what?" This book tries to give some answers.

My memoir, if honest, had to include my enduring passion—grappling with big questions about life's meaning. My abiding purpose in life being to educate, I invite readers to accompany me on my spiritual journey. In *Beyond Parochial Faith* I hope they find solace for hardships, motivation for challenges, and food for reflection.

"I feel naked," I cried more than once, while dredging up painful memories, finding words for the feelings, and sharing them. Now in my mid-seventies, I am still growing. I disclose my personal secrets here to spark self-reflection, to encourage self-respect that honors pain, and even to prompt chuckles while inspiring and informing.

As readers travel with me on my journey of self-discovery and expanding spiritual awareness, I hope they are prompted to see and accept themselves more fully and to allow new patterns of thought. May my reflections on life's purpose broaden horizons of imagination.

An interesting thing happened while I was trying to remember my past. It seemed I was creating my past along with creating my present and future. The facts matter less than how I interpret the past from my perspective today. But I had to remain faithful to my memories. I could not fictionalize if I wanted large truths to emerge.

Reared in Catholicism, I developed doubts about doctrine and tried to be an atheist. After reading books that explore ideas about ultimate reality, the logic of atheism seemed less compelling and my heart led me to something else. I obtained a master's degree in theology and regularly attend Mass in a Benedictine chapel. I still relish dialogues with atheist and agnostic friends, but life experiences made denial of what is called "God" impossible, although I object to religion personifying it exclusively as a humanlike male.

My faith in the inner realm is secular. While swimming in Catholic culture, my own interpretation of religious doctrines is informed by the findings of science and the challenges of atheists as well as the teachings of religion. Together, religion and science enlighten. Divided, each can devolve into calcified thought. I challenge fundamentalist belief in both.

Hundreds of authors unmask patriarchy in Catholicism and offer new interpretations of doctrines, showing humanity's hunger for spirituality free of religious indoctrination. Some authors who critique religious patriarchy stay in the Church and urge reform from within. I do this. Aiming to provoke thinking and questioning, I vigorously denounce what I call sexist God-talk.

Parts of this book triggered resistance from readers of my manuscript. I pressed on. The book demanded to be written.

Acknowledgments

I THANK ALL WHO mused with me about the past to awaken memories while this memoir was taking shape. Most names have been changed; actual names are used with permission. All opinions expressed are mine alone. I mean no harm to anyone and know that my memories may not accord with persons I write about. My siblings are among those who helped, although they would tell entirely different stories.

I thank Maxine Moe Rasmussen, Richard Hagenston, Vincent Smiles, Mariterese Woida, OSB, Katherine Kraft, OSB, Ann Machtemes, OSB, Karen Rose, OSB, Carol Landkamer, and Marilyn Rowan for reading parts of my manuscript, commenting, and supporting. I thank a reader who reviewed almost my entire manuscript but wishes to remain anonymous. I thank my writers group—Marilyn Salzl Brinkman, Bill Morgan, John Roscoe, Robert Roscoe, Marcia Neely, Arlys Krim, and Margaret Mandernach, OSB—for directing me away from cerebral language to concrete language understandable by general readers. Their questions, likes, and dislikes compelled me to clarify my purposes.

Jeanette Blonigen Clancy
December 2018

German–Catholic in Stearns County

Catholic Germans

Steeped in German-Catholic culture while growing up, I soon realized that the world around us did not live like us. Sometimes our way seemed wrong and I felt isolated, unacceptable, not "normal." A larger horizon than the one surrounding me beckoned from birth. How could I feel this before I saw the wider world? It's one of the mysteries I ponder, but the process of writing produced some insights.

Our family was so German that I didn't know my mother's first family name was hard to pronounce for English speakers until I was an adult teaching English. "Fuchs" rhymes with "books," means "fox," and is common in Germany. Our family was so Catholic that missing Mass on a *Sonntag* (Sunday) or *Feiertag* (Holy Day) was unthinkable. My farmer father considered Sundays the time to rest up for *Werktage* or workdays. If weather required bringing in the hay or harvesting wheat on Sundays, permission had to be obtained from the priest.

Beginning in the 1850s, German immigrants answered the call of Father Francis Xavier Pierz, a German-speaking missionary to Native Americans who came from Slovenia, part of the Austro-Hungarian Empire. Pierz read the signs of the times and knew that Europeans flooding America would dominate. He deemed Catholics the most desirable settlers to mix with the Native Americans he cared for. His promotional descriptions in German-language publications—downplaying Minnesota winters—attracted German immigrants to Stearns County from Wisconsin and eastern states as well as directly from Germany.

Stearns County stands out as an unusual example of German-Americans speaking and behaving like Germans for several generations after immigration. It had the heaviest rural concentration of Germans in Minnesota, which has more people of German than of Scandinavian ancestry. John Ireland, Archbishop of St. Paul from 1888 to 1918, wrote that "a new Germany was planted in Stearns County." The archbishop urged Catholic immigrants to adopt the language and customs of their new country to lessen the invective heaped on Catholics during the nineteenth century.

But some German-Catholics said he was too ardent an "Americanizer." They intended Americanization—today it's called assimilation—to proceed slowly. The Pennsylvania "Dutch" had tried to make German an official language of the United States, but in 1795 it failed in Congress. The Benedictines who founded St. John's Abbey and University in Collegeville deliberately kept it a German institution for years. They were instructed from "home" in Bavaria to accept only Germans. Today, St. John's has international connections. Germans still comprise the largest ethnic group in the United States, but they are so well assimilated that no one notices.

In 1884, a church council in Baltimore instructed Catholic parishes in the United States to build parochial schools. In Stearns County, this directive was carried out by public schools behaving like Catholic schools. Some public schools in Stearns County during the last part of the nineteenth century were staffed by Benedictine Sisters from St. Joseph. One such was in St. Martin, where I grew up. By the time my father, born in 1902, went to school, lay teachers had replaced religious Sisters, but Catholicism continued to reign.

Bernadette Weber, OSB, went to a one-room public grade school north of St. Martin, where the school day began with prayer, the teacher taught Bible study, and everybody prayed before and after they opened their lunch boxes at noon. "When I think about it," she wrote, "we were like a parochial school. We had a crucifix in the classroom and had Bible history classes twice a week and the Baltimore Catechism the other three days."

My public grade school in the village of St. Martin stood next to the church, the parish house (where the priest lived), and the church cemetery. Everyone was Catholic. Religious feasts were accommodated in the school calendar, and Father Cyril came into the public school to teach catechism. We ate our school lunch in the parish hall. This is the rich Catholic stew in which I grew up.

Gradually, slowly, church-state separation demanded by the Constitution took hold in Stearns County. After my second grade, Father Cyril no longer came into school. Between my sixth and seventh grades, we became a parochial school, but resistance by parishioners had to be overcome. "Why pay double taxes?" they wondered. They had expected the earlier arrangement of an essentially Catholic school funded by state taxes to continue.

Stearns is packed with Catholic churches. In *Legacies of Faith: The Catholic Churches of Stearns County*, Robert and John Roscoe write, "With a population approximately sixty-six percent Catholic, this county contains fifty-two Catholic churches, the majority of which were built between 1871 and 1931" (1). Many churches stand within ten miles of each other. The beauty of their architecture, reflecting styles and masonry skills of German builders, surpass in some cases "all but a few of the churches recently visited in northern Italy" (vii).

No parish encapsulates the unique Stearns County culture more than the Parish of St. Martin, where the old country's pull remained strong. Lying in the heart of the county, St. Martin has been mentioned in studies as typifying German-Catholic culture. The Flynns and other Irish families who moved in learned some German just to get along.

In St. Martin's parish, fewer than two hundred families produced over a hundred religious vocations over the course of a hundred years. One was my brother Arnold, who became Father Aloysius or Father Al. Our neighbor, Brother Roman Fleischhacker, produced a roster of religious in the parish—*The Fruit of Faith and Witness*. Using it, I figured out that within a half mile of our farm, eleven farm neighbors entered the religious life. Within a wider radius of approximately two miles, the count goes up to twenty. Close farm neighbors, the Mandernachs, gave three religious Sisters and two Brothers to the Church. The Weber family produced four Sisters and two priests.

The Seed from Which I Sprouted

My mother, Magdalena Fuchs Blonigen, was born in 1901, the great-granddaughter of German immigrants who settled along the Sauk River in 1855. Johann and Gertrud Fuchs answered the invitation of Fr. Francis Xavier Pierz, the Slovenian missionary credited with bringing German and Slovenian Catholics to Stearns County. He said Mass in the log cabin of Johann and Gertrud Fuchs, my great-great-grandparents. Mother's maternal grandparents, Johann and Elisabeth Weymann, also answered the call of Fr. Pierz and also settled near the Sauk River, at Spring Hill in western Stearns County.

My mother, Lena, a fourth-generation German-American, grew up in a solidly German world. Her mother tongue was the dialect of the German Rhineland, what she called *Preuss* (pronounced "prrrice"). She talked about hearing other dialects and one *Franzose*, a French person. In school Mother learned standard German and English. Outside of school, I think Mother rarely heard English while growing up. Standard German eased communication between neighbors who spoke different dialects.

Lena's mother, Mary Weymann Fuchs, could understand some English but did not learn to speak it and didn't need to. Her husband and children handled contacts with the outside world. Son Mike took over the farm and married an Irish lady from Eden Valley, Margaret Mc-Carney. Margaret hired a woman who knew both German and English to help her communicate with Mother-in-law Mary. This was after 1940.

When Grandpa Fuchs died, Grandma Mary stayed in the homes of her daughters. My cousin Betty tells of Grandma living with them, playing and talking with Betty's youngest brother, Johnnie. Grandma spoke only German and Johnnie spoke only English, but they understood each other.

My Fuchs and Blonigen forebears came from the same region in Germany. Called the Eifel, it is a low mountain range west of the Rhine known for its hilly terrain formed by volcanoes a million years ago. The Eifel is beautiful with its high hills and forests, but stony, and a grudging provider for farmers of the nineteenth century—*steinreich* ("stone-rich") it was called.

This area of the Rhineland was the poorest in Germany and sent more people to America than any other. Land was scarce, crops were failing, and families were large. Its inheritance custom added to problems. When a farmer died, the plot of land was divided between the sons, resulting in tiny parcels unable to support families.

My brother, Fr. Al, brought me to the Eifel to visit Fuchs and Blonigen relatives during the summer of 1997. There, Karl Fuchs told us so many family members migrated to America that he mourned what seemed to be his family's demise. Then the Fuchs family genealogist from America arrived and informed him of the scores of Fuchs relatives in the States.

We stayed with the Igelmunds, distant Blonigen relatives who put us up while preparing for their son Mark's wedding, at which Al officiated. Their speech patterns sounded like ours in Stearns County, with turns of phrase not acceptable in standard German. Al, who was eight years older than me, said it transported him back to the speech he heard from Mother and her sisters speaking what they called *Preuss*. I was struck by hearing *Mark sei Frau*, meaning "Mark's wife," but literally saying, "Mark his wife." It is not standard German but the way we in St. Martin also formed the possessive.

Rhinelanders who migrated to the New World in the middle of the nineteenth century did not tell immigration officials that they were *deutsch*. There was no *Deutschland*, although ethnic Germans populated much of Europe from France to Russia. For centuries, Germans lived in hundreds of independent states, some smaller than Stearns County, others large. By the middle of the nineteenth century, Austria and Prussia had become powerful German states that competed against each other.

Prussia (*Preussen*) gained control of the Rhineland in 1815 when treaties after the Napoleonic wars carved Europe into new chunks. This is the reason Stearns County Germans said they spoke *Preuss*. But they were not really from Prussia. Mother never learned that Prussia began in an area now part of Russia, between Poland and Lithuania. Its people were Slavs until German peasants were brought in and gradually became the majority. After a centuries-long march to power in Europe, Prussia became a Protestant kingdom in 1701.

Prussia had a militaristic reputation that intensified under Otto von Bismarck, its chancellor from 1862 to 1890. Bismarck suppressed Catholics. A master strategist, he secured secret alliances and provoked small wars to control ever more territory for Prussia, culminating in 1871 with the German Empire under a kaiser (etymologically related to "caesar" and "czar") in Berlin—finally a unified Germany. In WWI, half of Europe and the United States fought that German empire.

Many emigrants from Germany who landed in Stearns County fled the Prussian military draft. While doing research for my local history books, I learned that some immigrants were so fearful of the Prussian military they refused to divulge their original family names, making genealogical research impossible for their families in America. This does not apply to my family, but the draft also drove my great-grandfather Johann Blönnigen—John Blonigen in America—and his brother to America to avoid conscription. They were a little over twenty years old, prime material for the Prussian army.

In 1846 their parents followed with the rest of their children. They settled in Mount Calvary, Wisconsin, and from there John Blonigen and his wife, Elizabeth Heinen, my great-grandparents, migrated to St. Martin with their growing family in 1860. Their many descendants populated St. Martin and rippled outward to who knows where.

Around 1980, Al drove me and our father, Herman, to Mount Calvary to dig up information about our ancestors. Mount Calvary cemetery is on a steep hill, making it impossible for Dad, who was unsteady on his feet, to walk on it. After looking for Blonigen gravestones at the bottom of the hill, we drove halfway up the side of it, where Dad got out. He took some tottering steps but could not resist the pull of gravity, which sent him stumbling onto a gravestone. The inscription amazed us—Dad's great-grandparents, Johann and Anna (Schöttel) Blönnigen! "Excited" does not accurately describe my feeling. It felt like the hand of providence had directed him and us precisely to the spot, one of many incidents in my life that I interpret as direction from the invisible realm but that scientific materialists insist is only coincidence.

A word about the Blonigen name, variously spelled—Blönnigen, Blönigen, Blonien, Blonyen—and most recently Blonigan. A few relatives gave up correcting people and changed their legal name to "Blonigan," which looks more Irish. I was once introduced to the wife of a St. John's professor as "Jeanette Clancy." Looking at me intently, she asked, "What was your maiden name?"

"Blonigen but I'm not Irish," I said without pausing before "I'm not Irish" because I anticipated what was coming. During student days at St. Ben's and a few times after that, I had occasionally been mistaken for an "Irish lass."

"You're Irish," said the professor's wife.

"No," I corrected her. "Our family spoke German at home. We didn't even learn English until we went to school."

"You're Irish," she repeated firmly and knowingly. I protested, saying more about our family's German heritage, but she was not deterred. Confidently, she told me that a recessive gene poked up in me, explaining that Irish traits, buried for generations by intermarriage with Germans in the Rhineland, emerged to manifest in me.

"This explains people telling me I look Irish and seem Irish," I said. "Maybe this explains my marrying an Irish man and my interest in all things Irish. I wouldn't mind living an Irish life."

"You're living an Irish life right now."

I believe her and enjoy telling this story. The first wave of Irish migration was not triggered by the potato famine in the mid-nineteenth century. Irish missionaries to the Rhineland centuries ago were accompanied by Irish families. My brother Fr. Al looked for ancestors when he studied in Germany and was told that "Blonigen" is not a German name. His sources suggested that Blonigens might originally have migrated from Ireland.

Idiosyncratic

Large families—eight the average number of children in my grade school class—and marriage with fellow German-Americans resulted in an interesting web of relationships. My mother knew many of them. After her short-term memory started to fail, she retained her ability to trace relationships. She used to go into a detailed account of who married whom back to four generations, implicating, it seemed to me, half the population of Stearns County. Folks here like to say we're related to everybody in the county.

Close biological relationships developed when the county's pioneer population was small, German immigrant families were large, and travel was limited. My grandparents John and Mary (Weymann) Fuchs were one of three Fuchs/Weymann couples—three brothers married three sisters. And my great-grandmother, Elizabeth (Löhr) Weymann, was the niece of my great-great-grandmother Gertrude (Löhr) Fuchs, so that my grandparents were second cousins, once removed. Relationships like this were common, fueling talk of a "Stearns County Syndrome," the suspicion that German-Americans here developed mental inferiority because of inbreeding.

The "syndrome" was declared a fallacy at a conference in St. Cloud. No evidence was found for the alleged drop in IQ brought on by inbreeding. Bill Cofell, a sociologist at St. John's University, studied Stearns County culture and attributed the belief to "destructive stereotypes." A peculiar mixture of German and English in Stearns County speech fueled the belief. Cofell did not deny the fact of lower verbal skills in Stearns schools during the 1950s but attributed them to the county being deprived of its language and culture. The culprit was not mental retardation but residue from anti-Hun hysteria during World War I.

War propaganda fomented by the US government under Woodrow Wilson fueled suspicion that German-American spies lurked everywhere. It incited dreadfully cruel acts, such as tarring and feathering people. One German-American loyal to the United States was lynched, and a jury found the perpetrators "not guilty." Despite this, German-Americans allied with their new homeland rather than with the kaiser. Soldiers from Stearns County were valuable for their knowledge of German—they could translate.

Nationally, people were indicted for speaking out against the war, and in Minnesota the Benson School Bill of 1919 prohibited teaching school subjects in German. Bill Cofell interviewed my mother's cousin, teacher Lucy Weymann Reis, who said,

> Up to World War I, I taught German reading and grammar right along with the English. Then when the war came out, then, . . . you know how it went then. Anything that was German . . . we were traitors.

She encouraged her students to speak English on the playground by giving them merit cards. The county superintendent of schools complimented her because, on a surprise visit, he caught boys speaking English outside of class. "He thought that was rather unusual," she said.

Bishops, priests, and teachers urged people to stop speaking German and change to English. Levels of cooperation varied, but German sermons in church stopped, and religious instruction changed to English. Hardest for some people was having to confess in English.

The size of Stearns County protected its people somewhat from the worst consequences of war propaganda. My older brothers and sisters growing up in the middle of the county during the 1930s to '40s spoke German on the school playground without being punished, although all instruction was in English. A contrasting picture comes from Viola Rothstein, who grew up in Eden Valley, on the border with another county. She told me children got their hands slapped for saying German words. I heard similar accounts from others.

National hostility toward Germans created in Stearns County a kind of insularity and suspicion of outsiders. Adding to it was anti-Catholic sentiment—Catholics were despised and distrusted. In Stearns, people reacted by not trusting folks from outside the county. Shunning outsiders still flavored relationships when I was growing up in the 1950s. But what was it like for my parents and grandparents? Did they encounter hostility or were they insulated by the size of the county? I wish I could ask them.

I never heard a hint of disloyalty to our country, but two bits of conversation have stuck in my memory since childhood. We were sitting at table on the farm one evening when a neighbor came over. A small part of the conversation stays with me. He told my father, "One good thing about that Hitler—he got rid of the Jews." Daddy didn't say anything.

The other occasion happened when we were visiting relatives and I heard a man say clearly, *Hitler war ein guter Mann.* Again, Daddy did not say anything. My father read *Der Wanderer*, a German-Catholic paper that fiercely defended German immigrants and Catholic doctrine, but just as fiercely opposed Nazism.

Bill Cofell believes WWI prejudice slowed the pace of assimilation in Stearns. John Roscoe started teaching English in Albany High School when I did, in 1965. He reminded me, "Some of our students had never been in St. Cloud, twenty miles away."

Syl Welle, an informant for the Albany centennial history I wrote, recounted the story of bringing a visitor from Germany to the municipal liquor store of Albany in 1963. Bartender Harvey Beuning asked the German visitor, "What'll you have?"

Syl said, *"Du musst den Deutsch ansprechen"* (You have to speak German to him). From that point until Frank Katzner said, *"Noch eins, dann geh' ich heim"* (Another one, then I'll go home), all conversation in the bar from its six or seven Albany neighbors was in German. The visitor looked in astonishment from side to side. Americans often hear English spoken in Germany, but not often do Germans hear their language spoken in America.

Polish and Irish Catholic immigrants settled on the eastern side of Stearns County. South of Albany, a pocket of German Lutherans thrived in harmony with Catholic neighbors. And near Paynesville flourished German Methodists. Less than a quarter mile south of our farm were two Schulz farms owned by "non-Catholics" whom I never met, although geographically they were our closest neighbors. My father and older brothers might have made their acquaintance in the process of farming, but not the rest of our family. There was no antagonism. They simply had no part in our family life, in contrast to Catholic neighbors miles away with whom we interacted regularly.

German-Catholic culture is fading in Stearns County, but it hangs on. During the 1950s, business transactions like shopping and bringing milk to the creamery were conducted in German. My family listened to KASM, the local radio station, for agricultural news and old-time music. The station broadcast a weekly German language program into the 1990s. I was told the program, hosted by Clyde Weivoda on Sunday afternoon, was popular with German war brides in central Minnesota. Weivoda is a Slavic name, but the family came from the Austrian empire, where all citizens knew German. KASM ended each day at sunset by broadcasting a recording of the rosary. Today it plays music all night but still broadcasts the rosary at 6:00 every evening.

The hold of German culture in the twenty-first century manifests in making music together. Cold Spring has a *Männerchor*. Meier Grove and St. Martin still have town bands. Four brothers and one sister of mine played in the St. Martin Band at one time or another. My oldest brother, Adelbert, who proudly bore his unmistakably German first name, lived in St. Cloud but drove the thirty miles to St. Martin to play in the band through the 1990s. His son Florian joined him as a college student and continues after his father's death.

When I brought my future husband to the farm for the first time in 1963, Daddy asked, "Are you Cherman, too?" The proud answer, "No, Irish," brought a disappointed look, or did I imagine this because I did not want to disappoint Daddy?

Talk Funny

All eight of my great-grandparents and four great-great-grandparents lived in America, but we spoke German at home. We said German prayers before and after meals, prayed the rosary in German, and didn't learn English until we went to school. Gradually more English entered our speech. During my grade school years, we pressured our parents to say table prayers in English, and they finally gave in.

Even my youngest sister, Evelyn, who entered the first grade in 1951, spoke no English until she entered the first grade. There was no kindergarten—this significant German contribution to American education did not bless our community. By the time I went to school, however, English was not entirely foreign because I heard older siblings saying things in English.

During my pre-school days, I knew we were not doing a clean job of speaking German. The articles *der*, *die*, and *das* (meaning "the") often became just *da* or *duh* in our speech. I guessed that we corrupted more defined endings because I heard various endings on nouns and adjectives, which in German are inflected by gender and grammatical function. Knowing vaguely that our speech was not polished, I tried to talk to Evie in what I imagined to be correct German. She said I talked funny. She nailed it.

When I got to second grade, some pages of my reading book looked familiar. My older sister Celia had read them to me. I don't know how much I understood then, but I quickly picked up the connection between letters and their pronunciation. It made me impatient during laborious reading lessons in early grades. No member of our family found immersion in English difficult.

School work was easy, but I was frustrated on the playground, where English did not flow out easily. By that time, German no longer prevailed on the school playground. The discomfort of having to learn a new language has mostly slipped my memory, but in a later grade a classmate told me that in first grade I fell off the see-saw, cried, and asked, "*Wo ist Celia?*" (Where is Celia?).

I remember feeling awkwardly different because of rivalry between "towners" and farmers. And my classmates did not seem to be as German as I was. Their parents were younger than mine and their families spoke English. Wanting to fit in, I became a student of language. How to say, "*mach schnell*"? I was sure "make fast" would not do, having observed that word-for-word translation didn't always work. Listening for the phrase others used, I learned to say "hurry up." This habit of observing and teaching myself served me for a lifetime.

In first or second grade, Teacher had us sit in a circle to tell what we got for Christmas. My prize gift was a suitcase for doll clothes, but how to say it in English? Fortunately, the teacher's daughter was in line before me and said, "I got a doll suitcase." The same word we said at home—"suitcase"! This relieved but did not surprise me because I'd already figured out that English peppered our German sentences. I just didn't want to seem dumb by saying the German word.

Why, I wondered, was a feast day called a *Feiertag*? To my childish bilingual ears, it sounded like "fireday," which didn't fit the way grownups used the word. Though afraid of seeming stupid, I asked at home, "What does fire have to do with *Feiertag*?"

As I feared, my question met laughter, and Daddy added, "*Feiertag* has nothing to do with fire." Not until I studied German in college did I learn that *feiern* means "to celebrate."

I was ashamed of my parents because they didn't look or talk like other Americans. They called me "Chenette" and my brother "Cherald." They said things like "fife pount back" (five pound bag) and "*Das is zu tight*" (That is too tight) and "*Da fahrt kei'* train *mehr*" (There goes no train anymore), mixing English words with German dialect, pronunciation, and syntax. We never used the German words for "train" or "car." These inventions became widespread only after the middle of the nineteenth century when our forebears migrated.

The combination of English words with German word order created curious sentences. I wrote down examples spoken by my parents: "He threw over the fence the hay." "I raked many times the hay." "It gets early dark." "I got pictures too yet." "We're going next week to the farm." "I had that book always in here." "Then they had still the religion." "We went by their place." "They had in May a blizzard." "You had to put always all the straw in."

In English we might say, "Right?" when we want agreement. In Stearns County, we followed a statement by asking, "*Gel?*" (*g* as in "go"). *Gel* comes from a German dialect and is based on the word *gelten*, meaning "to be valid."

But another of our speech oddities has no basis either in standard German or a dialect. When we said, "*Ich gleich das*," we meant, "I like that" or "I enjoy it." In Germany *ich gleich das* means "I am similar to that" or "I resemble that." Stearns County folk twisted the meaning of *gleich* from "resemble" to "enjoy" because the English word "like" means both "resemble" and "enjoy." The melding of two languages created a new German word unique to Stearns County.

Working hard to be "normal" and rid my speech of German traces, I learned to say "colander" instead of "strainer" and "emery board" instead of "file." With effort I stopped making hair plural as in "My hair are too long. I have to get them cut." A classmate in boarding high school told me that I talked with an accent after a vacation at home. Disappointed, I worked harder to get rid of it. Only after years of living as an adult did I fully appreciate our bilingualism. I can understand young people wanting to wear what everyone's wearing and do what everyone's doing because I was captive of the same desire.

In college I chose German as the language to study, wanting to learn the standard forms. I pronounced the R as English-speaking classmates did. After listening to tapes, I learned that the way we pronounced it at home was correct. Today I like to roll the R when pronouncing foreign names. I cannot speak the dialect of my childhood anymore, but I enjoy hearing it when I get the opportunity.

In 2005 the Igelmunds, Blonigen relatives in Germany befriended by Father Al, visited us when he celebrated the fortieth anniversary of his ordination. They also were friends of Raymond and Darlene Blonigen, whose daughter Shirley had researched Blonigen genealogy and written *The Blonigen Tree.* Together we hosted our relatives and I heard Ray speak Stearns County German, an amalgamation of dialects. It tickled me enormously, as I time-traveled back a half century. Our German relatives had no difficulty understanding him, which first surprised me, then made sense.

Language fascinates me. When Al brought me to Germany, I strove so mightily to speak German correctly that my efforts amused our German hosts. In retrospect, I realize that I was entertaining them somewhat as Raymond later entertained me. I imagine word-conscious strangers being amused by the German inflecting our English sentences. In faraway places, folks from here are told, "You must be from Stearns County."

My observations of language differences sharpened when I became an English and German teacher. Betty Sporleder, a fellow English teacher at Albany High School, told me that when she started teaching there, she honestly thought North Lake was "Nord Lake." Dr. Richard Salk knew he had entered a unique culture when he brought his car to a garage for repair. "*Wo ist die Schpark pluck wrrrench?*" asked one repairman of another. Viola Rothstein married Irishman James Flynn and became a teacher in Albany. Aware of language confusion, she told of having some fly poison standing out in her schoolroom. When a student came near it, another one cried out, "Don't touch it. That's gift." In German *Gift* means "poison."

German influence on language constructions has taken over more than Stearns County. Minnesotans give evidence of heavy German migration when they ask, "Are you coming with?" echoing the German *Kommst du mit?* I mentioned this once as an example of incorrect usage in the teachers' lounge of a Stearns County school. Looks of bewilderment greeted it. Not wanting to embarrass the teachers, I didn't inform them of the standard form: "Are you coming along?"

Prohibition

Stearns County gained notoriety during Prohibition. Its German-Catholic setting provided the perfect habitat for resisting the ban on alcoholic drinks, but resisting meant participating in the notorious, lawless decade of the 1920s.

Prohibition began in 1919 with the Volstead Act, a federal law drafted by a Minnesota Congressman that put into effect the Eighteenth Amendment to the Constitution of the United States, which prohibited making, selling, and transporting alcoholic beverages. It ended in December of 1933 when the Twenty-First Amendment repealed the Eighteenth Amendment. Prohibition's ban on alcohol reduced consumption but did not stop Americans from drinking, and it created an upsurge of criminal activity in which organized crime flourished.

American breweries have German names for a reason. Making and imbibing spirits was an integral part of culture in the old country. While researching and writing my centennial histories of Albany and Avon, the vague knowledge I'd had about Prohibition took on flaming details in lives of people close to me. Some of them I am not allowed to divulge because fear lingers that "the Feds" will find out. One man drove the getaway truck in a crime that ended in death. His wife threatened him with divorce if he would not quit trafficking in liquor. I was taking notes while interviewing their son, but he blurted, "Don't write this down!"

The prohibited beverages were called "moonshine" (produced while the moon was shining), and the transporters were called "bootleggers" (hiding a bottle in the leg of a boot). They dominated economic activity in Avon Township, my home today. The liquor was called "Minnesota 13," a hybrid seed corn developed at the University of Minnesota for a short growing season. Residents of the Avon area learned of the drink's renown and the area's renown when traveling out of state. A story of dubious verity illustrates. A Minnesotan is in a Chicago bar (sometimes he's farther away, maybe in Asia during World War II). He sees the sign, "If you can order a drink the bartender doesn't recognize, you get one free." He orders Minnesota 13, and the bartender asks, "Where do you want it from? St. Wendel, Holdingford, Avon, or Opole?"

Catholics in Stearns County considered moonshining illegal but not immoral because brewing spirits was a respected profession in the old country. My Avon history, *Nestled between Lakes and Wooded Hills*, features the Himsl family. Alois Himsl, a brewer from Upper Austria, migrated to St. John's, where he expected to continue practicing his profession. Sadly for him and his family, St. John's did not have the brewery customary in European monasteries.

Economic necessity and the status of brewing in German-Catholic culture spurred riotous moonshine activity here. I was told everybody did it. I learned that my sixth-grade teacher in St. Martin had lived near Avon and participated. Examples abounded of moonshine stored behind the altar in church. Sellers of the stuff escaped detection by hiding behind a clerical collar. A monk at St. John's built stills out of compassion for the desperately poor farmers in the area. Those were drought years.

Frances Budde, an Avon woman I interviewed when she was around a hundred years old, said, "I sure wouldn't want to live them days over again. We were always afraid of getting caught." She voiced the refrain, "The Feds are coming, the Feds are coming." When her husband was caught and doing time in jail, he wrote to her that she should "start in again." She explained, "We had to make up what it cost us for the jail fine."

"It was to survive," added her son Cyril. "There were eight kids to feed. What else was there to do?" They took whiskey to Avon and traded it for groceries. "The cows," said Cyril, "milked enough for the kids to drink. The rest came out of moonshine." Their land in the hills south of Avon was little suited to farming.

Despite her dread of the Feds, Frances had no guilt. "I never confessed it," she said. "It wasn't against Church laws."

As if fear of getting caught did not cause enough misery, the dangers of brewing brought other calamities. One night someone in the Budde farmhouse yelled, "Fire." They had five kegs of whiskey stacked in the basement and beneath them a steady, blue gas flame artificially aging the liquor. One keg was too full. Its cork popped, and the alcoholic beverage leaking out caught fire. It spread through the basement. "Dad had to run through the fire to save my brother," said Cyril. "You couldn't breathe, the fumes from the alcohol cut out the air. We were afraid the house would go down."

Hazards afflicted farm animals as well. Buddes dug a shallow, open well, down which buckets were dropped to get the great quantity of water needed for cooking the brew. This saved them the work of digging a normal well by hand. One time they were missing a horse and found it stuck in the well. It was unhurt, and they rescued it with the help of neighbors and planks to pry it out. Animals also could be overcome by mash, a by-product of making moonshine. They might be fed mash or wander to it accidentally, and if they ate too much of it, they got drunk. On the Budde farm, cows, chickens, ducks, and pigs consumed the mash at various times, occasionally with remarkable results.

While writing this memoir I learned that two of my great-grand-fathers were alcoholics. At least three great uncles were in the business of making moonshine. One died a horrible death from drinking it. An older cousin described it as the worst death imaginable because he saw pus oozing out of his great uncle's dying body. The poisonous stuff was eating up the man's insides.

One of my great-grandfather's sons, Joe Fuchs, died young and left a widow with ten children. His brothers, my grandfather John among them, obtained a small farm for her near upper Spunk Lake in rural Avon, where poverty clung to the family. "We lived on water," his grand-daughter told me. The offspring of Joe also cooked moonshine. Frances Budde, their neighbor, reported that they built a chicken coop that held a small number of chickens and a large still in its basement. "And that chicken manure," she said, "that kind of deadened the smell."

From my oral sources I heard it estimated that only about 5 percent of those cooking or selling liquor were caught. Avon's telephone switch-board operator had a clear view of Main Street and alerted bootleggers when she spotted strange cars in town. Local sheriffs cooperated—the whole community cooperated—in thwarting the Feds who came poking around. When someone got caught, his sentence could be commuted if he snitched on someone else. This, the Buddes are sure, accounts for the raid on them.

Information I gathered for my local histories haunts me when I think about my largely-unknown family history with alcohol. It forges a psychic connection between me and my maternal kin-women. I think my mother saw a connection because she mentioned the alcoholics in her family when I said my husband was an alcoholic.

What was it like for my foremothers married to moonshining men? What was it like for women who desperately tried to hold things together while their men cooked moon, drank it, or killed themselves with drink? Frances Budde revealed some of the pain for women who always feared a raid and whose men went to prison. These women could not escape. Di-vorce was not an option for them. Prohibition stories entertain us today, but it was no fun for those who endured the era's worst consequences.

Present Day

German names still dominate obituary columns, even in the city of St. Cloud. During school hours, Crossroads Mall in St. Cloud is the hangout of retirees. Walking through it, I heard two elderly men take leave of each other by saying, "*Mach's gut*" (Make it good or Have a good day) and "*Du auch*" (You also). When I attend family reunions, I hear cousins of my generation say phrases in the Stearns County dialect and feel a bit sad that the dialect will die out as speakers of it die.

We used to sing *Grosser Gott* ("Holy God, we praise Thy name") at the end of a festive Mass, some verses in German, some in English. I remember singing *Grosser Gott* after the year 2000, but in more recent years the song is sung only in English. It disappoints me. In 1965 I introduced the study of German to Albany High School, but some years after I left it was discontinued and is no longer offered there. The same is true of other high schools in our county, while study of Spanish has expanded. I applaud study of Spanish but would like to see young people also learning their own heritage. I believe it would give them more understanding of immigrants today.

Blonigen/Fuchs seeds planted in Europe were dispersed in America for the same reasons that bring immigrants today—to flee poverty and violence. Germans from the Rhineland came for economic survival, as do Hispanics and Somalis today. My forebears avoided conscription for Bismarck's wars. Today Somalis flee al-Shabab and Hispanics flee the violence of drug gangs that force kids to kill or be killed. In the nineteenth century, Catholics were trashed by Americans, as Muslims are trashed today. Resentment against Muslim prayers in schools today parallels the school fight of 1896—all about prayer in school—that I relate in my centennial history of Avon.

Today, however, Hispanics and Somalis are expected to assimilate much more rapidly than my forebears and I did. When I hear, "Why can't they learn English?" I like to mention that I am a fifth-generation German-American who did not know English before going to school.

In 2002 to 2003, I taught English to adult immigrants, most of them Somalis. After that, one of my adult students asked me for help in writing official letters. I invited him to my home so that I could work on my own computer. Abdi became a cultural navigator in the St. Cloud schools and continues occasional visits to my home. Our friendship spread to his family and a few of my neighbors.

To build understanding and solidarity with those who look different, sound different, wear different clothes, and practice a different religion, I proposed having a potluck picnic in our neighborhood. We would
share food and conversation with Somali guests bringing Somali food.
To explain and promote it, I started going door to door and soon came
to a house where I interrupted a party of card-players. One of them dis-
gorged a stream of hatred against Somalis. That stopped my door-to-door
visits. At home one day, the doorbell rang. Two couples stood there with
complaints about Somalis and immigrants in general. Their objections
confirmed it—Somalis were not welcome at a neighborhood party.

I got a greater shock when around 2010 I gave a presentation
about Muslims and Islam for St. Cloud Community Education. At the
end of my prepared talk—at least he waited that long—a man let loose a
stream of invective. I could feel my face flashing red. Caught off guard,
I could think of nothing to address his biases but stumbled around with
mollifying statements. Later, I wished I had corrected him, but still
later—today—I know that nothing I might have said could have made
a difference. I don't know what about Somalis disturbed him more, their
race or their religion.

In 2016, St. Cloud received national attention when a Somali man
stabbed people in Crossroads Mall. It topped a series of incidents expos-
ing hostility toward newly arriving Africans. Among the heroes who prevented ill feelings between cultures from escalating further were Catholic
leaders. The bishop of St. Cloud Diocese and the prioress of St. Benedict's
Monastery received Catholic of the Year awards for promoting interfaith
dialogue. They joined civic leaders, other religious leaders, and ordinary
citizens working to smother backlash and instead build a welcoming
place for Somali and Hispanic refugees.

I tell people from other parts of the country that I live in Lake
Wobegon, the "place that time forgot." Garrison Keillor featured Avon
in his stories and captured the mind-set of Stearns County culture when
he said things like, "We have so many ways to not talk about things in
Lake Wobegon, and so many things to not talk about." Keillor started
Prairie Home Companion while he was living north of St. Martin. He
often mentioned Norwegian Lutherans, the stock he came from, but I
recognize German Catholics in his stories that poke gentle fun. Identifying us unmistakably are German names and jello "salads" containing
marshmallows and whipped cream.

A scene in Avon about 1994 illustrates our culture. My neighbors Lee and Mazie Schmid had their married children visiting from around the country—daughters and sons from East and West Coasts, Colorado, and Utah, all home on vacation. They attended the Avon parish bazaar. Close to the church entrance stood the beer stand, an inevitable and essential part of festivities. The crowd around it included children. In front of church an old-time band played, led by the concertina. Couples of various ages were dancing the polka on the pavement as Fr. Simon stood on the church steps taking pictures. Everyone was singing, "In heaven there is no beer. That's why we drink it here." Wide-eyed, the daughter-in-law from South Carolina turned to her husband and asked in her Southern drawl, "Ron, are they singing in a foreign language?"

Both cherishing and critiquing the milieu of my childhood, I reflect on its lessons. Religions speak in distinct languages and cultures, each with a unique view of reality but all mediating the inner realm. Our accustomed way of thinking about spiritual matters is not the only or necessarily the best way. Christianity is one brand of spirituality, one spiritual language among many just as legitimate, if unfamiliar. From a child encased in a culture foreign to most Americans, I have become one who likes to nudge us out of parochial grooves of thought toward more inclusive frames of thought.

2

Family Wounds

Grandma Thekla

In my home I display an aged 12 by 18-inch photo surrounded by a golden, intricately carved frame that I grew up seeing on the wall at Grandma's. It is of her wedding in 1899. I love history, I love old things, I love the frame and the picture on my wall, but I can't say I loved Grandma Thekla Blonigen, and I don't believe she much loved any of us.

We grew up hearing our mother seething with indignation over her mother-in-law. When older sister Celia first saw the framed photo on my wall, she asked what people coming into my home thought of Grandma in the photo. Her face changed even before I had a chance to say what she immediately realized upon asking. The young bride in the photo had not yet turned into the ogre haunting our family while we were growing up.

Grandma Thekla Blonigen was the only grandparent in my life. My grandfathers both died before I came along. Grandma Mary Fuchs died when I was five, but dementia had confused her for years and I don't remember ever seeing her. My three sisters talked about visiting her in St. Cloud. They got to go on trips to St. Cloud because they needed an eye doctor. I slightly envied their need for glasses, which brought them to the big city.

My mother and father married on October 1, 1929, a few weeks before the stock market crash triggered the Great Depression. It seems a fitting metaphor for at least part of their marriage. Mother was twenty-eight, in those days old for marrying and beginning a family. Worse, the first two children died a few weeks after their healthy birth, for which Mother blamed her mother in-law. Births happened at home. After birth, mothers were confined to bed and another woman took care of baby and mother. The woman there for Mother was her mother-in-law Thekla.

For years afterward, Mother talked about that time. Her breasts were full and she asked that the baby be brought to her for nursing. But Thekla refused to bring the baby for breastfeeding. Instead, Mother saw her spooning well water from a bucket into the baby's mouth. My mother concluded that this well water, not boiled, led to the baby's death. Mother recounted another memory. Thekla intended to bathe the baby before Mass but didn't have time to heat the water and get to Mass on time. Mother told her to skip the bath, but Thekla bathed the baby in cold water. The baby got pneumonia and died. How often cold baths happened and whether Grandma Thekla ever let Mother nurse, we do not know.

Still mourning the death of her first baby, my mother got pregnant again. Thekla said, "Just wait. This baby will die too yet." It happened. Years later, our oldest living brother, Adelbert, heard neighbors describe how downhearted Dad was. Brother Roman Fleischhacker told me he saw the mourning firsthand as cross-bearer for both funerals. "So terribly sad! It was so hard for your parents." Listening to him after my parents died, sixty-six years later, impressed on me as never before how deeply wounded they must have been.

Devastated, they got a priest to perform an exorcism and prayed they would still have lots of living children. They hoped one would become a priest. The third baby born to them lived—Adelbert. Alverna followed and then Arnold, who became a priest. I was the first of eight living children to be born in a hospital, when Mother was forty-one years old. A week after she turned forty-four, Evelyn arrived, the "baby of the family." Evie and I were "da kits."

I conclude from listening to older family members and neighbors that my parents' first years of marriage united them in love despite the severe strain of losing their first two babies. They were named Florian and Leroy. We grew up knowing about Florian and Leroy. I do not recall ever not knowing, and we visited their graves in the St. Martin cemetery. They were not buried together, but for us they were one unit—Florian and Leroy. Adelbert named his firstborn child "Florian," and it happened that Alverna married a man named LeRoy. His siblings call him "Roy" but we always say "Leeroy."

Brother Michael and Sister Margaret Mandernach told me that Thekla Blonigen served as their family's midwife. It is hard for me to imagine her performing this admirable service, having grown up with Mother's resentment. Did Grandma Thekla deliver Florian and Leroy? Did my parents perhaps switch to doctors after their deaths? Thekla had given birth to seven babies of her own. Were they not breastfed? I wish there were someone alive who could answer my questions.

My father, Herman, was the only one in his family who married. His mother did not let her daughters interact with men. Their unusual behavior was remembered by Br. Michael, who grew up as their close neighbor. He said, "If a man came near while they were working outside, they stopped and hid. I think my father was the only man allowed to talk to them."

In the 1950s, Bill Cofell conducted a sociological survey in Stearns County. He told me years later of the contrasts he observed when he visited families in our neighborhood. In the Stang family children felt free to participate, inserting comments and even correcting their dad while he was answering questions. In Grandma's house, she was the only one who answered Cofell's questions. Her daughters were grown women, but Cofell said they "peeked around the corner from rooms where they were hiding."

My aunts could not do what other young women did—go to dances and work as maids. Dances were the way to find husbands. Jobs helping mothers with babies and toddlers were the way to earn money and learn mothering skills. (Only religious Sisters had intellectual or professional jobs.) My five aunts did not go to dances and none got married. They dutifully accompanied their mother to church for Mass every morning. "You could tell the time by their passing on the road," said Br. Michael.

In our home, my father's sisters were called *die Mädchen* ("the girls"), his term for them. *Die Mädchen* never defied their mother, but my father was not deterred from what he wanted to do. Br. Michael admires him for getting out from under his mother's domination. The Mandernach place earlier was owned by relatives of the Fuchses. Working there as a maid was Lena Fuchs. This is how our parents met. Their marriage evidently infuriated Thekla. How much would be revealed later.

Our family narrative stressed Grandma Thekla's puritan, unreasonable piety. We heard our mother repeating her mother-in-law's insistence that she should walk to church for Mass every morning (Mom couldn't drive), followed by retorts Mom wished she had given.

Grandma haunted our family, but she never talked to us children. My only memory of her being in our home happened when I was around six years old. It was after Christmas and we were to show our Christmas presents to Grandma and the two *Mädchen* who came. As I was displaying something to the aunts, one of them said I should bring it to "Mam." I hesitated. Did she mean my mama or hers? I guessed correctly and brought it to Grandma. Now I know that she wanted to feel things because she was nearly blind from glaucoma, but this did not cross my mind at the time. I intuited that my child's point of view did not count right then.

Grandma died when I was eight years old, but *die Mädchen* assured her continuing influence on our lives by plaguing us with their freakish prudery. Dad and older brothers worked their farm just a half mile from ours, so there was constant back-and-forth. My aunts' car in the driveway sent us scrambling upstairs to put on clothes that covered more of our bodies. Sheet music on our piano showing Patti Page in a low-cut gown drew a disapproving remark. After Mass on Sundays, *die Mädchen* discussed which girls were dressed sinfully in church—sleeves too short or neckline too low. Weddings provided more opportunities to cluck over improper dress.

In his book, *Discovering My Inner Child*, written by Fr. Al while ministering at Marriage Encounter weekends, he describes an incident that gives the flavor of puritanism infecting our family life. The aunts brought a cow to be inseminated by our bull. When the bull was mounting the cow in the barnyard, windows in house and barn flew up—Mother from the house and Father from the barn—shouting to kids in the yard to get into the house immediately.

Still, I have fond memories of going to Grandma's on the Sunday after Christmas. Being one of "da kits," I didn't feel oppressed by the annual visit but looked forward to it because I liked the yellow brick house. Wainscoting lined the large kitchen, and a lovely built-in cabinet separated pantry from kitchen. Its glass doors showed half-doilies hanging from shelves holding chinaware. Hooks for outdoor clothes lined one corner of the kitchen. Next to the outside door hung a sink with a pump. Instead of turning on a faucet for water, they pumped water into large bowls—no indoor plumbing. Going potty in their outhouse in the middle of winter was miserable, but they always had homemade candy and served a delicious meal. That is, our five aunts did. Grandma sat in a corner chair, an austere presence who said nothing.

Their parlor or "front room," like ours, was unused except for special occasions. It was opened for our Christmas visit. There hung the photo that charms visitors to my home. Near the parlor, a beautiful, rose-colored clock occupied its own shelf high on the kitchen wall. Sometimes Grandma Thekla sat under it. Younger sister Evie recalls being afraid when she passed by while going to the parlor. Grandma reached out to her. She may have wanted to feel baby Evie because of her near-blindness, but it frightened Evie.

A book of Mother Goose nursery rhymes captivated me in that house. English nursery rhymes could make little sense to any American child, let alone a child who knew little English. But my introduction to the book was my introduction to the music of poetry. Before or shortly after I started first grade, my brother Jerry read aloud rhymes from the book. The verses enchanted me.

Arnold had no fond memories of going to Grandma's. From his book written when he was Fr. Al, I learned that the Christmas visit had earlier taken place on Christmas Day. It bothered him so much that he persuaded Mother and Father to reserve the big day for our family alone. He wrote:

> I recall the absolute fear of going into the parlor where Grand-mother was sitting when I was very small. She seemed like a queen sitting on her throne who had a distant and scowling look on her countenance . . . we would hide behind the large heating stove. . . . She did not address one single word to me ever, as far as I can recall. There was simply no interaction between her and her grandchildren. (Blonigen, *Discovering*, 18)

His negative feelings about Grandma Blonigen may have been influenced by Mother because she confided in Arnold.

My Mother

My mother, Lena, got little schooling because her father demanded her help on the farm. The third oldest of ten children, she was used as a workhorse because she had a big body and was a good worker. Wearing too-small and worn-out shoes cast off by her mother, she had to walk on rough, uneven clumps of dirt turned over by the horse-drawn plow that she guided through fields. She hated it. Her slightly younger brother had asthma and got to go to school while she was kept home to do farm work. For the rest of her life she resented having to do man's work. Al wrote that she "cherished the dream of becoming a nun and music teacher."

Her father forced farm work onto her, but when she mentioned him during my youth, it was with respect. Her resentment was directed at mother-in-law and sisters-in-law. They received her strongest invective— *die Luder* ("bitch").

I grew up hearing her schooling summed up as about a fourth-grade education. In the early decades of the twentieth century, the school year lasted eight months. She missed many days of school beginning in the fourth grade and was taken out entirely after the sixth. When I grew older, I tried to reconcile stories about her lack of education with her reading of magazines as an adult. Bits of her writing indicate that she educated herself.

I was born a dozen years and six living babies after Mother and Father lost their second baby son. A year before I was born, Grandpa Blonigen died. And a year and a half after my birth, Dad's only brother, Aloysius, died of brain cancer. This death had dreadful consequences for our family. I was ten months old, so I am reconstructing this from the words of siblings and Mother's complaints. Who would work Grandma's farm after Alois died? The aunts and their mother shined up to the only man left in their family—Herman, our father. They persuaded him to work for them. In referring to this, Mother used the word *schmeicheln*. My English-German dictionary explains what was going on—"coax, flatter, cajole, wheedle, fawn upon."

Dad decided he had to manage both his and his mother's farms, with his sisters and his four sons working as they were able. He and his sons would receive wages for the work of only one person. When Arnold had become Al, he speculated on Dad's decision to work for his mother:

> I suspect that he was trying to regain her favor which he had lost when he got married despite her command not to. Or, he may have reacted on the guilt he felt deep inside for not obeying his mother . . .
>
> He was always on the defensive justifying the decision he had made about working his mother's farm.

Dad's decision to take responsibility for the farm of his mother and five unmarried sisters knocked a hole in marital harmony between him and his wife.

Then Grandma died and her will poured salt onto the wound. Her entire estate went to *die Mädchen*. Nothing to her son and his family. Dad's loyalty to his mother and sisters, his labor and financial support, were not rewarded, but he and my brothers continued the work called for in the earlier agreement.

Mama never got over the blows. "Mama" was her name in our family, but she was not a mama in the common sense of that word. Her resentment and hostility toward Thekla and *die Mädchen* pervaded our family life.

In my earliest memories, close to babyhood, Mama is a distant, dark, brooding figure, always around but not much involved in my life. She is the big person in the house but not the one to go to for requests or questions. I never tell Mama, "I want a drink," or ask, "Where are we going?" much less tell her my thoughts. She does little mothering. Older siblings are the ones who answer me.

One of her sons noticed her neglect—Arnold. A born psychologist even before he became Father Aloysius, Arnold worried about the consequences for his youngest siblings. As Al, he recalled times Mama would suddenly dissolve in tears, leave the kitchen, and disappear into her bedroom. He wrote,

> My mother seemed to be on the verge of a nervous breakdown much of the time. . . . My older sister and I became the surrogate parents of the family.

From my adult perspective, I can see that it was so, but even unusually mature teenagers cannot correct the dynamics in a family holding so much hurt.

I do not recall a back-and-forth conversation alone with Mama in childhood, not even a shallow one, much less absorbing thoughts and desires. Mama was a stranger, not an intimate. *She doesn't know me,* I thought to myself. She was not interested in me, did not know what I was thinking and would not understand it. I certainly couldn't talk to Daddy. He was focused on farm work and even more unapproachable. She was the one always there.

When I wanted an answer from Mama that an older sibling could not give, I'd say "Hey," throw the question into the air around her, and hope she'd notice. If she did, the answer might come indirectly, not looking at or speaking to me personally.

I am guessing I was seven or eight when I wanted to ask Celia—the most approachable older person because she was the closest—why we couldn't talk to Mama or say "Mama" to her. I could not draw up the courage to ask. This seems so weird to me now that I have difficulty recalling or describing it. As I was processing these things with Al, he wrote,

> You are right, we never called her "Mom" or "Mama" to her face, although we referred to her as "Mama" when speaking of her to another. I remember that most of the time we called each other in the family "Hey."

The "Hey!" habit in our family makes it hard for me to tolerate our popular culture's verbal fad of substituting "Hey!" for "Hi."

I rejected Mama. When she put me with Evie into the back-porch sink to bathe us, I resented it. It was embarrassing to be treated like a baby—I wanted to be more grown up—but it was more than that. I felt she had no right to do this. I felt alienated from her. *Why?* I puzzled over this when the memory rose in later life. And how did my brother Jerry's memory fit? He told me that when I saw the baby crib being taken down from the attic for the next baby, Evelyn, I cried disconsolately, long and hard.

I often prayed in bed at night, cringing from loud arguments in the kitchen below. During the day, we heard again and again the same plaints from Mama. She stood at the kitchen sink doing mindless work, reciting monologues of indignation at *die Luder*, who seemed to have stolen away her husband. On and on she complained, oblivious of her children being drenched by it.

Decades later, Al explained in an email to me,

> Mom felt abandoned by Dad; she in effect lost her husband emotionally. That is what all their arguments were about. . . . Since you were still so young, her cutting herself off from everyone affected you more than us older ones. I do remember heart to heart talks with her. However they turned into monologues of complaining later on.

Her anguished laments formed the backdrop for my childhood and youth. Absorbed in her own pain, Mama had little energy for mothering us. I believe this formed my lifelong orientation toward deprivation. I disliked Mama's vulnerability but copied it in later life.

While I was swimming in the water I could not say it was water. If someone had asked me during my youth to describe my mother, I would have started by mentioning her arthritis and her difficulty walking, both attributed to the mis-fitting shoes and field work. I could not have spoken about her damaged emotional state, even if I'd wanted to, but Mama's eternal complaining left a deeper mark. We, like she, were starved for loving affection.

She assumed that neighbors and relatives disdained us, and in Al's words, we had to "prove ourselves in the eyes of others." Her wounds, I now know, were passed on to us, suffusing our self-perception. I suspect our family also was infected by the weirdness of "the Blonigen sisters," as they were called by others. A vague family shame grew in us. As an adult, I fight the feeling that my natural place is subordinate to others and having less than others.

As I work through this memoir, my understanding of Mother grows. Along with in-law torments, a feeling of unfair treatment in her family of origin blocked attention from the needs of her youngest children.

My perspective today lets me see the consequences in my compli-cated interior life. Mama's absorption in her own pain, her emotional dis-tance from us, was more devastating for us younger kids than Dad's harsh work ethic, which burdened my brothers. Now I know that Mother loved me, even in a biased way, according to siblings. She fought for my educa-tion. But she seemed a stranger to my real self, and I did not let her in.

One Sunday after church, Mama was visiting with a friend. As I ap-proached, I could tell that her friend was saying something about me and they smiled lovingly at me. Mama grabbed me and hugged me fiercely. I yearned for hugs but squirmed out of her embrace, while knowing it hurt her. What brought on her sudden, strange embrace? Was this about my singing in the family band? I don't know.

Pondering my childhood in later years, I could not completely ac-count for my strange dislike of her, beginning in my pre-school years. Not until I was in my sixties did I learn the biggest reason for my dam-aged relationship with my mother.

My Father

Someone who saw their wedding photo made a frowning face and said, "Wow, he looks serious!" I knew immediately that she was referring to my father and not his brother, the groomsman. Mama said Daddy had the flu. I see both an upset stomach and determination in his face. It makes sense. He was opposing a powerful force in his life—his mother. The look in his eyes could be read as defiance.

For us he was a more distant authority than Mama, but she called him "Daddy" to us, so that was our term for him. Daddy always was all business. Sundays meant time to rest up for *Werktage*. No fishing or hunting—too much like fun. My four older brothers lived with the consequences of his decision to work for his mother and sisters, while we younger sisters were spared the demands of his supervising. Daddy was an exacting overseer of their work; things had to be done his way. Punctuating our family life were angry exchanges between him and Arnold, who dared to argue with him.

While I was growing up, I did not dare talk to Daddy. I was not one of his workers and had little contact with him. Rare memories of being with Daddy alone are pleasant because the harshness I expected did not come. In our house, enclosed stairs led from kitchen to "the upstairs." One time when I was a little girl, I came downstairs into the kitchen and discovered no one there but my father sitting at the table. *I wonder if he knows my name. Should I walk back up?* I stayed but didn't say anything and he didn't. But he was not scary. It surprised me.

An earlier memory comes—before I started school. We are at our parish festival after dark. It gets cold and Mama tells Daddy to keep me warm by picking me up and holding me. It is not an intentionally loving embrace, but it feels heavenly.

Despite lots of anger and loud arguing in our home, there was no corporal punishment, although it was widely accepted when my parents were growing up. I never heard of beatings in their families of origin either. When Dad was in his eighties and I was visiting him in a Good Samaritan home, he told me that he saw his grade school teacher beat kids—not himself, others—and Dad resolved never to hit his kids. The teacher whose bad example motivated him to avoid corporal punishment was Conrad Diekmann, the father of Father Godfrey Diekmann, who would be a world-renowned expert at Vatican II and a favorite professor of mine.

Arnold

As I reflect on our farm life, I grow more aware of the disproportionate role Arnold played in our family. Today I realize how much I depend on his accounts to interpret events before I came along. Conversations he had with Mother about the in-laws formed our view of them. His narrative of our family guided my perceptions while I was growing up and guides them still. As I write this memoir, I miss his astute observations. He was the one who confronted Dad about Grandma Blonigen's effect on our family, and he chafed under Dad's single-minded focus—working the farms. There were raging arguments when creative son protested demands of prosaic father.

Arnold enlivened our family life. As his younger sister by eight years, I enjoyed his ability to make things happen. When he was around, things moved, nothing stood still, life was exciting. He drew things, made things, argued about things, inserted novel ideas into family conversations, was different from the rest of us.

Little scenes with him play out in my memory, times when he made life interesting and fun. His creativity seemed to spill out uncontrollably. He made up games, learned how to cook, led my big brothers in projects. He produced drawings, paintings, and figures. For Christmas he created an outdoor crèche with three-foot figures that he placed with lights on our front steps. In summer he made lawn ornaments for a 4-H project, designing the patterns himself, cutting and painting the wood figures.

I enjoyed his boundless creativity as a child and more as an adult. Br. Michael says on quiet evenings they could hear Arnold across the fields playing his accordion. Ceaselessly, Arnold was making music or listening to music. During Metropolitan Opera broadcasts he put his ear to the radio, while his family wondered why he listened to such noise. Arnold drew me in to appreciating classical music, still my favorite type of music.

His talent benefited our St. Martin Sunnysiders 4-H club. For a talent competition, clubs could enter a musical performance and a play or skit. One 4-H talent show stands out. I was just a little girl, but I remember the evening when the play and music entries by the Sunnysiders' club wowed the audience. Arnold led his three brothers in a band as the music entry and he played a leading role in planning the play. He picked it, assigned roles, himself in a supporting role, and persuaded his grade-school teacher to direct the play. It was a huge hit.

At the end of the evening when winners in both categories were announced, our band won, but long faces greeted the announcement of the play winner. Not ours. Its quality had obviously surpassed that of the others and been the audience favorite, but the judges wanted to give honors to more than one club.

Arnold was my third oldest sibling but acted like the oldest. He was the initiator, the innovator, the one leading others, the one driven to achieve. I used to think he refuted the birth-order theory that says these traits belong to the firstborn. Then I learned that you include deceased children, and after the fourth child you begin counting with number one again. Arnold, the fifth born, was a "firstborn." Whatever science decides about the birth-order theory, Arnold became a conspicuous example of it—a super performer.

In fact, Arnold was protective of our terribly shy oldest brother, Adelbert. Our oldest siblings went to dances and the next day we younger ones heard what happened at those dances. Bert was smitten over a certain girl but too shy to ask her to dance. Arnold schemed to get him over his fear of asking her or any other girls to dance. His efforts produced more frustration than anything else.

Arnold's artistry apparently impressed teachers in our grade school. In one of the primary grades, I was approached by a teacher on the playground—not my teacher or a sibling's—with a request that mystified me. I should take it home, she directed, and she was confident the request would be fulfilled. I took it home and Arnold drew a large cartoon figure that I brought back to her the next day. As thanks, she handed me a bag full of candy bars. Stupidly, I handed some out to kids around me clamoring for them, but I did bring home a few and confessed there had been more.

Arnold's face fell. He had a huge weight problem and loved sweets, although his nickname *Dicke* (fatso) caused him much misery. When I started grade school, a boy taunted me by yelling, "Fatso, Fatso." It hurt, but I was confused as much as hurt because I was a scrawny thing. At night I used to pray that I'd gain weight. Later I figured out what drove the heckler. By my reckoning, that boy was in primary grades when Arnold was in seventh and eighth. Needing a victim, the boy copied the taunting he'd heard in school earlier, assuming it would fit a member of the same family.

I was embarrassed by my family. Embarrassed by the way my mother looked, embarrassed when members of our family spoke in public, embarrassed when people saw the inside of our house and we hadn't cleaned before they came. I wanted things to look nice; appearances counted a lot with me. Evie tells me I did a lot of weeding in the garden. In the house I became more of a cleaner than a cook. My three sisters learned the arts of canning and making sauerkraut. I didn't.

As an adult, I came to realize the distortions in my perception. Marilyn, a schoolmate in St. Martin, said about my mother, "She wore her hats very correctly, never a hair out of place." *Huh?* I doubted she knew which woman was my mother. At a school reunion, I was reminiscing with a male classmate and slyly asked him whether he had a crush on the girl I thought the most desirable. He said, "No, some of us boys liked you. Bet you didn't know that!" He enjoyed my astonishment. Another classmate told me I was "pretty, poised, and smart, a perfect little girl who had everything." What a contrast between my self-image and others' images of me!

3

ON THE FARM

Missing Affection

MY PARENTS DID NOT show love, to each other or to their children—no kisses or hugs, no pats of praise, no words of affection. We grew up without smiles of appreciation or how-are-you's or "Good morning" or "How do you feel?" or "How was school?" or "What would you like?" Birthdays were hardly acknowledged. I blame the lack of social niceties for my tendency in later life to skip greetings and consider common pleasantries a chore. Kisses and hugs were so foreign to our life that I was well into adulthood before realizing that they were normal in all cultures and not a modern development. I did not know this.

In a family of eight living children, my younger sister, Evelyn, and I trailed as "da kits." Older siblings were the work force and expected to care for us. Sometimes I felt in the way of parents, brothers, and sisters, for whom "da kits" were a responsibility, not human persons with thoughts and feelings. Our parents talked about us in third person—about "da kits" or *das Kind*. Daddy said, "*Das Kind guckt krank aus*" (The child looks sick), instead of asking me how I felt.

Both parents seemed distant, inaccessible authorities, and no other adults were available for listening and talking to me as a person—no grandparent, aunt or uncle, no teacher or family friend. We called our father "Daddy" because that is what Mama called him with us, but we only heard him and talked about him. We didn't exchange words with him. I could talk comfortably with Celia, only three years older, and with Evie, but Evie didn't count because she and I were "da kits." Today I realize that Arnold, eight years older, was paying attention to family dynamics.

One time, Celia came home from a dance on a cold winter night and climbed into the bed we shared. I let her come close to my warm body and drink in my warmth. We were like spoons in a drawer. Sweetly I exchanged my warmth for her enfolding touch—balm for our touch-deprived lives. When I grew older and was at a dance, a young man, a neighbor who had a bit to drink, put his arm around my waist in a jolly gesture that didn't mean much to him. To me it brought that same wonderful feeling of being held. I wanted it to go on and on.

I wondered why older siblings got only socks and such for Christmas, when Evie and I got toys. We grew up both ignored and spoiled, oblivious of the favors given us "kits"—extravagance at Christmas, oldest sister Alverna arranging my natural curls into locks every morning, older brothers driving us places. I am still discovering ways this played out. Years after Verna died, her husband, Leroy, revealed that before they got married she had to come home once a week from St. Cloud, where she worked, to do the family wash because I was away in boarding school. I should have been taking my turn as oldest girl at home.

As I rake my memory for times alone with Daddy, I come up with hardly any. In one, I am walking behind him on the forty acres, a separate parcel of land that tagged along when he bought "the other farm." It's Sunday. I know this because Daddy's not hard at work, just surveying his property. From older siblings, I've heard it has Indian burial mounds. This excites me. I recall no one else being with Daddy then and I'd like to think I asked to go along because I wanted to see them. I didn't see any, and they held no special interest for Daddy. I'm guessing he wanted to see what crop he could grow on the little piece of land not covered by mounds.

In another memory, I am walking behind Daddy in the St. Cloud Gamble's store and he tells me to stop walking behind him. He hasn't been talking to me and he doesn't hold my hand. How can I walk beside him when I don't know where he's headed? Uncomfortably I do my best.

Direct communication in our family was rare, as unacknowledged feelings were repressed. I became an actor pretending not to have feelings. I'm guessing I was eight or nine when the following happened. I had been away from home for a day. The next morning Celia pointed out tire tracks in our farmyard made by someone other than Dad or older brother, rare enough on our farm to be noticed. Celia pretended she didn't want me to ask who made them, and I pretended not to be curious. She broke down and told me. All I remember about this is our avoidance of straight talk.

We did have the security of family heritage. Mama talked about her family and Daddy's family, anchoring us in German-American stability. But that came later. In my earliest memories Mama pays little attention to me. *She doesn't know me.* When she grew more attentive after the earliest years, I refused her love. Not until after she died did I learn how she unintentionally marked me with emotional insecurity when I was a baby.

Today older siblings tell me that Mama had real conversations with them. Verna said she was a communicator, and Al said he had good talks with her. But he described the prevailing attitude: "Children didn't have feelings, serious thoughts, or rights." I add that adults did not talk about their own feelings either, although daily we saw them painfully displayed.

In my twenties, I attended a wedding at which the groom shed tears while hugging his friends. I was confused. What was he crying about? The simple welling up of feelings too powerful for verbal expression was unfamiliar to me, but an intuitive glimmer of understanding rose in me. My future husband confirmed it. "He's not crying for sad. He's crying for happy." I knew about crying for happy. When my oldest siblings started earning money, they bought Mama a vacuum cleaner. As everyone watched her unwrapping it, I left the room because I was embarrassed by my tears.

Dawning Consciousness

I can recapture the feeling of sitting at table and wanting to contribute to the conversation but knowing my words might trigger condescending laughter. I wanted the power of words. I minded not being one who could receive or make a comment instead of one who would be talked *about*. I think being one of "da kits" motivated me to become a writer.

We had no bikes or pets, although some of us made pets of dogs and cats. I liked to sit in the barn, letting a passel of kittens sleep on my lap. They would do this much too long for comfort, but I endured the pain in my legs. One time I fed the dog a pan of table-leavings and returned to the house with a kitty in the pan. Its crusted-shut eye had drawn my pity. Mama shrieked and ordered it out of the house—no animals in the house was the rule.

My brothers and sisters knew I liked cats and cats liked me. The year before I started school I favored a pretty white kitty. One morning, I thought older siblings had left with Daddy for the daily drive to school and creamery, milk cans in the back of the blue Dodge pickup. They came back into the house. "You have to come and hold Kitty. She keeps following us."

"No," I didn't feel like interrupting my breakfast—*Leberwurst* with syrup, delicious.

They kept urging, "Hold Kitty so we don't drive over her." I refused their appeals. After breakfast I went outside to look and saw her beautiful, white, mangled body. It was awful. How could I be so stubborn? My first experience with guilt, leaving me with regret that hangs on to this day.

Because Mama had been forced to miss school and do what she considered man's work, she resisted letting her girls do farm work. Generally, she succeeded. Oldest daughter Verna she claimed for housework and, because the youngest three of her eight living children were daughters, she could indulge her wish to treat us as girls and not farm hands. Our four older brothers did the farm work, and we washed dishes—no big deal. I enjoyed singing as we worked, sometimes harmonizing in three-part rounds.

One advantage of being a "kit" was having free time, but occasionally we two youngest had to do noon chores during threshing time. It meant lugging feed and heavy pails of water out to the young chicks in the pasture. One on each side of a pail, we lifted and carried it as far as we could, before letting it down to rest. Slowly, with stops and starts, we got the water out there.

Another challenge was collecting eggs, because some hens resented it and pecked at the hand reaching for eggs under them. I held the heads of menacing hens with a corncob before snatching their eggs. I liked being given responsibility. I also liked to entertain and provoke a response. One time we greeted the car of workers coming home for lunch and I reported that we got the noon chores done except for gathering eggs in the top row of cubicles. Two aunts in the car exchanged a glance. I savored their amusement, had even hoped for it. Entertaining an audience was a way to assuage my feeling of inadequacy.

There were times I envied girl schoolmates who worked in fields and barns. I admired them but would have been worthless at that kind of work. Dad persuaded Mama to let Celia drive tractor for threshing and haymaking, and she could do it. But when he tried me at it, I drove over a fencepost. He gave up. Evie, also inept at farm work, laughs that after she drove a car into a ditch, Daddy mumbled, *"Hab' nett gemeint dasz du so dumm wärst"* (Didn't think you were so dumb).

Cleaning was Verna's constant task. If she rested from it, Verna complained years later, Mama would say, *"Tu dei' Arbeit"* (Do your work). I'm sure Mama heard this from her parents. When I became the oldest girl at home on the farm, I was washing the floor one day in our dining/sewing/television/music/family room, a room used for everything and full of everything. Verna arrived from St. Cloud, saw I was cutting corners by washing only traffic areas, and let me know it was not acceptable.

Despite this, after Verna left home I became the cleaner because I didn't want to be caught with an embarrassing house if "company" came. A 4-H club meeting was scheduled at our house on a day our grade school had no classes. Celia came home from high school expecting to scrub floors and get rid of clutter. She found the house looking presentable already—floors scrubbed and little heavy work left for her. I took pride in her pleased surprise. When Verna got married, her wedding reception took place on our farm. I was the oldest girl at home. Loving the responsibility of making house and yard look attractive, I painted rooms in the house, cleaned the attic, pulled brush out of "the bush" and burned it in huge fires.

Emotionally distant from parents and siblings, I separated from my surroundings. No one available to hear me, I had no words for thoughts or feelings, but wordless questions and emotions seethed in me. My inward-looking personality put up a phony front to hide my secret inadequacy. I escaped into daydreaming, designing scenes where my unacceptable self could shine. I sought approval where I could get it, by being a good girl and being smart. School provided a place where I could excel. In school I stopped calling my mother "Mama."

Recess was my least favorite time. That's when bold children ruled, those who were good at playing ball and fearless in clambering on playground equipment. I dreaded recess. I didn't know how to play like other kids. On a visit to relatives one day, my cousin gamely tried to find something I could play. Nothing worked. I couldn't roller skate, ride bike, or play her kind of games. She gave up and guiltily told me she was going to play with her friends. I was ashamed but also relieved that she gave up. She and other girls seemed better than me in every way except school-smarts. They were normal; I wasn't.

Little traffic flowed on the dirt road that passed our farm in the 1950s. The isolation honed my contemplative tendency. As a sickly child, I had long swatches of time alone, letting my thoughts play out in awake-dreaming time. Besides daydreaming wishfully, I developed powers of observation and analysis. I still luxuriate in solitary times when I can find my true thoughts and feelings, which often I do not know until I get some distance from an incident.

As a child I always had my nose in a book if I could find one, at times preferring that to playing games with siblings. My parents could not see the point of my incessant reading. They thought I should do something productive with my time. So Mom came up with something useful—embroidery. I didn't like it and never became good at it but still have a dish towel I embroidered. Summers were book droughts. Free of school, I had time but nothing to read. I prowled through magazines in the house, read cereal boxes, anything I could find. *Readers Digest* was good. I loved the vocabulary quizzes.

One summer I found a rich trove of magazines in the attic; some even had short stories! Treasure! I combed every single one for stories, and some articles also interested me. To this day, reading replaces travel as a means of learning about unfamiliar places and people. Through reading I learned about the Holocaust before it became well known by the American public. It made me sensitive for a lifetime to torture and extreme deprivation. It may have helped to orient me toward hardship. Because others suffered horribly, it didn't seem right to want good fortune for myself. Stories of making do with almost nothing still affect me deeply.

Reading and my zealous cleaning saved me some anguish at puberty. My first experience with menstruation was short and light—just staining in the panties. I wondered what it was but didn't tell anyone and didn't worry much. I already knew cold water takes care of blood stains. One day, while cleaning out the top shelves of the broom cabinet, I came upon a pamphlet explaining menstruation. It could not have happened more providentially. When I got a real case of menstrual flow along with cramps, Celia observed my body language and started to educate me. I could say, "I know what it is." She told me where Mom kept the rags to put in our panties.

It was not reading but kittens that gave me the best education about birth. My parents brought us along when they went visiting. We had to find playmates or entertain ourselves, giving me more practice in keeping my mind occupied without external stimuli. On one visit, an older daughter invited all kids to the hayloft of the barn. There, a mother cat was giving birth. She continued her labor while her privileged audience watched, as kitten after kitten emerged. *So that's how it happens!* This newfound knowledge was not wasted on me. I applied it to other farm animals and then to humans, grateful for this sex education decades before the term "sex education" entered my vocabulary.

Music

In my youth, songs were always playing in me and I was always singing. My musical ear heard melody, pitch, and harmony at an early age. As a pre-schooler one day I was walking along in our farmyard, singing to myself, when I came up to an older cousin who smiled at my singing. Abruptly I stopped in embarrassment. This self-consciousness around "company" faded as I grew older and my family paraded me as a singer. In retrospect, I realize childhood singing accounts for my lifetime comfort in front of an audience.

I loved singing in the children's choir at Christmastime, but off-key singing by peers hurt my ears. At times, the children's choir sank down as much as a half note below the key played on the organ. One time, indignant, I persisted in singing the right pitch, loudly. Organist Henry Haehn winced in pain at the dissonance. I quit, knowing that what I'd done was worse than a whole choir singing flat in unison.

I sang with Verna when she played the guitar. More memorable was singing at dances with the Harmony Knights, a band of my four brothers led by Arnold. At the age of sixteen, he transposed music for the instruments of the band. He had not gone to high school but taught himself by observing key relationships while playing in the St. Martin Band. Arnold conceived and named the Harmony Knights, built and painted music stands that folded up, led rehearsals, and did all announcing when the Harmony Knights played at events. Other young men joined rehearsals in our house. We "kits" went to bed and fell asleep while the house was rocking with the music of the band.

Youngest brother Victor was the drummer. He remembers "the day it all started, when Dad came home from an auction with a piano." After that came home-study courses in reading music. Dad was tight with money, but besides the piano our family had an accordion, woodwind and brass instruments, and a set of drums. When my older siblings were children, Dad bought them children's flutes, harmonicas, a ukulele, a xylophone, drums, and a little piano. Victor remembers Dad playing the accordion some evenings. "He couldn't play but he went on playing anyway."

When I was nine or ten, Arnold used to call me onto the stage to sing with the band. These were wedding and shower dances, community gatherings at which children might be present. I sang some songs alone and Arnold harmonized with me in "Blue Skirt Walz" and "Mocking-bird Hill." I imagine a little girl singing in her brothers' band must have charmed adults, but it did not raise my status with schoolmates.

In school I was bullied. Not until writing this memoir did I figure out the reason it happened and its effect on me. The bully must have seen me singing at dances and envied me. She was a cousin. At home my sisters asked why I wasn't standing straight. "Stop stooping. Stop rounding your shoulders." Today I attribute to singing with the Harmony Knights followed by school bullying for my lifelong ease in front of an audience—where I'm safe—contrasting with my lifelong insecurity in social situations—where I'm not safe from a female rival.

As adults, every member of our family continued playing musical instruments, or singing, or both. When Arnold became Fr. Al, he got a degree in music, played many instruments, led choirs, and wrote musical compositions besides ministering spiritually.

Christmas

Our German-Catholic culture blossomed most profusely at Christmas, the season German immigrants taught Americans how to celebrate. German devotion to St. Nicholas came to America by way of the Dutch *Sinterklaas*, which derives from St. Nicholas and became "Santa Claus." For us, the Christmas season began with the feast of St. Nicholas on December 6. In the evening on December 5, we put plates on the table for each of us, and in the morning every plate had a pile of candy, nuts, maybe an orange or apple.

During the weeks before Christmas Day, we prayed to *Christkind-chen* (Christ Child). In our family *he* brought the gifts, not Santa Claus. Instead of letters to Santa, we prayed to *Christkindchen*. A classmate in school slyly told me that Santas in town were fake, showing me the dictionary entry for Santa Claus. I wondered how he could ever have believed Santa was real. Our family miracle was much more believable, and it was wrong not to believe miracles.

But that dictionary entry raised my suspicion. I noticed older siblings getting fewer toys at Christmas. Arnold kept adjusting tree decorations, and I knew that he, not *Christkindchen*, created the outdoor crèche on our front steps. The facts became obvious, but I played along so as not to spoil the fun for the family.

Christkindchen brought the presents, decorated the tree and house, baked and decorated the cut-out cookies, enough one year to last nearly 'til Easter. All appeared at one time—on Christmas Eve. What a job, not only to do it but to keep it secret! Tree and goodies were kept in the "front room," which was closed and unused all year except for company.

From Christmas Day through early January was visiting time. That's when parties happened, not before Christmas. A lunch with newly made sausage finished the evening, usually midnight or later. We went along to parties and slept in the car on the way home. In the 1950s it was still possible to hear Christmas music on the radio after Christmas Day. I miss that. We celebrated Christmas through most of January, reveling in the music in church and at home. *Stille Nacht* was a staple. As an adult, I still enjoy singing traditional Christmas songs, although the words imagining God to be a set of male gods annoy me.

In Church

Church pervaded our lives. At Mass, the priest faced away from us in the sanctuary, which rose a few steps higher than the rest of the church. We watched Father Cyril's back while he moved his arms and hands in ceremonial positions and recited prayers in Latin. Boys vested in cassock and surplice served Mass. Standing or kneeling on steps behind and lower than the priest, they answered his Latin prayers with memorized Latin responses. They got to ring bells at the Consecration to dramatize moments when the priest raised host and chalice.

Usually Father Cyril stood at the center of the altar, but he had to read the epistle on the right side and gospel on the left. Priest and servers bowed or genuflected every time they passed the center of the altar where the tabernacle held the consecrated Eucharist. Moving the Lectionary from side to side was the job of a server. He had to be strong enough to carry the heavy book with its holder down the steps, genuflect, and carry it up the steps to the other side. I held my breath when a little altar boy teetered down the steps carrying the load nearly as big as himself.

The show was performed by an all-male cast upon the stage of the sanctuary for us silent spectators in the congregation. Women and girls stood, knelt, or sat on the left side of the church, men and boys on the right, youngest children in front, then teenagers, then adults in back. I never questioned gender roles when I was growing up. But a college class-mate said she was disappointed when she visited relatives in St. Martin. "I couldn't be with Uncle Matty in church," she complained. She said St. Martin's gender division reminded her of the gospel verse saying to those on Jesus' left: "Out of my sight you condemned, into the everlasting fire prepared for the devil and his angels" (Matt 25:41).

Women were allowed in the choir loft. The choir sang Latin Masses in four-part harmony accompanied by organist and director Henry Haehn. He was married to a first cousin of my father, and half of the choir were Blonigens. Haehn earned high status as the premier educator and musician in St. Martin for half a century. He had taught in the school and, when we children were growing up, he owned a store with a children's library. My brother Jerry happily borrowed books from that library and said of Henry Haehn, "He was the town."

Besides Sunday and holy day Masses, there were Benedictions, Lenten Stations of the Cross, First Fridays novenas, and processions in church and cemetery. Processions included incense and men carrying canopies that identified their *Vereinen* or parish societies. In the cemetery were tiny chapels with altars at each of the four corners where the priest stopped the procession to lead prayers.

Corpus Christi brought the only females who ever marched in processions, little girls in white strewing flowers. It was a big deal. If lilacs were not in bloom for the Corpus Christi procession, it was hard to fill the basket with flowers. German communities in Minnesota called the feast *Blumenstreuen* (strewing blooms).

First Friday novenas sent us to confession and communion. These were pre-Vatican II days, when scrupulosity was rampant. It bloomed riotously in me, imbued with the puritanism of Grandma Blonigen and the aunts. On the morning before receiving communion, we had to fast. And that presented a problem when I had a cough at bedtime. I could get to sleep if I tucked a cough drop into the side of my mouth and let it dissolve as I dropped off.

But what if some of it did not dissolve before midnight? That would violate my fast for First Friday communion! I went to the communion rail anyway because I didn't want to stick out among schoolmates in this public school that acted like a Catholic school. Fortunately, Father Cyril had his priorities straight. When I confessed this, he dismissed my worry about breaking communion fast and gave me a little sermon about choking on a cough drop. I wasn't worried about that.

Another time, I'd gone to confession and was ready for communion. While reading a book, I came upon a picture of women wearing dresses that revealed a tiny bit of cleavage. Naturally my eye fell on the damned spots. Quickly I turned the page because I didn't want to look at them. But I agonized. Had I committed a mortal sin? Would I compound the wrong by receiving communion? If I didn't, everyone would notice. Not summoning the courage to be conspicuous, I lined up with the rest at the communion railing, and I don't remember feeling guilty afterward. Maybe common sense rescued me.

Summer Sundays in church posed another problem. I have difficulty standing for long. The air being close and hot in summer, I grew faint during long standing periods. Sitting would relieve my problem instantly, but I didn't want to call attention to myself by sitting before the Mass rubric directed the congregation to kneel or sit down. Kneeling would have been fine because it let me lean on the pew in front. Holding out long as I could, I hoped positions would change before I fainted and became conspicuous. There were times when the scene around me grew black, like a photograph negative. Always I got relief just in time.

At home we played church, mimicking the only theater we knew, beginning with priest and servers processing out of the sacristy with the tinkling of a bell. There were moments in the Mass when Father Cyril turned around to face us, majestically opened his arms wide, and proclaimed, "*Dominus vobiscum!*" (The Lord be with you). In play I made the motions and said cleverly, "*Dominus, wo bist du?*" (Lord, where are you?) It's the part I remember best because it was naughty, but I don't recall it wracking me with guilt. My soul was saturated with prudish talk, but sacrilege was a relative stranger.

Lent was big in those days. We always gave up candy because there was nothing else we could think of to give up. Doing without was normal. Sometimes I forgot it was Lent and ate candy that came my way because getting it was so rare. I liked Stations of the Cross better than Mass because we got to move positions frequently—standing, kneeling, or sitting—and the plaintive song we sang at stations appealed to me. I can still hear the melody that conveyed deep sadness, a feeling familiar to me.

Before we became a parochial school, we had a few weeks of religious summer school. A group of us on the playground broke into one of the songs we had just learned to impress a teacher happening by. She listened intently, looking at each of us in turn. Later I figured out what she was looking for. Which voice was clearly singing the melody in the muddled cacophony of children's voices? Pride in incidents like this didn't help me feel socially acceptable with peers.

Priests' sermons meant nothing to me, Mass was boring, prayers were rote and meaningless, litanies tedious, but I can't say I hated church. Why? I don't have an answer. Our grade school was close to the parish church. During recess I sometimes had the urge to go into church just to be there for a while, especially during Lent. I never did it, lacking the strength to be different from my peers. I still love churches. Every church pulls me at least a little.

Father Cyril was sure I was destined to be a nun. He tried planting in me this desire and expectation by teasing, "Have you decided what name you'll take?" I liked his attention and took it seriously. What made him so sure I would fit in a convent? Did he intuit an inner trait, my fascination with the inner realm? Later I learned he knew of Arnold's wish to be a priest. For whatever reason, Father Cyril thought I belonged in a convent.

Religion was the only spiritual avenue available when I was a child. Drawn to something exalted, I used the religious terms given me to express my faith—the Christian Catholic brand. But I do not remember praying to Jesus when I was little. I sought closeness to God but not to Jesus, knowing in a vague way that the something we call God is infinitely greater. In a nonverbal, inchoate way I understood God to be infinitely beyond human beings.

Out of this childhood mysticism came the knowledge that references to God as "He" did not mean God was more masculine than feminine. While knowing nothing about pronouns then, I might have preferred "It" to "Him" or "Her." A child's question like, "Does God have a wife?" or "Where is Lady God," did not occur to me. Such questions would have seemed to be jokes, not questions seriously begging answers. It would take many years of living before I would realize the harm in male-centered language.

Seeking spiritual depth as I grew older, I was told to achieve it by developing a personal relationship with Jesus. I tried but could not do it. Jesus was a man, and I was looking for infinity/divinity/sublimity—something higher than humanity, although I could not have put words to it. So began my dislike of worshipping Jesus. It would evolve into recognition of religious indoctrination.

On the radio was "The Greatest Story Ever Told," a program telling stories that ended with Jesus speaking and inspiring the crowd. In this radio series, he always said the Beatitudes. The words had little meaning for me, but their utterance did. I waited for the moment and thrilled when Jesus' sacred presence produced the powerful effect on listeners. Such moments when the inner world breaks into physical reality still thrill me, but they are not confined to the Christian context.

Warm Memories

As a child I knew I could never live on a farm for the rest of my life, but today I remember the farm of my childhood with fondness. In strange surroundings, the smell of newly mown alfalfa can throw me into ecstasy that mystifies people around me. Nostalgically, I recall the flowers Mom nurtured, the garden with a long row of rhubarb, the glorious lilac, the granary with its "rooms" for grains on the second floor, "the bush" where we played as children and where gigantic boulders at the bottom of a rock pile intrigued me, and the barn. When cows were out to pasture, it still held kittens and a bull. His massive head threatened only when he thrust it out to feed on the newly cut grass we put into his trough.

We had a wind-charger for electricity. It stood next to the silo and had to be secured every evening or when a storm threatened. Power from the wind-charger depended on weather—wind—but too much would bring down the charger. It supplied electricity for us when other farms yet had none, but by the time wind took it down, most farms around us had gotten electricity through REA, Rural Electrical Association.

Close to the edge of the grove we called "the bush" was the *Beckhaus* or outhouse, a two-seater with a little hole for little ones. It was not used much after we got indoor plumbing in my early childhood. The first times I climbed up to use the big hole I was afraid of falling in. Sears Roebuck and Montgomery Ward's catalogs lay alongside the holes. Everyone hoped soft pages in the back would be left when they sat there.

As an adult, I looked up the word *Beckhaus* but couldn't find it in any German-English dictionary. I found colloquial terms for outhouse and learned that *Becken* means pelvis, but no dictionary had *Beckhaus*. Then I checked with German immigrants and experts in the language—they'd never heard it. Then I asked people who grew up in this county, and they said, "*Ja*, that's what we called it," but they didn't know more than that.

I got a new idea when visiting my elderly neighbor. Lee Schmid did not speak German as a child because his Irish mother wouldn't allow it. But he learned enough to sell goods for his dad's and grandpa's lumber company. He thought the word was "backhouse." Was that it? Now I know it was, another instance of two languages merging into confusion.

I recall summer weekends that culminated in the Sunday roast chicken dinner. On Saturday we watched headless chickens dance on the grass after Arnold chopped off their heads. Then we helped pluck their feathers, loosened by dips of the carcasses into hot water. We watched as Arnold skillfully cut open the carcasses and pulled out the guts, saving the edible parts and flinging the intestines to the ground where cats swarmed in anticipation of devouring the mess.

When I grew older, I had the job of assembling the food grinder and fastening it onto the seat of a kitchen chair. Kneeling on the floor, I stuffed hearts, kidneys, livers, gizzards, celery, onion, and bread into the grinder with one hand, while turning the handle with the other. This was for the stuffing, which would be mixed with bread crumbs Mom had been saving. The bird's vital organs—nutritious meat—supplied the foundation of the stuffing. Nothing like it is available today, either in food value or taste.

Mom coated the meat, including the neck (no piece was more fun to chew on), with flour and spices, then fried it. She placed the fried pieces around the outside of a large roaster, filled the middle with stuffing, and placed the roaster in the oven. When it was done—when all the flavors had sufficient time to mingle—she scooped up the excess chicken fat and discarded that but used the yummy juices to make gravy.

Mom's roast chicken resembled the ravishing chicken prepared for church fundraisers in Stearns County. They served hundreds and required hours of preparation by men and women. Such free labor became rare as people got jobs outside the home, which is the reason Stearns County chicken at church festivals became obsolete. St. Martin's Parish may be the last in the county to succumb to this sad fact of twenty-first-century life.

One unforgettable piece of my childhood was winter sausage-making. *Die Mädchen* supplied a pig. And Brown Swiss cows no longer good "milkers" were butchered for beef. I don't associate guns with my father because he did not go hunting. Only recently did it occur to me that he must have had a firearm to kill the bull, pig, or cow. I have a vague early-childhood image of a carcass hanging close to the barn, but later Dad had the butchering done by others.

Mom rendered the lard and mixed meats for sausage. The first stage—Mom patiently scraping out the contents of pig intestines—revolted us. Long she labored, with many fresh bowls of clean water, to scrape the intestines and transform them into casings. The next stage was mixing ground-up meat and spices in a washtub. I can still see my dad kneeling on the floor, mixing it with his hands and tasting to see what spices were needed.

What had begun in filth ended in glory. *Die Wurstmaschine*, that mysterious, wonderful apparatus, reigned on our kitchen table in majestic splendor to perform its little miracles. As Dad fed the machine and turned the handle, older siblings jockeyed for position to turn the long sausages as they emerged from the spout. My favorite sausage was *Leberwurst*, which we ate at breakfast with syrup. This was nothing like what Americans calls liverwurst—ours was much more delicious. Another meat delicacy produced by my parents was dried beef, and again, beef jerky is nothing like it. What we ate was cured in the smokehouse and melt-in-your-mouth tender.

We did not live on a well-traveled road. Some summer evenings were so quiet we could hear cars on the county road half a mile away. Sitting on the front steps (hardly ever used), I heard a neighbor singing as he worked a field on his tractor. I watched another neighbor in a field across the road pound in fence posts, noting that I could see his post pounder landing before I heard the thud. Most startling and gratifying, a hummingbird appeared and darted among flowers just a few feet away, my first sighting of this natural wonder.

There was time to think, to contemplate—mindless physical work provided opportunities for that. Using the freedom to explore, I found places on the farm high enough to let me look down on familiar buildings and spaces from a new perspective. This fascinated me, a stranger to skyscrapers. High up in the haybarn was an opening for the rope and pulley used to pull in loads of hay. Once, when the piles of hay were high enough, I stood on top of the hay, peered out of the opening, and looked down over the farmyard. Familiar things from an unfamiliar perspective—new, high, and broad. A perspective that presaged my love today of reaching for the new, the broadest way to see things.

Another spot allowed this. The square attic on top of our square house was accessed by a staircase and, above the staircase, a ladder with comfortable steps reached up to a trapdoor in the roof. It beckoned me. When I got the courage to climb that ladder so that I could touch the rooftop, I could see two stories beneath me to the bottom of the attic stairs. Two times, only two, I unlatched the trap door in the center of the roof and pushed it aside. Climbing more steps to peer over our rooftop, I was rewarded by the sight of blue hills in the distance. Marvelous! I did not tell anyone. They would have warned me away from doing it. When an adult, I figured out that the blue hills were north of Richmond, toward Avon, my future home.

Each of the four bedrooms on the second story of our square house had two windows looking out in two different directions, except the room I shared with Celia. It had a door that opened to the roof over our back porch. On moonlit nights I sat there and surveyed our farm in the ethereal light of the moon, another unfamiliar perspective. It was peaceful, mysterious, and intriguing.

4

___

High School

Arnold

ARNOLD STARVED HIMSELF BEFORE he turned twenty and turned into a handsome young man. In about four months, his weight dropped from 245 pounds to 175 pounds. Two family photos on top of my dresser tell the story. One taken earlier shows Arnold fat and older brother Adelbert a handsome young man beside him. In a photo five years later, slim Arnold stands out in back, taller and more impressive than Adelbert. In this second photo, brother Gerald, only a year-and-a-half younger than Arnold, wears the same suit that fit Arnold in the photo taken five years earlier.

Besides slimming down, Arnold developed a magnetic personality. He was popular in Stearns County as a band leader. Soon Verna's friend Linda became his girlfriend. Rumors of marriage circulated, a possibility with romantic appeal to us kids. One Sunday afternoon, Linda drove into our farmyard, astonishing everyone. Arnold went to the car looking stunned, serious, and scared. They had a long talk, after which he came back into the house and went upstairs without saying anything. She drove off. Later we learned he had broken up with her, but not the reason for it.

After Arnold had become Father Al, he related a life-directing incident that must have happened before I was born. The family was at Grandma Blonigen's and so was Leni Blonigen, a priest's housekeeper and cousin of the aunts, outspoken, widely known, and respected. She singled

Arnold out from the other kids, saying, "He will be a priest." The prediction became a beacon calling him to the priesthood. But at the age other young men in the parish entered the seminary, Dad didn't let him go to high school, much less enter a seminary. He insisted Arnold was needed on the farm. While attending the ordination of another young man in our parish, Arnold heard an inner voice saying, "Someday you will be kneeling there before the bishop." The voice, he wrote, was "so pronounced that I actually looked around to see where it came from."

When Linda drove to our farm, she was responding to a letter Arnold had written to her, explaining why he could not marry her, including that he was considering the priesthood. She wanted to get married and came to plead with him. In *Discovering My Inner Child*, Al relates his anguish when he could no longer avoid the question of whether he was really in love or just enjoyed being popular as a band leader and feeling normal by having a girlfriend.

> I decided that if I were to marry now I would be trapped into being a farmer for the rest of my life. . . . To marry this girl at this time would be for me converting a temporary prison sentence into a life sentence. . . . What was so frightening to me was that I didn't want to hurt her. (62)

To solve his dilemma and determine his life course, he decided to use the draft notice he had recently been sent. The army would draft him unless he joined another branch of the service. To avoid the draft, he would join the Air Force, requiring a longer term but offering skills unrelated to farming.

In the evening after breaking up with Linda, he announced to Mom and Dad his decision to join the Air Force. Both thought it foolish. Arnold was twenty, not old enough to leave without his parents' permission. Crestfallen that not even Mom supported his idea of joining the Air Force, he angrily accused Dad of objecting to everything he wanted to do. "If I would want to go to the seminary now, would you let me go?" He had not planned the question. It came, he wrote, "spontaneously . . . out of my unconscious."

Dad surprised him by saying, "Yes." He even would pay for it. Arnold was ecstatic.

> I could hardly believe that I had heard correctly. My mother had a peaceful smile on her face now. . . . She was the one who had

kept alive in me the vocation to the priesthood. . . . Suddenly I
felt as if a tremendous load was lifted off my shoulders.

Arnold joined the Mariannhill Mission Society, a German religious
order of men that he'd read about in their *Leaves* magazine. He dreamed
of being a missionary in Africa. Mariannhill had only two houses in
North America, one in Dearborn, Michigan, the other in Sherbrooke, a
city near Detroit in Canada's Quebec province.

When this conversation in the kitchen happened, I was there, only
twelve years old, but I felt the electricity. Al's account of those fateful days
in his life reminds me of how small my world was then, but already I
knew that I did not want to live on a farm for the rest of my life. Immediate surroundings did not bind my imagination.

In years to come, Arnold's visits home to Minnesota would become
windows to the world beyond. He studied in Germany and visited famous places in Europe that I learned about in my high school art class.
He had experiences to tell about, photos and films to show. When he
came back from Germany he projected an unfamiliar aura, and his German was different. Jerry asked him a question, and spontaneously out of
Al's mouth came *Nein* instead of "No." It sounded so much better than
our Stearns County German.

From Public to Parochial

Our public grade school became a parochial school in time for my seventh grade. This was put to a vote in a parish meeting. Dad approved of
it. I surmise he read in *Der Wanderer* that stricter separation of church
and state was coming and increased the need for parochial schools. Rose
and Veronica (called "Froni") usually represented *die Mädchen* in public
gatherings because they were the youngest and could drive. Like other
parishioners they didn't see the need to pay for a Catholic school—it was
Catholic already. The vote was so close that their two votes changed from
No to Yes would have tied it. Dad told his sisters they should have voted
for it. Few parishioners attended that meeting, and later Father Cyril's
push for a parochial school brought the parish around.

Before, Benedictine Sisters had taught us religion on Saturdays
and in summer school. Now, they were the only teachers we had. Sister
Bethany, the principal and teacher of seventh and eighth grades, won the
respect and affection of the parish. In December she told us, "If you don't

know yet who gives presents at Christmas, it's time you learn." Then she told us to ask our parents for a Mass missal so that she could teach us how to attend Mass. I was glad I'd figured out the secret of Christmas.

At home it was awkward. I had to reveal my lack of belief in *Christkindchen*, knowing Mom would be disappointed. When I reported Sister Bethany's order to buy me a Mass missal for Christmas, Mom shushed me quickly, afraid Evelyn would overhear. I hoped Mom had heard the order despite her fear that the Christmas secret was out. The missal arrived, and Evie went on believing.

Bethany was an excellent teacher. Vigorously she taught religion as if to make up for lack of it during previous grades. One thing she said did not seem right. She said our religion is the one true faith that everyone must accept. What about people in the world who never heard things our religion teaches? In China, for instance? I'm pleased this thought occurred to me then, but I didn't voice it, lacking clarity to put it into words.

Another memory hints of theological questioning. We were taught at what point in the gospels Jesus instituted each of the seven sacraments. I disappointed Sister by not knowing the answer to the test question, "When did Jesus institute Ordination?" I should have answered, "At the Last Supper." Quite a stretch, it seemed to me, to claim this is when Jesus established the priesthood. In later years, I learned it was a pre-Vatican II argument to support the Catholic position that there are seven sacraments. Martin Luther said the only sacraments instituted by Christ are Baptism and Eucharist. Other Protestants followed Luther in this.

Bethany had a goal in mind with her energetic teaching of religion. In my eighth grade, she entered me and a male classmate in a diocesan catechetical contest sponsored by the Knights of Columbus. I remember nothing about the contest except one of the KCs afterward shaking hands with Daddy and telling him he should congratulate me on my performance. With an awkward laugh my father shook my hand and said, "Congratulations." I was as embarrassed as he.

In school the next week, Sister kept asking me if I got a card in the mail giving the result of the contest. No, I hadn't, and why did she keep asking? Finally, she sent me to the village post office. Our farm was on a rural Paynesville route, but in the St. Martin post office was the card she wanted, telling me I'd won. As Sister was announcing it to the class, I felt a stirring inside me, a strange knowing that some power was directing my life, an inner thread pulling me to where I needed to go. The prize was a scholarship to a Catholic high school.

I wonder how my parents felt about this. It must have made them proud—especially Mom—but I'm guessing Dad was not entirely happy. Despite Mom's pleas, he had not even allowed my four oldest siblings to attend public high school, keeping them home to work on the farm. Born in 1902, Dad was certain that his children needed no more education than he did—eight grades. Because he did well, didn't he? That finally changed when the principal of Paynesville High School drove to our farm and explained that state law required attendance until age sixteen. By that time it was too late for my four oldest siblings, but Victor and Celia attended Paynesville High School.

Now I, one of "da kits," had a scholarship to attend a Catholic school. Dad let me go to St. Benedict's High School and even let Evie follow me—more astonishing. But after two years she was pulled out and finished in Paynesville. Why my dad let me stay at St. Ben's for four years is still a mystery. I strongly suspect he did not pay the cost of that schooling after the scholarship and work-study money ran out. I suspect the Sisters and my mother talked him into letting me stay. It was two years after Arnold entered the seminary. Had that broken new ground in Daddy's mind?

Convent High School

I entered St. Benedict's High School in 1957, when the most educated women in our world belonged to religious orders. The school had been opened to girls not intending to become nuns only the year before. Father Cyril must have assumed that his expectation for me was now being fulfilled. Was that in my parents' minds too? I don't know how or when I knew that the convent was not for me. After leaving Father Cyril's influence, I really didn't think about it, even though I now lived in a convent school.

We were in a four-story building with dormitories on the top two floors. They held four dorm rooms, each holding eight girls, and a porch on the top floors held six more. White curtains on a track created separate alcoves at night. My alcove on the top floor was closest to the St. Joseph parish church. The knell of its bell sounding each quarter hour accompanied my sleep and dreams, pleasantly. Besides a bed, every student had a dresser with a wash basin, a chair, and a locker in the hall outside. The bathroom with its toilet stalls, a few more sinks, and three tubs but no showers, served forty girls plus a prefect. Upper classes roomed on the third floor.

Mass attendance on Sunday was required and strongly encouraged on weekdays. In my dorm, Liz Weber, a St. Martin girl who had four sisters in the convent, went to Mass every morning. The clanging of her wash basin brought grumbling from our dormmate Ginny about "the one-man band" waking her in the morning.

The first two floors had schoolrooms, library, offices, locker rooms, music rooms, and community room. The basement had a laundry room with pay machines, but I used a scrub board to wash clothes, not having any money to spend. I must have taken laundry home, too. For my work-study job, I was one of three girls assigned to clean the large community room in the basement where all-school events were held. We didn't meet Sister Carmita's standard and got scolded. I was not used to cleaning a clean room. On the farm, cleaning resulted in a satisfying difference between before and after.

Also in the basement was a room that opened to a tunnel that led to St. Walburg's, where senior Sisters lived, including Sister Prudentia. She was our lovable and unforgettable Latin teacher, a teensy, tiny nun with a teensy high voice. In Latin class, S. Prudentia said it's best not to make your bed first thing after you get up. She insisted it's better to let it air awhile. Our infirmary was on the side of the building facing St. Walburg's. One day in class, S. Prudentia disapproved of the "sick" girls she saw braiding the curtains.

The high school facility was tiny and inadequate, even by standards of the time. For our three meals, we walked outside past the chapel—a grand edifice with a dome—and into the basement of the college building. We walked to a different building for art class on top of a garage, and to biology class in a former laundry building. I did not mind any of the living arrangements—it was a world apart from the farm I wanted to escape. Institutional rules and food did not disagree with me. Since then, I feel comfortable inside every convent I enter.

After school we got time to play, a sweet or salty treat if it was not Lent, and time to carry out work-study assignments. After that we had a supervised study hall and another one after supper. Study halls required us to sit in a room on second floor and be quiet in assigned desks—no talking or whispering. Every day ended with Compline, the Church's night prayer recited together in the dorm hall.

In fall, we had a picnic in St. Benedict's woods, Maple leaves on trees above and ground below enthralled me. Our farm sat on the plains, south of St. Martin, which sits on the boundary separating Minnesota's woodland from the plains. I had never seen maples blooming in autumnal splendor.

When parents were invited for certain events, I was ashamed of mine—a meanness that shames me now—but I always was eager to go home when it came time for that. As the summer before senior year matured and a new school year approached, we got a letter at the farm giving us a later starting date, because a new high school was being built. Then another letter giving a still later date. School finally began on September 25. Making up missed schooldays on Saturdays went on for months. My high school class was the first to use a new, unattached residence building and to graduate from a new school building.

Our dorms still held eight girls but were roomier, and the school facility was large and lovely, complete with chemistry lab, several music rooms, and a real stage plus auditorium. Before, we'd had to use the St. Joseph Grade School's stage. Performances in the auditorium could be viewed from the floor above, where a fireplace lounge was served from a small kitchen nearby. We still had to walk to the college building for meals, farther away now, past the grotto, past the monastery and St. Joseph cemeteries, and past the pond, but our new school felt luxurious.

St. Ben's gave me a good education. I most appreciate the foundation in literacy given us by Latin, which we studied our first three years. It helped to make S. Prudentia unforgettable and showed how proficiency in more than one language eases the learning of other languages. My classmates groaned over Latin, but my background had prepared me with clues to how language works. Changes in word order, inflections, and phrasing were no strangers to me, and they assumed satisfying clarity in Latin class. More than monolinguists, I appreciate geniuses who master multiple languages.

We were not taught to use Latin as a language, only to read and understand it. This didn't satisfy me. I played with composing sentences in Latin but can remember only one to tease my sister: *Evelina porcus est.* Knowing it was mean, I never actually said it to her, but privately I could entertain myself by substituting names of people in the sentence.

Junior year we got a new English teacher. Sister Judine liked to direct plays, which added new zest to school life. Plays provided a way to pretend I was someone else, and they didn't require the same amount of breath control as singing. I joined every play activity S. Judine directed, although I didn't get the roles I wanted. In the play *Murder in a Nunnery*, I aspired to be the prioress but had to play an elderly murderer, a role much harder to play, but I did not stop wanting to be prioress.

Solo singing was no longer the effortless thing it had been with the Harmony Knights. Self-consciousness spoiled it, but singing in choirs and small groups remained an important ingredient in my life through high school, college, and after college.

Lifelong leanings were forecast in high school. The occasional column I wrote for the school paper focused on content I found in *Time*, *Newsweek*, and *U.S. News and World Report*. A teacher flattered me by saying I was going to be another Pauline Frederick, a well-known journalist at the time.

My predilection for teaching showed up. When a classmate asked for help with English grammar, I enjoyed making it clear for her. I was asked to teach my Latin class when Prudentia became sick, because this parochial school did not pay substitute teachers. Teaching Latin was immensely satisfying.

Later, Sister Idamarie asked me to teach geometry. I'm not good at math. Numbers "fly in and out of my head," to quote Carl Sandburg, but geometry required little work with numbers. I thought of it as basically logic, which I can handle. Because I think in words and logic, numbers revealing comparisons, as in percentages, mean more to me. The evening before I was to teach, S. Idamarie taught me the lesson and the next day I taught it visually—the way I grasped it best. One student told me she got it better after I taught it than when Sister was teaching—probably someone with a brain more like mine and Carl Sandburg's.

Calculations—picky work with numbers, what an accountant does—invite vexing mistakes besides being tedious. My preference in math applies to other subjects. I prefer the overarching flow of an issue to the details. Not the nuts and bolts, but the broad implications interest me. I hated Algebra II and struggled in that class. Our teacher made us do calculations with a slide rule for no reason I could see. Other math calculations were no fun, but at least I could see their logic. Years later, the new math entered schools with the aim of teaching math understanding instead of memorizing and following formulas, but we were stuck with meaningless formulas.

Idamarie knew I aspired to be a teacher. "Your struggles with higher algebra will make you a good teacher."

"I could never teach this stuff!" I said, bewildered. That's not what she meant. She told me I could now understand students struggling to learn something. A revelation: to teach, I not only have to know the content to be taught, I need to see the content through the students' eyes. It was a valuable lesson for a future educator.

I flopped in sports and physical education, no good at physical games and not interested. Observing my lack of attention during the basketball unit, Sister Annerose assigned me the role of referee for a while—an excellent move, I admit as a later supervisor of student teachers. She was forcing me to pay attention. I failed miserably. In retrospect, I speculate that Annerose saw the irony in my reputation of being smart.

One day a Sister came to me with an urgent message. She had found Evelyn sobbing disconsolately and Evie refused to tell her why. Sister evidently wanted me to do something. I didn't see anything I could do. Evie didn't want to tell me either.

As an adult, Evie told me she'd been rejected by a classmate. I had a parallel experience. Feeling socially unacceptable, I clung to anyone who would let me. I got into the habit of going to the room of a friend every morning and together we'd go to breakfast. One morning I arrived, and she had left without me. It stunned me, but I knew the reason. She felt stifled. I learned a lesson and we continued to be friends.

At one point, the high school administration conceived the bright idea of teaching us table manners, evidently thinking we missed something by going through a cafeteria line and eating off trays. On the feast of the Epiphany we got out of school uniforms and dressed up—this was before women and girls started wearing pants. Sitting down at tables in a college dining room, we learned proper table setting and use of tableware. Waitresses brought dishes of food that we had to politely pass around.

The school recognized another element missing in our experience—boys. For me it was the only disadvantage of being at St. Benedict's. There were mixers that must have been forgettable, as I don't remember a single one. More memorable were the boys Judine borrowed from a local high school for our plays. I certainly was interested in boys but didn't know how to be social with them. Summers between school years included hardly any contact with boys. My older brothers didn't want me tagging along to dances in case they wanted to take a girl home after the dance.

Marilyn, the schoolmate from St. Martin, was attending public high school and told me a secret. "If you want boys to notice you in a crowd, stare at them for a while. They'll always turn around and look at you."

Her honesty shocked me. I wasn't admitting even to myself that I wanted boys to notice me.

There was a prom. A classmate tells me today that we could invite someone both junior and senior years, but I screwed up the courage for only the senior prom, determined to meet that challenge. But whom to ask? Guys I would have liked to ask might turn me down. It was too risky. I asked John Kolb, my almost-brother who played sax in our family band. I figured he would be more likely to accept if I lined up a girl to go with my real brother Jerry. It was a relief when all three agreed and even seemed happy to do it.

Afterward, Sister Norbert Ann asked, "Was your brother at the prom?" She didn't really ask; she knew. How? We don't look alike at all. She agreed that there's no physical resemblance. She just knew we came from the same family.

St. Ben's was where I belonged, but it did not cure my feelings of emotional insecurity and social inadequacy. Grade school bullying had left its mark. I enjoyed the learning part of high school but being smart and talented did not erase my feeling during playtimes that I was not normal. To make myself acceptable, I pretended to like certain rock-n-roll groups like the Beatles and other teeny-bopper idols. Now I know that the only unacceptable thing was my feeling that way.

As I reflect on schooldays today, I see my penchant for living in my head, with its disdain for physical skills and predilection for abstractions. I pay more attention to ideas than to concrete objects and events happening around me. Gadgets tend to flummox and intimidate me. Shopping is a burdensome chore, whereas a lot of women love shopping. I mind being different but wouldn't want to stop thinking about large issues, trends, and ideas. As I grew older, I found more women and men with my preferences. Maybe we didn't find each other earlier because we all were afraid to go against the grain.

I wish I could say I questioned religion in high school but that would not be true. I was a good Catholic girl from a parochial school, intent on conforming to Catholic doctrine. As a child whose farmer father had to get permission from a priest to work on Sunday, I did not shake the habit of getting permission from religious authority. I went to Father Jerome, our chaplain, to ask about a daring religious idea in a book. All I remember about his response is that he wasn't disturbed by it. His relaxed attitude surprised me, told me to be less doctrinaire.

I was a melancholic young person with periods of illness. Childhood scrupulosity traveled with me to high school, where I had spells of trying to be holy. Consistent with my training, I thought I should deny myself, sure that God would not want what I want. To please God, I should not desire honor and success. Suppressing natural impulses contributed to my depressive tendency.

One moment sticks in my memory. I was sitting in class severely downcast and wishing Teacher would notice. She ignored my signs. After this I heard the term "self-contempt" and applied it to myself, glad I'd found a word for it. But there was no one to listen to me and draw out more words to express what was inside me.

In the wider world of Catholicism, dissidence was little known. The Vatican warned American Catholics against applying to religion the principles of democracy and freedom. It wanted Catholics to believe what it wanted Catholics to believe. Pope Pius IX attacked progressive ideas in the middle of the nineteenth century, and Pope Leo XIII criticized progressive efforts in the United States in an 1899 encyclical. They effectively produced a Catholic ghetto mentality for half of the twentieth century. This mentality formed me. And gone was the earlier childhood mysticism.

Since then I've learned that under the placid surface of 1950s Catholicism raged vigorous debates. The fiercest in the United States were sparked by John Courtney Murray, an advocate of religious freedom and separation of church and state. Murray's religious freedom differed vastly from demands made by the religious right today. Some of them strike me less as calls for religious freedom than denying freedom of conscience to others. Murray's thought was condemned by the Vatican, although not officially. Later he was vindicated by Vatican II. Ecclesiastical flares between church authorities held no place in my awareness, but now I wonder whether any cinders drifted into the minds of certain high school teachers.

Die Mädchen

S. Judine's teaching of English meant less to me than her directing of declamation and plays. I was tall, but she gave me the role in *Room for One More* of an orphan taken in by a family. I understood perfectly my character's feeling of being unwanted. Knowing how to cry out feelings,

I gave the part all I had for the last performance. My parents surprised and pleased me by seeing the play that evening because in the afternoon they attended an agricultural meeting in the same building, the St. Joseph Grade School. Two *Mädchen*—Rose and Froni—came along.

The play required girls to wear prom dresses. Days later, Judine asked me about a written complaint sent to the school, disapproving of so much flesh showing on girls. I tried to allay Judine's concern. "They're very prudish. My family is always talking about that. They even send letters to the bishop complaining about low-cut wedding gowns." I was not going to let the aunts ruin my triumph in having played my part well. Judine never brought it up again.

My grade school mate Marilyn says that my fashion-police aunts were *the* old maids of St. Martin and girls were afraid of them. Red toenails or immodest dress would be *verboten* around them. Kids played pranks on them. They'd call the aunts' number and ask, "Can I talk to your husband, please?"

Marilyn was in a car full of teenagers who tipped over their mailbox. She crouched low in the back seat to avoid being recognized. It was dark; there was nothing for Marilyn to fear. But the next morning her dad reported with a frown of disapproval, "Last night people were tipping mailboxes again."

Die Mädchen listened in on party-line conversations. We said their own lives must have been boring. My family scorned their prudery, but I think it helped to form my scrupulosity. And I think their anti-body views exacerbated the absence of loving touch in our family. Mom complained that *die Luder* disapproved of kissing and caressing babies.

During threshing and haymaking, older brothers came home from working and eating at Grandma's with reports of religious opinions *die Mädchen* had. They disapproved of anything new in religion and would have been aghast had they learned of the later evolution in my religious views.

On the other hand, I also have pleasant remembrances of Grandma and the aunts. Regina, Monika, Agnes, Rose, and Froni were nice women. I learned to hate their views while liking them. They were family. They didn't give us Blonigen cousins, but we were closer to them than to our Fuchs aunts who gave us sixty cousins. As one of "da kits," I never had arguments with them and enjoyed being with them. I remember Evie and me being babysat there and expecting to be given a treat. When none was forthcoming, I screwed up the courage to ask for one and we got it.

Celia remembers walking home from school with our brothers and stopping at Grandma's farm for a drink from the outdoor pump. Occasionally, Grandma came out to offer them cookies. In fact, Celia said the hope of getting cookies motivated their stopping by the pump for a drink. It's not the Grandma I knew.

Celia enjoyed going there and watching Regina feed the hogs and chickens. She got permanents from one of the aunts. *Die Mädchen* sewed dresses for Verna and Celia. They gave us lettuce and apples from their huge garden. They made horseradish Daddy liked. They supplied flowers and arranged bouquets to decorate the church. They kept their house and farmyard neat, clean, and attractive. Rose, the second youngest, was energetic and full of opinions. By my calculation, Rose was still climbing a ladder in her late sixties to change storm windows on second-floor windows.

We had no phone on our farm in the earliest years of my childhood. Occasionally, messages for us were called to the aunts, which they passed on to us. I remember a winter storm before we got a phone. Rose walked a half mile through deep snow—the road was impassable by car—to deliver a message called to them because we had no phone. So dutiful were they.

By the time I came of age to have opinions, I had no occasion to argue with them. Their eccentric puritanism leaves me with mixed memories and feelings. They introduced me when young to the paradox of good people having harmful views. Despite their association with our family's heartache, I had affection for them.

My Mother

The year I graduated from high school, Mom reached sixty years of age, worn out from carrying a load of resentments, having ten children plus a miscarriage, and losing her first babies, Florian and Leroy. My summers between boarding school terms at St. Benedict's High School were spent at home. I was the oldest daughter in the house, listening to her grievances. She had to give up school and do the work of men on the farm. Her feet and legs hurt because she had to follow the plow in shoes too small. Her father imposed these hardships, but I never heard her voice resentment against him. She blamed her in-laws, *die Luder*.

On and on she whimpered, oblivious of consequences for her daughters. Distress, resentment, and hurt filled the house and me, but even in my distaste over her outpourings, I could not criticize a person so openly hurting. Following the model of older siblings, I felt sorry for Mama. I started emotionally parenting her when I was a child, her complaints a backdrop for my life. I disliked her victim mentality but learned to be a victim.

My earliest memory of a non-mother absorbed in her pain differs from recollections of older siblings, born before our uncle died of a brain tumor. Reconstructing our family life as an adult, I have concluded that Mama talked to Bert, Verna, and Arnold while they were growing up—not the case for us "kits." Al said all the older children received more loving attention as infants and youths than we did. I once said to Celia after she recounted a memory, "You had a different mother than I did."

During my high school years, I felt ashamed of Mom and ashamed of my shame. As an adult looking back, I am replacing my distaste with sorrow. I know Mom persuaded Dad to let me continue high school at St. Ben's. Jerry and Evie, the only siblings still home then, tell me that she bragged about me when I was away in boarding school. I hate hearing this, but in retrospect it looks right. I was living the life she had wanted. We didn't celebrate birthdays in our family, but she had a birthday party for me. I cringe as I realize her favoritism.

One time I came home from St. Benedict's High School to a house looking unusually clean and orderly. A beautiful plant was strategically placed to capture admiring attention from a person walking in, and Mom was finishing up sweeping. I exclaimed. "It looks so nice! Is someone coming?" A shrug of her shoulders told me she'd cleaned for me. I was speechless. I hope she read some gratitude in my astonished look of recognition at what she was doing.

My second-cousin Maryann Blonigen reminded me of a typical summer scene in St. Martin when we were kids. My mom and her mom visited animatedly after Mass for long stretches of time. They talked and talked, while both families sat waiting in cars. Cousin Maryann thought that our wait one time grew to a half hour. Where was Dad when this happened? Maybe in Rothstein Implement or Mondloch Hardware? Mary's recollection set me to thinking about topics of women when they confide in each other. I wonder if Mom vented about in-laws with another woman married to a Blonigen. Each must have been balm for the soul of the other.

Mom was an adult leader in our 4-H club. She was a gardener and conservationist, a tree planter, a woman who preferred working with plants to doing housework. With pleased surprise I noted that 4-H club members treated her with respect. It suggested there was something wrong with my feeling ashamed of her.

I think my passionate advocacy for justice came from Mom because she used to rail against "the middle man" or capitalists who exploit the labor of farmers. In my adult life, outrage is a familiar feeling. I am more affected by workers preyed on by Wall Street than by families suffering from earthquakes, floods, fire, or drought. Any type of injustice raises righteous anger in me. My model for this may be my mother.

I also recall her love of lore about the old days. While telling stories about the past, her face would light up and a fun-loving personality shone. One story appealed to me so much that I retold it in German for a graduate paper at the University of Minnesota. I cannot verify the details but tend to trust oral history from seniors. Mom heard it from her mother and recounted it when I interviewed her shortly before dementia confused her.

Her Grandpa and Grandma Weymann, our maternal great-grandparents, lived in Spring Hill in the 1860s, among the earliest pioneers in Stearns County. Grandma washed clothes in the spring and Grandpa, graciously and cautiously, let Indians take what they would. A full pail of water obtained from the spring in the evening might be empty the next morning. "You had to be good to them," Mother said.

For service in the Civil War, Grandpa Weymann received some wooded acres near St. Martin. Mother's storytelling ability shows:

> It was a nice morning, bright sun, no breeze, sunshine, and Grampa said to Gramma, "I think I'll go to the woods, because we don't have much wood on hand anymore."

Hitching the oxen to a wagon, he went to "make wood." The bright sunny day turned cloudy and a fierce northwest wind told Grandpa a blizzard was coming. Quickly as possible he loaded the logs he'd harvested, hitched up the oxen, and headed home, about seven miles away. He walked on the lee side of the load to escape the worst of the wind.

The oxen walked very slowly—he trusted them to find the way—and he had to keep encouraging them, but one time they stopped, and no amount of encouraging could prod them on. Checking on the problem, Grandpa discovered that discharge dripping from their noses had formed a continuous stream, reached the ground, and froze, stopping the oxen. He took the ax and hacked away the frozen stream fastening them to the ground.

> And then he wanted to start again, and they were so all in [exhausted], they couldn't anymore. He tried and he tried. They couldn't. Well, he waited a little while and he tried again, tried again . . . and then finally he got them started again, and they kept on going, and going and going, and ah going, and going and going, and he thought, "I wonder what's gonna happen."

> He never . . . he never expected that he would come alive home. Gramma, she never . . . she thought he is frozen to death someplace. And they were going, and it was pitch dark, and all a da sudden, Boom! "Now," he thought, "here we have to die." He went around the oxen in front. Was the house!

The oxen had found their way home.

During the four-day blizzard, Mother's grandpa had to leave the cabin a few times to chop wood from the logs the oxen hauled home. Without those they might have frozen to death. The oxen had to fend for themselves, although Grandpa anxiously waited for the storm to abate so that he could go to them.

> The third day he tried. He put a scarf around his mouth and he tried to go down to the barn. A few steps from the house, he just could not make it. Had to go back and wait another day. Four days and four nights. Then the next . . . after that the next morning he finally, finally could make it down there. It was still blowing pretty good yet.

> [laugh] The barn was made out of straw. The cows were standing up to the belly in snow, and they ate the straw. They were hungry from all that pulling wood. *Ja*, then they had the snow, too, for water.

The oxen survived by eating their own barn and eating snow for water. Reading my transcript today, I see Mother's dramatic flourish. She relished being a storyteller.

I now see depth in my mother that I could not see as a child. In my parents' bedroom, I saw devotional literature suggesting an interior life that probably resembled mine today, seeking respite from daily disquieting events. She often sat with spiritual reading of some type. Although her choice of readings bore little resemblance to mine, my orientation toward the spiritual world was instilled by her and Catholicism. I appreciate it.

5

COLLEGE

Essential

AFTER HIGH SCHOOL, LIFE without college was inconceivable, but so was the possibility of financing it. I matriculated at the College of St. Benedict during my senior year of high school anyway, without my father's permission. I can still see him looking down at me and informing me that he would not pay the difference between tuition and my scholarships plus on-campus jobs. He didn't say it in a cross way and I knew this was just. Having been allowed to stay in boarding high school after my oldest siblings were denied high school, I'd already gotten more than my siblings. But quitting college was not an option. It would have ended meaningful life for me.

Today my matriculating for college seems unbelievable. Where did that daring come from? My bold self didn't go so far as to consider college *any*where, only at St. Ben's, the campus that had become a home. I needed it for security. Attending college elsewhere never entered my mind.

In the early 1960s, the only post-college careers offered women at St. Ben's were teaching and social work. Not a problem because I was born to teach. In second grade I wanted to be a second-grade teacher, in third grade I wanted to be a third-grade teacher, and so on up the grades. Teaching elementary school had no appeal. I was interested in subjects for older minds. But which secondary major to choose? Many in the humanities interested me, although at that time I could not have used the term "humanities" to describe my area of interest. Social studies looked inviting, but English seemed to cover its content plus more. It became my major.

What about my minor? I loved being in plays and was good at acting. It brought positive attention I craved. So I chose speech and drama as my minor. While wrestling with a required class assignment in theater mechanics—all the technical stuff required to make a play happen—I realized I didn't give a hoot about it. The annoying theater class turned out to be a blessing. The only way to get out of it was to drop the minor and choose another immediately, with no time to decide. I was studying German for our language requirement, and it was easy. Switching to German, I was unaware of how it would enrich my life.

I didn't try out for many plays, although they had filled me with pleasure and excitement in high school. It puzzles me somewhat, but I recall not wanting to take time away from studies. Singing continued, however, so much that I was mistaken for a music major. My knowledge of music theory was extremely limited. All I could do was sing. The little bit of piano I'd taught myself on the farm using the home-study course bought for my brothers didn't amount to much. It helped me to read notes and musical notations during choir rehearsals, but I didn't progress in reading music because I lazily relied on my musical ear to learn songs.

To fulfill a science requirement, first-year students usually took biology. I'd had biology and chemistry in high school, where no physics was offered. To learn something new, I took physics, not knowing what I was getting into. No problem, I thought, because I'd been the valedictorian in high school.

I was directed to physical science, a requirement for science majors. The only first-year student in the small class, I was the only one not headed toward a science degree. It was hard. This challenged my assumption that mental ability differs only in being smart or less smart. Now I was beginning to see varied kinds of intelligence. Mine is not a scientific mind.

The class didn't help my grade point average, but I didn't regret taking it. Sister Pascal, the professor, encouraged me, and later she became my boss for a work-study contract. It was interesting work, much better than dusting furniture that didn't look dusty. Besides correcting objective parts of her students' tests, she had me typing science anomalies she found in science publications. They were fun, but at the time I couldn't see the point of gathering them. Now I do. They were great brain teasers for students.

Tired of maintaining a high grade point average during senior year, I rebelled, though with fleeting moments of regret. An English teacher I liked gave us a list of novels we could read as part of a class requirement. All we had to do was say we read certain novels to indicate which grade we expected. I'd performed well enough to earn the usual A if I read enough. As easy and pleasurable as that. I did not do it, didn't read the required amount and didn't lie to say I had. Why? I hope I'm correct in remembering that, besides just plain study fatigue, there was a measure of integrity in my impulse to stop working for a grade.

Refusing to let grades drive me also motivated my refusal to do what classmates did before finals—study late into the night. I'd kept up in classes because they were interesting, so that review the evening before went quickly. I wanted sleep and went to bed. My grades on those tests say I made much the wiser choice. In my various roles as an educator throughout life, I often passed on the lesson of this experience. I told my classes and later my student teachers to tell *their* classes that studying the morning before a test or cramming before a test has little worth. The way to retain knowledge is to review often and sleep on it. Sleep is the great cognitive aid.

To complete my English major, I started a creative writing class, for which I wrote a short story that was harder to write than academic papers. Titled "Wounds," the story displays my mixed feelings of sympathy and dislike for my mother. It shows her wounds becoming my wounds. Reading the story today brings pangs of pain like those triggered when I read parts of this memoir. I feel naked. Although the act of writing brought some satisfaction, I dropped the course and took another after telling the instructor honestly my reason for doing it. Creative writing required self-exposure, which brought pain.

Social Misfit

Illness dogged me in college as it did during the rest of life. My first bouts with laryngitis showed up, a condition that would afflict me for years. During one bout, a select group of nine to which I belonged—Campus Singers—were scheduled to sing on the public TV station in St. Paul. Despite everyone's worries, I was able to sing with them. During another bout, I had a small part in a play at St. John's. Other cast members warned the director that I couldn't talk, but during practice he put me on stage anyway. When I got on stage my voice worked. *My laryngitis must be psychological.* This suspicion did not help me to express myself in ordinary conversations.

Academic study gave me more pleasure and was easier than social life. Trying to fit in, I went to local joints where classmates met Johnnies, feeling unequal to them all, male and female. Without being aware of it, I weirdly separated classmates into those cool and those uncool like me. The ones from Stearns County intimidated me less than classmates who lived farther away. Strangeness gave them status in my eyes. When in later life these classmates complimented me on my writing, I was seized by cognitive dissonance and encouraged to change my self-image from social misfit to normal and acceptable.

Every time friends went to a so-called beerbust, I hesitated. I wanted to be normal, but beerbusts sounded unappealing. I always found something better to do. Another normal experience I missed was being "campused" for breaking a rule. I never broke curfew—11:00 p.m. on Fridays for first-year students. On Sunday evenings we had to be back from weekends in time to attend an educational convocation—hard for some classmates. But I looked forward to the presentations and nothing tempted me to break rules. Today my dissenting self finds amusement in my good-girl past.

My desire to be like everyone else took extreme form when I joined the sunbathing craze. Tanning was not allowed just anywhere. Students had to stay modestly away from male maintenance workers on campus by using the flat roof of the main building. Good tans were admired—tanning was the thing to do. Although I hated lying in the sun, I followed this crowd as another way to erase my background. But I could not tan, no matter how much time I sacrificed to it. Others could spend less time and get a nice tan. Blonds tanned more easily than I did. It was frustrating. What was the matter with me?

Determined to conquer the problem, I spent hours in the sun one day and broiled myself long as I could take the heat. Out of the sun, the pain arrived and grew worse in ensuing hours. My compassionate friend Gidge nursed me for days. Fortunately, my foolishness did not sprout skin cancer, but it may have contributed to my lifetime sun sensitivity. Or did this come from the Irish "recessive gene" identified by the professor's wife?

I didn't want classmates to know what kind of family I came from. I was different. My low self-evaluation made college men seem socially out of reach. A telling incident reveals more about this self-perception. We played characters in costume for an event with a historical theme. I did what I do well—played the part of a Roman wearing a toga. And surprised myself by attracting a Johnnie. It was easy. The difference was that in this scene I was not myself. Nothing came of this little exchange, but it stuck in my memory because of what it told me about myself.

Money for fun, even for things most would consider necessities, did not exist for me. I marveled at college students who spent money to eat somewhere besides the school cafeteria, which was covered by registration. Why would they spend money they didn't need to spend? And self-indulgence seemed wrong; our religion encouraged brave suffering. My Depression-age parents bred frugality in me. Even today, when I unwrap a stick of butter I carefully scrape off tiny spots of butter on the wrapping.

Jim

I emerged from school and farm life utterly inexperienced at relating with boys. Intense self-consciousness bound me during adolescence. There were few opportunities to go to dances in summer, and dances required mingling in an obvious search for partners. I wanted to pretend it wasn't important, afraid that no guy would want to dance with me. Having a boyfriend was not in my realm of possibilities. A college senior, a psychology major, briefly dated me but broke it off by telling me I was immature. I accepted his assessment because it matched mine. Why was I so insecure in boy-girl matters? My looks were good enough, and I was not a pariah. While writing this memoir, I am finding reasons.

After my first year in college I was fortunate to be given a summer job at the college. I and another student were even given a place to live in a house the college owned. She worked in the kitchen, and one of the workers there arranged a blind date for her with Jim. His friend Tom and I went along to make it a foursome. During the evening, it became obvious to all four of us that the spark was not between Jim and her but between Jim and me.

He lived in St. Cloud and started taking me to bars with music for dancing. In people's eyes I could see that we looked great when we danced together. I didn't feel inferior to him because he was not a college guy. A friend of his commented approvingly that I listened to him a lot. Jim's talk about his life in the Marines was interesting. It didn't occur to me to talk about myself or subjects I was learning about. We continued dating through my college years.

Having a boyfriend gave me a sort of security. Now I didn't have to join classmates at beerbusts and local joints to meet Johnnies. It was a relief. But Sister Pascal, my physical science teacher and work-study boss, had known the gang Jim ran with when she taught at Cathedral High School in St. Cloud. She didn't say much, but her tacit disapproval spoke a vague warning.

Jim attended a few events on campus with me. The Benedicta Arts Center was built during my college years, and the first events in the building were scheduled before all construction was finished. We planned to attend one in the little theater on the west side of the building. My unreliable memory tells me it was a musical performance on a Sunday evening. I checked with archivist Peggy Roske and she dug up items in a campus paper, but we never found a performance that matches both my memory and weather reports at the time. It doesn't matter. We performed our own drama.

The new arts center was built on land that used to be the Sisters' farm, and the parking lot west of it was an unpaved field some distance from residences on campus. It was a nice walk in nice weather, but that day it was raining relentlessly. Sister Pascal and my German teacher, Sister Margretta, were close friends and wanted to attend the performance. I offered them a ride in Jim's car.

As we approached the west side of the BAC, we met a small lake. Jim hesitated, then proceeded to drive through. We got hopelessly stuck. Water all around us and more coming down and, from Jim's point of view, three women depending on him to do something. He took off his shoes and socks, rolled up his pant legs, and waded out to get help, leaving me in the front seat and the Sisters in the back seat to wait and bemoan our situation. "Oh Sister!" said Margretta, leaning into Pascal's lap.

After what seemed an hour, Jim came back with his friend John, who had driven out from St. Cloud armed with galoshes for the Sisters to wade to John's car. Jim carried me out, which Margretta thought was romantic. We never saw any performance on stage. Our little drama had enough tragedy, suspense, and comedy.

By the time I got back to my room, I was laughing so hard I could hardly tell my roommates what happened. There is a photo taken the next day, of a nun wearing her habit sitting on a tractor chained to Jim's car. She looks back while she pulls his car out of the mud hole.

Evolving Belief

In college I gained some freedom to question Catholic authority. Women educated me in Catholic high school and college, by itself a challenge to the hierarchy. Most of our instructors were religious Sisters, but these Catholic Sisters did not fit the stereotypes of naïve piety and docile compliance. As a liberal arts college, St. Ben's exposed us to fine expressions of great thinkers from outside of our tradition.

Few high school or grade school moments had steered me away from accepting Catholic authority. College classes gave more reasons to veer from it. I cannot track my slide toward questioning the Catholic line, but learning history must have prepared the ground.

A favorite course was the Survey of Western Civilization taught by Sister Emmanuel. As we surveyed the history of the "Holy" Roman Empire and the religious Thirty Years' War, I saw the Vatican competing for power against political rivals. Supposedly holy men were cut down to human size as popes and princes of the Church vied for worldly power against each other and against secular princes. The Protestant Reformation was particularly engrossing. Luther's alleged words *"Hier stehe ich; ich kann nicht anders"* (Here I stand; I can do no other) spoke powerfully to me then and now, despite his cruel response to the Peasants Revolt. Luther encouraged oppressors of the peasants to "smite, slay, and stab" them, denying peasants the right of conscience he claimed for himself.

Literature classes introduced me to religious cultures radically different from my parochial upbringing. Through them I could look at my religion from the outside in. Their ways of imagining the invisible realm looked unfamiliar on the surface but had familiar themes. In Homer's narrative of the Trojan War, *The Iliad*, Lord Zeus is called "Father Zeus." He resembles the Bible's Lord and Father. Both encourage their favorites to kill enemies. The Lord of the Bible seems more bloodthirsty, though. He commands his people to exterminate entire tribes and cities, leaving none alive (examples in Exodus, Leviticus, Numbers, Deuteronomy, and Joshua).

I noticed that prayers of Odysseus, Achilles, and Hector to their gods and goddesses resemble prayers of Christians to Christian gods. While in college, however, I was far from having the courage to call Father, Son, and Holy Spirit "Christian gods," even to myself. I had no vocabulary to distinguish between Christian images and spiritual reality.

In my present adult life, a college classmate asked if I remember when I started thinking that Jesus is not God. This set me on the path of remembering. It began early in life. As a child, I sought closeness to God, never to Jesus, because I knew that God was infinitely greater than the man Jesus. This was not a clear thought; I simply did not pray to Jesus. As a voracious reader, I kept running into the figure of Jesus assuming a position that he did not have for me. Occasionally I felt vaguely inadequate for not relating with Jesus in the way Catholic literature told me I should.

The same friend told me that I declared in college, "God is not just a man!" It surprised me, then reminded me that in college I was annoyed that God-talk always refers to "Him." I did not dare confess my difficulty with the belief that Jesus is God because the Catholic climate around me would not tolerate it. I could say, "God is not just a man!" because it aligns with Christian theology and does not necessarily say anything about Jesus. The question of Jesus' divinity still lay buried, a muddle I didn't want to confront.

I wrote a poem after a snowfall dazzled me by transforming our lovely campus.

LAUDATE

How much
Whiteness of wet
New-falling snow can I
Bear, without crying for sheer joy?
Praise Him.

Although it was printed in our college literary magazine, the poem's end never satisfied me. In vain I had searched for a way to express gratitude without referring to God as a male. "Praise Him" had two syllables that *sounded* good and "Praise Her" would not be accepted by the people around me. No solution coming to mind, I reluctantly settled for "Praise Him." When compliments came I didn't mention my difficulty with it. Today I'd write simply, "Thank You."

In our senior year, Father Reinhold taught us theology and introduced us to historical-critical research coming from Bible scholars independent of Church authority. We had been taught that God did not dictate the Bible, but this went further. Using historical, archaeological, and textual clues, scholars showed that humans who produced the scriptures were shaped by human cultures. They composed in a variety of genres, using a variety of literary devices without intending to write accurate history or science. Much of the Bible contains myth, we learned.

These studies had the blessing of the Vatican. Years later I learned that German Lutherans had begun the research in the eighteenth century, but Vatican approval had not come until 1943. Now, even Catholic authority was acknowledging the presence of myth in the Bible, a provocative opening for me. I could ask commonsense questions about dogmatic claims. But I had not moved much past goody-two-shoes morality.

Family

During my high school and college years, my distance from the farm widened. Between school years in college, I got jobs, which reduced time on the farm and separated me further from family members still there—Jerry and Evie besides Mom and Dad now in their sixties. I did not think or care much about how life was evolving for them. A few years after I graduated, Evie entered the College of St. Benedict.

Dad had the reputation of being a successful farmer because he had bought another farm, even though he and his sons were already raising crops on two farms. I am sure he was a competent farmer, but he counted on free labor from his sons. Al wrote that Dad was inventive. The one example I noticed was something he rigged up in the barn to force cows into defecating where they were supposed to, in the gutter. When they humped their backs they dropped feces where it dirtied their udders as they lay down. Dad ran a thin wire across their backs to shock them out of humping their backs.

He wanted to leave farms for his sons, never questioning that they would be farmers. In this he was badly mistaken. Only Jerry continued farming, and he said it was just that farming was all he learned to do. Being one of the older siblings, he was not allowed to go to high school, and unlike my other brothers, he had not escaped farming by joining one of the services. I think his real aptitude was intellectual work, which he applied to farming. He, Dad, and *die Mädchen* joined the National Farmers Organization. Jerry did research, wrote articles, gave presentations, and held national office in the NFO. Many years later he wrote a book arguing that the too-low parity price set for farm commodities caused the demise of family farms.

During my college years, Arnold was on a journey that had echoes of my own. He and I didn't communicate much while I was in college and he was in seminary, but his book, *Discovering My Inner Child*, discloses the painful course of his preparations for the priesthood. Wanting to become holy, he read about saints who stressed extreme self-denial—Adolphe Tanquerey, Teresa of Avila, John of the Cross, and Aloysius, the saint whose name he chose as his religious name. "Aloysius" also was the name of our father's brother whose death from brain cancer wrought such havoc in our family. St. Aloysius wore a rough rope close to his skin. By imitating such models, Arnold reinforced precisely the pattern from which he needed release.

Returning to the farm for a summer vacation, Arnold dove back into heavy farm work to assuage his guilt for costing money as a seminarian. His muscle tone had deteriorated, but he lifted the combine to hitch it to the tractor. This badly wrenched his back. Mother and Father urged him to go to a chiropractor, but he refused. In his book he explained,

> I had developed a strange method of punishing others by hurting myself. It was most likely a way of projecting guilt unto them. (81)

He continued doing farm work and returned to the seminary wracked with excruciating pain compounded by shame and the fear of admitting to superiors that he needed relief.

Finally, he could not avoid telling Father Rector and came under the care of a doctor. But trying to become holy interfered with Arnold's recovery.

> I felt at times special to God. . . . The severe penances were for me the means of earning God's love. My adult child projected the same attitude toward God as I had learned to behave with my father, earning his approval by achieving.
>
> In meditating on the sufferings of Jesus and imitating them I could more easily identify with him. . . . With the most intense fervor I could muster, I gave myself to Christ and offered all my pain. I even asked him to give me more suffering. (83)

He would get what he asked for.

Years of torture from back pain and treatments dogged him. Persistent headaches developed from imitating a saint who tried to think of God at every moment of every day. Stopping the practice put an end to his headaches. At another point he experienced dizziness and blackouts in class, suffering feelings of guilt, shame, and unworthiness to be a priest. His body was manifesting suppressed and unresolved rage and resentment at his father for keeping him tethered to the farm.

He joined in recreation times, he wrote, "as a matter of obedience." Only duty took him away from his goal of becoming a saint. If he inadvertently experienced pleasure, he felt guilty because fun is bad and every moment should be spent in serious work.

> At home I had lost the ability to be playful. My father had always frowned upon having fun. . . . I regarded play as an imperfection, not proper for a saint. (84)

Not surprisingly, Arnold sank into depression. Feeling unworthy of joining Mariannhill, he told Father Rector that he'd decided to leave, but he could not come up with a suitable reason for leaving.

Although our spiritual journeys evolved along parallel lines, Al never indicated in talks or writing that the exclusively male God-image of Christianity gave him difficulty, despite his anger at our father for keeping him on the farm so long and Mother supporting his desire to be a priest. Arnold never questioned the belief that Jesus is God. I do not think being male was the reason. Arnold did not think philosophically, although he excelled in psychological understanding.

I see his relationship with our human father as a metaphor for humanity relating to the Christian Lord-Father. Arnold felt trapped by Dad's "dream of his empire with his four sons all farming with him." In *Discovering My Inner Child*, he wrote that, although seminary physically separated him from the farm, he still was tied to the farm psychologically. In the seminary, he explained, he continued to hear his father's voice. Driven to meet expectations, he was afraid his superiors would say he hadn't done it right. He knew he needed to shed the image of God as a dictator in charge, a lawgiver like our father and Grandma Thekla. His solution was Jesus.

> It was easier to identify with Jesus as a personal God, rather than Father. The distance I experienced with my own father made it difficult to experience closeness to God as Father. (83)

Finally, Arnold decided that Mariannhill would have to accept him because he had tried so hard to be a good member of the community.

I had, after all, earned that. To be accepted for simply being myself was not part of life's experience for me. (84)

One outlet for expressing his creativity came in the form of directing
plays, but his greatest solace came from music. This he allowed himself,
I think, because our father had given permission to indulge that love on
the farm. Daddy had bought instruments, supported the family band, and
even hired a music teacher for Arnold on the farm. When Arnold faced
two months of having to lie hospitalized after back surgery, he brought
along his supply of classical music tapes, granting him a healing respite.

After a year in the novitiate, he became a professed member of
Mariannhill and received his religious name, Aloysius. He was slated
to continue studies in Germany. Before leaving for Montreal, where he
would board the ship to Germany with two confreres, he came home for
a last visit. On the farm he couldn't sleep in the "boys' room" because his
back brace required him to sleep in the spare room. He wrote that it made
him feel like a stranger in his old home. We were uncomfortable calling
him by a new name, so we didn't say any name at all, which added to his
discomfort. He told us to call him "Arnold." To this day, in our family
talk we still refer to him as Arnold. When I developed relationships with
friends of his in Michigan, I developed the habit of using his new name,
"Al."

Music was the great and abiding love of Al's life. My respect for
and then love of classical music was nurtured by him. His musical gift
found expression in Würzburg, Germany, as choir director and soon-to-
become chief organist, if that is, he stayed in Germany. He chose instead
to continue studies at St. Meinrad, Indiana, for two reasons. One was
language. If he stayed in Germany to complete his studies, he wondered
whether he would be able to preach and teach smoothly in America or
in South Africa, where Mariannhill had missions and English was an official language. German had been his conversational language for more
years than English. He had worked on the farm until he was twenty. By
comparison, I left the farm at age thirteen.

Al might have stayed in Europe, though, if a confrere had not given
him a powerful reason to return to the States. His friend told him about
a spiritual director at St. Meinrad, an extraordinarily compassionate and
insightful counselor. Arnold hoped this person would lift him out of the
depression caused by his overachieving, over-performing personality.
That indeed would happen. But first, more pain.

During the summer before his first semester at St. Meinrad, he nearly drowned in a swimming accident. Fortunately, a companion who was a good swimmer noticed he was missing, found him on the bottom of the lake, and brought him to the surface. Together he and a fellow seminarian lifted Al onto a raft. Coughing up water from his lungs, Al regained consciousness. He was hauled back to the house in a tractor and trailer, "feeling guilty all the way to the house," he wrote. Despite wearing a back brace, he endured pain so severe that it interfered with his studies. Al begged his doctor to consider surgery, which was granted. This is when he spent two months in the hospital with his precious musical tapes.

The emotional pain caused by childhood experiences continued during his four years at St. Meinrad, but there he grew in the ability to release patterns of feeling and thought learned in the first twenty years of his life. His spiritual director recognized Al's hidden anger at Dad for keeping him on the farm and gave him permission to feel it. Al had been suppressing anger and confessing it as a "sin." His director asked, "Where were you born and raised?"

"Central Minnesota, around St. Cloud."

"No wonder!" The director had conducted retreats in this area for priests, religious Brothers, and Sisters who manifested similar hang-ups.

By the time of his ordination, Al had grown in self-esteem and stopped doubting that he was worthy of the priesthood. He was freed of false guilt, resentment, and anger at our father, who, Al now believed, was proud of him like the rest of our family.

We celebrated with St. Martin's Parish on the day of his first Mass, an event momentous for our whole family. Our Arnold was a priest! Years later, Al apologized to me for that time. Why? He was ordained the day after I graduated from college, depriving me of my moment of glory. I hadn't seen it that way at all.

6

AFTER COLLEGE

Place in Society

AFTER COLLEGE I EASILY got a teaching position because teachers were in demand then. I am profoundly grateful as I observe the bleak expectations of today's college students. A position opened in Albany, close to my farm home and St. Ben's. My college methods teacher, the one who prepared us to teach English, had held this very position before she became a professor at St. Ben's. I surmise that her recommendation made it the only teaching position for which I had to apply.

The summer after graduation, my college friends toured Europe. Would I join them? I had college loans to pay back, and family training in austerity made it impossible for me to join them. I have often thought with regret about that trip I should have taken. What an opportunity gone by! I ought to have borrowed the money—worries be damned. My college loans for four years amounted to less than students today owe after a single semester. In just a few years I paid back the NDEA (National Defense Education Act) loan the financial services office had helped me to get, paid it so quickly that I got a letter commending me for it. Apparently, swift repayment of such a loan was rare.

I had the job. That was in place. Now, to finish building a safe and respectable identity I moved toward marriage. I had to persuade a reluctant Jim, who had not yet found a line of work that suited him. He had come home from military service in the Marine Corps, but not with training typical of Marine service. After boot camp, Jim played trumpet in the Marine Corps Band for Eisenhower's Goodwill Tours. He got a beautifully smooth sound out of his trumpet. This promotional piece describes the tours:

> Ambassadors of Good Will supporting Eisenhower's People to People Program, displaying music and precision marching, this small group of marines attained a performance schedule unheard of in the annals of military music.

The Goodwill tours made Jim a world traveler, but they had not prepared him for life.

He needed a skill that would make a living, which school and the Marine Corps had not provided. After his year in kindergarten, his teacher told Jim's mom that he should repeat kindergarten because he was not ready for first grade. He was the youngest member of his class and not ready to focus on cognitive skills. He wanted to play (and needed to). But his mom considered the suggestion shameful and sent him on to first grade. Guys like him were passed from grade to grade during the 1950s without mastering the academic content. By automatic grade promotion they barely squeezed through high school graduation and went to work in construction, trades, or other kinds of manual labor.

Jim was a slight man with an artistic temperament not suited to heavy physical work, though his artistry was not apparent to me during our first years together. While we dated, he worked at a variety of jobs, none leading to a stable occupation or career. He knew he was not ready for marriage although he was turning twenty-six. I didn't care, I didn't think, I just wanted to get hitched, driven by insecurity.

To get more distance from the farm, I pushed to have our wedding take place in Jim's St. Cloud parish instead of St. Martin. My parents cannot have felt good about it, although they would move off the farm in a few years to that very parish in St. Cloud. In retrospect, I see the tremendous stresses on Mother. She was nearly sixty-four when I graduated in June and Al was ordained. One of my brothers married in September, another in November, and we married in December. And she was preparing to leave the farm. How heedless I was!

But the wedding a few days after Christmas was joyful, bridesmaids and flower girl wearing red with white muffs to carry out the winter theme. I still like looking at photos to see how young and beautiful we all looked, including our parents. How sweet the flower girl and ring bearer!

How sweet the positive attention from relatives and friends closest to Jim and me! We both enjoyed it.

On our wedding night, a brief thought flitted through my mind. I had committed to spending alone time with this man for the rest of my life and wondered if I had made a mistake. This was not about sex; the intimacy I yearned for was mutual understanding. Not ready for regret, however, I shoved the thought to the back of my mind. After we married, Jim behaved like the single man he had been, going out alone night after night. I was occupying myself with teaching, reading, and deluding myself.

My dissatisfying marriage went onto a shelf, because teaching satisfied me. Legally married to Jim, I was emotionally married to teaching. It challenged me, but I enjoyed leading classes and relating with students and staff. The teaching position I'd landed in perfectly fitted my abilities, let me feel accomplished and attractive. The invisible thread continued to guide me, but I was not ready to deal with emotional issues.

After Mother and Father retired to a house in St. Cloud, Dad drove to "the other farm" near Paynesville to fix up the old house for renters there. The house in St. Cloud was tiny, and he needed to keep busy, although he was close to seventy years old. City life was not right for either Dad or Mom. After a few years he began to build a new house for themselves near the old house for renters. When it was finished, they returned to their rural roots. The brief years they spent in St. Cloud were strangely simultaneous with the brief years Jim and I lived there. I often visited them.

Recognizing my own disquiet, I turned to pop psychology books. They told me to be honest with parents. My zeal to do that resulted in a conversation I remember with acute shame. Seeking to confront my demons, I unwisely thought it would mend something to confront Mother and Father. I went to their house and tried to express my dissatisfaction with their parenting. It was awful. The only detail I remember is saying something about not being loved.

"Luff?" asked Dad in bewilderment. Mature reflection later in life tells me their love was shown in sacrifice instead of words or physical affection.

Teaching

Years after I'd left the faculty at Albany, I met another former teacher in a grocery store. "You were *so young*," he said. People would come into my classroom and ask, "Where's the teacher?" I look back on those years aware of my immaturity then. In those early years of teaching, however, I had the perspicacity to observe a bias in education. The school counselor stressed vocational studies to prepare students for jobs. Coming from my liberal arts education, I told him we should teach students not just how to make a living, but also how to live.

I still think so. Reflecting on my years right after college, I consider this observation of mine an example of something in myself. My IQ or intellectual maturity was high, my EQ or emotional intelligence not so high. I was a good thinker, but socially insecure and immature.

In 1965, colleges and universities were starting to require for admission two years of a world language in high school. My minor in German gave me the credentials to teach it besides teaching English. No world languages were being taught at Albany High School before I came, and German was appropriate for that thoroughly German culture.

My childhood experience of learning English motivated me to do more than was usually done in high school language classes. Sister Margretta had taught us a method that linguists were promoting. Variously called the audio-lingual, oral-aural, or structured approach, it taught the target language by having students repeat patterns of its structure. Instead of learning *about* the language, they were speaking and writing it. Drawing from my own experience of learning English, I set out to get students communicating in German. If they were motivated, we achieved gratifying results.

Occasionally students came into my class already able to speak words and phrases in German. Other students had the language living in their bones from hearing parents speak it. Many said their parents spoke German when they didn't want their children to hear. But one of my star pupils had only Irish-American roots. Former students who traveled to Germany tell me how well they could handle the language there.

To teach German culture, I focused on history. Using *The Rise and Fall of the Third Reich*, by William L. Shirer, I tried to find in events before the Holocaust the reasons for it. At one point a student complained that we spent too much time on history, and I realized he was right. I had been following my own quest for knowledge and my love of history, not planning the course as seen from the students' eyes. Responding to his appeal, I stopped devoting as much time to German history.

When I made the acquaintance of native Germans in our area, I invited them to speak to my classes. Among the native speakers was Ilse, who had lived through World War II. Her older brother died in Russia. Her mother sought safety for herself and her little Ilse by moving out of Berlin to the country. Ilse tried to entertain her severely depressed mother by turning cartwheels. I pushed Ilse to talk about her war experience in front of my class, although she resisted. It gave her great pain. I'm afraid my persistence was insensitive. However, it may have prevented students from blaming all German people for the atrocities of Nazism, a tendency I observed in America during the 1960s, even among students steeped in German culture.

I also invited as a speaker my brother Al, home for a visit. An experienced entertainer familiar with both Stearns County and postwar Germany, he delighted my classes as an engaging speaker. He got them laughing.

Most German culture in my classroom came in the form of singing German songs. The students seemed to enjoy it as much as I did. After school one day, the school band leader came into my room and asked me to direct the school choir. I declined, saying I could not read music well enough and couldn't play piano. He said the piano playing was no problem; someone else could accompany the choir. I felt sorry that he had total responsibility for all music instruction in the school, but I didn't give in to his pleas, knowing that my singing did not make me capable of directing a choir. I could not relieve him.

During my early years of teaching I did not fully appreciate the difficulty of learning for students very different from myself. I did well in school because schools catered to my intellectual type. I taught the same way I had learned—appealing to verbal, left-brain skills. It left out mechanical and technical genius, artistic genius, entrepreneurial skills, and students who need hands-on experience, not just readings and presentations by a teacher. In my private life, I soon learned that a man (usually it *was* a man) who could not understand a simple paragraph could excel in mechanical ability. The handyman geniuses who help me with house and yard today might have struggled as much in my English and German classes as I do around machines.

My teaching contract included directing declamation and a class play. The first play I directed was *Room for One More*, the play that introduced me to drama in high school. Later I directed *Pygmalion*, and my sister-in-law helped me to spruce up our play by giving me the script of its Broadway adaptation, *My Fair Lady*, because she had been the fair lady in her high school musical. I added a few scenes from it to our production. In ours, the fair lady wore my wedding dress, adjusted and bedangled for the grand scene at the ball. I wondered, *Does this mean I don't value my marriage?*

I was good at interpretation but challenged by another aspect of theater. The part about directing that tested me most had propelled me out of a drama minor in college, the technical aspect—lights, props, set, and so on. For one play, a fellow teacher took pity on me and commanded her son to serve as my technician. Somehow, I muddled through the technical elements for plays I had to direct.

To interpret literature for my English classes, I used my acting ability to unlock the meaning, feeling, and passion in the words by reading them aloud. I always insisted students look at the book, not at me, because I wanted them to see the connection between oral speech and written word so that they could learn to interpret written words by themselves. It would also improve their spelling and writing mechanics. One time several students looked up to see if I was crying. After finishing the poem, I quickly changed my face and manner to let them know I had been acting.

Some poems would have been impenetrable if students had not heard them interpreted orally. The power of short stories, novels, and Shakespeare was enhanced when students heard the written word interpreted. I wish now that I had given in to students begging me to read aloud more prose works because it would have increased their understanding and reading ability. I felt guilty doing it because my students and I enjoyed it so much and it was making their job of learning too easy. This seems crazy to me now, but such was my damaged attitude.

I had favorite classes and favorite students. I believe any teacher who does not admit to it is lying. With self-awareness and self-discipline, I believe a teacher can manage with fairness students both agreeable and disagreeable. In one of my favorite classes, college-prep composition, a favorite student won my fondness when he dissolved in helpless laughter as I read examples of sentences that misstate the intended message, such as, "I am forwarding my marriage certificate and my six children one died which was baptized on a half sheet of paper."

This student observed that I put up with student misbehavior for a long time before finally putting a firm stop to it. His astute observation would come to mind years later when I saw myself enduring unacceptable conditions in my personal circumstances. I waited too long before finally making a change.

During a poetry unit, one of my students told me that she loved listening to Simon and Garfunkel because their songs were really poetry. I listened, agreed, and bought an album of theirs. Listening to it repeatedly, I caught the lyrics and typed them, then brought them with my album to school. The mimeographed lyrics in front of them, students and I listened to Paul Simon's poetry in music. I still enjoy hearing Simon and Garfunkel songs, and I still have the vinyl LP record.

Expanding Awareness

I taught for five and a half years before our first child arrived. How should I fill my summers? No yard work filled my days because we were renting. Doing volunteer work never entered my mind. Consistent with my mind-set of deprivation, I thought I should earn more money, but how? I tried being a Fuller Brush man. Really. It ended with a whimper, not a bang. After talking to my first prospective customers—two nice senior women in the neighborhood—I returned the Fuller Brush kit.

Selling was not my vocation, and nothing else seemed possible. The Civil Rights Movement was roiling national consciousness, but I was not ready to become the activist I became later in life. The possibility of joining protests against racial injustice never occurred to me.

Having dismissed my perceived obligation to make money, I gave in to my addiction—I binged on reading. Ensconced on my couch with sweets to tease my teeth, I read for escape and entertainment. I also followed serious interests. When Father Reinhold introduced us college seniors to historical-critical research on the Bible, we got permission to stop believing that Jonah lived in a whale for three days, that Noah's ark held representatives of every species, that Joshua's trumpet struck down the walls of Jericho—Old Testament stories—but this gave rise to more serious questioning of New Testament passages.

A year or so after graduating from college, I rejected belief in the Christian creed and left the church. The logical step after this seemed to be atheism. I tried to be a good atheist by denying the existence of spiritual reality but noticed something comical. While perusing headlines in a newspaper to look for interesting stories, I might see the word "Catholic" or "Christian" or "religion." Instantly my eyes would be riveted to the story. The irony became obvious to me. Despite my rejection of religion, I was captivated by its subject—spiritual reality. Atheism increased my interest in it, rather than directing me away from it.

Trying to buttress my atheism, I expanded on the skepticism planted by Fr. Reinhold. That Christians condemned all things pagan excited my curiosity, which led me to books about pagan religions, mythology, and the Goddess. One book led to another. Seeing an author mentioned a few times, I'd check out his or her work in libraries. Among others, J. J. Bachofen, Robert Briffault, and Mircea Eliade educated me about ancient myths. Later, Joseph Campbell would satisfy my curiosity about beliefs that preceded and influenced Christianity.

I inferred a difference between religious myth and the word "myth" as used in American discourse. Americans think of "myth" as a lie, but religious myths bear deep symbolic and motivational power. While learning to respect religious myth, I was simultaneously learning that the Christian story is myth—not factual history but true on another plane.

I do not recall what I read when but wish I could reenter my state of mind during those early years and trace the sequence of information entering my awareness. I was unlearning things I thought I knew but didn't have anyone to talk to, no one to share my burgeoning knowledge. The information went into a cubbyhole, but it changed my thoughts when I went back to church.

I could not go back to accepting church-talk uncritically. "Three persons in one God" had to share the stage with Hera and Zeus, the Buddha, Athena, and Krishna. In churches, Lord and Christ were part of the mental furniture, but they were not what drew me to church. I put up with them because I wanted contact with a church community and the reverent ambience that speaks of sacred presence.

A new perspective—non-Christian cultures—took residence in my mind. Ancients resented Christians for destabilizing society, disrespecting the Roman emperor, and desecrating holy places. I learned that the word "pagans" originally meant country people, those slowest to adopt the new religion that was invading the empire and disrupting traditions. Eventually the upstart Christian religion, rival of the old pagan religions, won the contest and wrote history.

Christians belittled pagans for worshipping gods and goddesses, but books gave me evidence that Christians made a god out of Jesus parallel to pagan gods. Like Apollo, Attis, Mithras, and Dionysus, Jesus was born of a virgin at the winter solstice. Today church leaders admit that we don't know when Jesus was born, but I have not seen an admission that Christmas copies birthday feasts honoring pagan gods and that, before Jesus of Nazareth, pagan gods had twelve disciples, died and rose in three days, were commemorated in rituals involving wine and bread, and so on. As these facts emerged in my reading, the whole myth of Christ came into focus.

Wanting distance from Christian stuff but drawn to spiritual content, I turned to writings about the Goddess. Accounts of faith in *Mater Magna*, the Great Mother, creator of the universe, overrode the Christian teaching that the Goddess is an abomination. I learned that She of the many names manifests the feminine face of the divine, simply an alternative way to think of what is called "God." That She reigned under many names in prehistoric times extinguished the Judeo-Christian claim to being the first monotheistic religion.

All this was gradually replacing the old furniture in my mind, but when feminism broke out in the late 1960s and '70s, I scoffed at it. Media reports of bra-burning made me dislike and deride feminists. Not until I started reading about religious and emotional/spiritual implications did I come around to embracing the movement, then becoming a passionate advocate. One of the first books proving the worth of feminism to me was edited by Charlene Spretnak: *The Politics of Women's Spirituality*. Its authors ripped me out of our male-dominant culture, almost disorienting me with their unfamiliar and non-Christian perspective.

Catholic nuns were among my best teachers in feminist thought. They taught me to distinguish between symbol and fact and to apply this to the Christian Trinity. I am a little embarrassed that I, an English teacher, had not thought of this before it was pointed out in feminist writings: Father and Son are symbols, not facts. We are not going to meet these guys after we die.

I became a feminist because it made sense; it was an intellectual thing for me, separate from my personal married life. Other myth systems made it obvious that father and son gods without any feminine deities create a lopsided heaven and therefore earth. I became aware that imagining males on top in the sacred realm makes it impossible to have females in charge anywhere. In our family, Mother did not make the big decisions, Father did. And God was "Father" and "Lord," evidence to me now that always praying to *him* and never to *her* deforms human relationships.

Gradually, dimly, applications of this reality expanded and reached thoughts about my marriage. I could easily see the impact of religious sexism on society, but problems with Jim didn't quite fit this male-female dynamic.

Jim

We didn't have a honeymoon. No money for that. The first day we went back to work, I waited for Jim to come home from work, but he didn't come. And didn't come. He had not said he was going somewhere after work. I was so worried that I called my parents. When Jim finally came home, it was after midnight. He acted surprised that not coming home sooner was a big deal and made it clear that he would keep doing it. My home-alone marriage had begun.

It wasn't his job that kept him away. He went bowling or played some other sport, then stayed out long after play was done. He was very good at every sport he took up—in his youth, hockey and basketball. When we were dating it was bowling. He confided that he'd aspired to become a professional bowler but gave it up as unrealistic. Night after night, he was gone. If he was home, he watched television, still absent to me. I was used to being alone with my thoughts, but this wasn't right. Didn't married people have conversations and plan things together?

After marriage, affection dried up. A few months into marriage I noticed, crestfallen, that Jim's tone with me was exactly the one he had used in talking about his mother—full of resentment and scorn. Soon I realized I was having thoughts I did not want to share with him, whereas before I'd felt I could tell him everything. I realized this need to have secrets indicated trouble in our marriage. His immaturity became apparent. I was immature, too, or I would not have married him, but I was growing. Why wasn't he growing up?

One night, Jim came home from his usual nightly bar time and woke me up to gush with affection for me, beyond anything I had experienced during courtship or, so far, marriage. He rambled on about something the bartender said, something about appreciating his wife alone at home. It took me years before I figured out what the bartender had figured out.

Our first baby, Patrick, arrived. I felt a rush of kinship with all mothers, having joined the great bond of womanhood. When it was time to bring Pat home to our basement apartment, Jim's mom and sister accompanied us. It was a relief not to be left alone with my baby right away. After they left, I sat on the couch holding Pat and wondering, "Now what?" I knew nothing about caring for an infant. Dr. Spock's book didn't give me confidence. I can still see my baby looking at me with old wise eyes as if he knew how I felt.

Despite my smarts in academic matters, I was naïve in matters of daily living. Getting Jim out of bed and to work in the morning was a chore I dreaded, but that he was having a hangover did not occur to me. Besides being unobservant, I was nonassertive, lazily going along with Jim's social crowd, his buddies and their wives. I knew how to discuss the Enlightenment in class, not how to discuss drapes with married women. Feeling like a misfit, I reddened when their attention was on me.

Men's talk could be interesting if they got off the boring subject of sports. I would have liked to chime in when they talked about politics and national issues, but their wives didn't participate. I thought they weren't interested. I decided, *My mind is more like a man's than a woman's.*

Those early years of marriage and teaching, however, contain some pleasant memories. We went camping near Itasca State Park with Bob and Sue, one summer nearly every weekend. Watching Sue's high-quality mothering and helping her to care for their two little boys helped to prepare me for motherhood.

On one camping trip, we invited friends Jeb and Mona to come with us and find out about the great life of camping. That weekend, camp owners told us a bad storm was forecast for the area. They suggested sheltering in the bathhouse. The storm didn't amount to much, just added some excitement, but Mona was terrified. Her trembling amazed me because I rather enjoy storms. This set me to thinking. My fears might seem as silly to her as her fear of storms seemed to me. *Hmm.* My observer self would recall this incident in subsequent years when I panicked over money worries.

We spent a lot of time with Bob and Sue, often at their house. She was feistier than I. One day she went on a rant against Bob, complaining about his spending. I liked what she said. *Yes, and Jim wastes money in the same ways.* But then came words that she seemed to know would shock, but she didn't hesitate. At that point I think she was talking to Jim and me as much as to Bob.

"When Jim and Jeanie are here, they expect to get drinks." *What?* It was a knock on my head. I hated all the drinking and often had forced myself to take a drink just to go along, to fit in, a convent-bred child following what I thought was the social norm. Her comment made me feel stupid and became a worm in me. *What, really, is normal social drinking?*

Some months after we married, I tearfully told my doctor that my husband seemed to have no interest in me. What was wrong with me? Jim was not pursuing other women but left me alone night after night. The doctor assured me there was nothing wrong with me. "Most men would chase you around the bedroom." He happened to live in the same neighborhood as Jim's family. "You're married to an alcoholic," he said. "You have to grow strong." I didn't want to believe it and grew adept at denying. I definitely did not want to grow strong. I had married for security, not more challenges.

Under the surface I did not respect my husband and he sensed this. He was not a good provider and did not meet my intellectual standard. While my respect for nonacademic skills was growing, it had not climbed high enough to cancel my feeling that I had "married down." Today I suspect that he sensed my secret scorn, and it may have contributed to his difficulty in finding his way.

When he was about thirty years old, Jim got an ulcer over concern that he hadn't yet found a suitable path in life. He came home from a doctor's visit unhappy from learning that alcoholic drinks make a stomach ulcer worse. The doctor also said milk and milk products would help to soothe his stomach. This gave Jim an idea he was proud of. When I had felt forced to order drinks in bars, I sometimes splurged on Brandy Alexanders and Grasshoppers. Jim bought a blender and made ice cream drinks with liqueurs for himself. This made his need for alcohol more apparent to me and I wondered if it wasn't apparent to others.

We clashed in personality traits. He looked for ways to play. I stoically deferred pleasure. He indulged in spur-of-the-moment spending. I fit the description "so tight she squeaks." His thoughts never strayed past material surroundings. I lived in my head, oblivious of surroundings. He escaped daily responsibility. I took it all on and worried about things.

Stupidly, I let him take care of our financial affairs simply because I hated dealing with money matters and he briefly worked in a bank. I turned my salary checks over to him, assuming we were saving up for a house. When he arranged a loan to buy a boat and needed me to cosign, I balked. This I would not stand for. I was making most of our money. I told him I would not cosign the loan agreement. We were living in a tiny basement apartment and I was pregnant. "I want a house!" I shouted angrily.

Teilhard de Chardin and Jung

Things were tolerable when my life revolved around reading and teaching, which satisfied my need for bookish work, being creative, and feeling worthy, before we had children. Book reviews directed my hunger for knowledge to writings that link religion with science and philosophy. This pulled me toward Pierre Teilhard de Chardin and Carl Jung, who fed me delicious and wholesome spiritual food, whetting my appetite for more.

Teilhard de Chardin, a Jesuit priest, paleontologist, and geologist, wrote *The Phenomenon of Man*, which thrilled me with its marriage of science and spirituality. That it was authored by a Catholic priest satisfied my respect for Catholic thought. I felt safe in the bosom of Catholic theology, even while I was flirting with atheism. The irony—feeling safe in the religion I criticize—occurred to me then, too.

I had spent life in a Catholic bosom larger than my Catholic family, had been educated, housed, and fed by Catholicism. The intellectual rigor of its theology was known to me, not yet the shabby behavior of its officials. Shaped by Catholic teachers in grade school, high school, and college, I developed trust in them, and my trust was not misplaced. They surrounded me and held me secure. They, not the power-driven hierarchs perpetuating patriarchy, were the Catholics I knew best. They were home.

Teilhard de Chardin's mind-expanding vision electrified me as I read *The Phenomenon of Man* in the late 1960s. Teilhard taught me to identify the spiritual or nonphysical aspect of humans as consciousness—all mind activity. He traced the rise of consciousness from inanimate matter through the living species—primitive life forms, plants, insects, fish, reptiles, mammals—evolving from the less complex and conscious to the more complex and conscious. This evolution of consciousness culminated in humans and collective, global intelligence—the Omega Point toward which all is heading.

When I came upon Teilhard's writings, the word "consciousness" was unfamiliar. His use of it led to clarity.

> We have only got to look at ourselves in order to understand
> the dynamic relationships existing between the *within* and the
> *without* of things. (63, italics Teilhard's)

With time, I realized that we manifest our *within* by our knowledge, thoughts, beliefs, feelings, imaginings, expectations, and attitudes—the consciousness that Teilhard identified.

In Teilhard's writings the word *within* means the immaterial or nonphysical aspect of everything. This shot a small bolt of electricity into me. The *within* is spiritual reality inside, behind, over, underneath, *within* all physical existence. With Teilhard's help, I could see physical and nonphysical reality emanating from the Creator/Source that I and others in the West call "God." This connects science with religion! I was mesmerized. Blown over by the thought of Teilhard de Chardin, I was to be led by it for the rest of my life.

Teilhard's intoxicating synthesis of evolutionary science with spiritual reality spoke a prophetic wisdom that far surpasses Christian limits. It stirred me profoundly. But the end of the book let me down with a disappointing thud. He stuffed his exhilarating concepts into the Christian frame by identifying the Omega Point as Jesus Christ, making human history crawl through one man—not at all what Jesus preached. A deflating return to what I'd questioned in grade school when S. Bethany taught that we have the one, true faith. Back to the same old Christian claim of privileged access to God.

Teilhard's loyalty to it seems sadder in light of the Vatican censoring his writings because he abandoned literal belief in the creation stories of Genesis. Teilhard's books did not appear until after his death in 1955. Since then, he has gained universal admiration, been favorably mentioned by four popes, and continues to be studied and quoted. I learned to ignore his Christian Omega Point because commentaries by scholars who also were awed by his synthesis ignored the Christian frame. Apparently, they were not wrestling with church dictates, as I still was.

The English translation of Teilhard's title, *The Phenomenon of Man* annoys me today. *Le phénomène humain*, published in 1956, should be translated the "Phenomenon of Humanity" because "man" does not include all humanity. The claim that it does insults women. I don't remember, however, reacting strongly to the English translation when I first read it in the late 1960s. My awareness has grown over time.

Carl Jung, a Swiss psychiatrist and psychotherapist, was another thinker whose seminal thought I met around 1970. He also spoke of inner realities invisible to the outer world, but Jung focused on emotional/spiritual health. He wanted us to become aware of our unconscious motivations—what's really driving us. He and other psychologists want us to ask, "Why do I do what I do?"—the question suggested by spiritual masters going back to the Delphic oracle, who advised, "Know thyself."

Freud opened awareness of our unseen minds—the hidden part of consciousness. Jung was Freud's disciple but broke away when he observed that Freud was making a dogma of sex. Jung regarded spiritual reality the main driver of human behavior, and sex only part of it. He identified spiritual patterns in us that he called archetypes, psychic patterns appearing in various forms. Zeus and the Christian Father, for instance, represent the same archetype, as do the Goddess and the Virgin Mary. Jung's thought revealed religion's role in human life and invited exploration of unknown human depth.

The book that introduced me to Jung was Anthony Storr's *The Essential Jung*. Out of the writings shone truth I had intuited but could not put into words. I did not understand all of it, but I was hooked. It took me years to get into Jung's thought, but my immediate reaction was feeling vindicated because this erudite thinker with awe-inspiring breadth of knowledge rejected literal religious belief. Almost immediately I started calling Jung's works "theology" because they filled that role for me.

Jung informs us that religious trinities preceded the Christian Father, Son, and Holy Spirit by several thousand years. He calls Jesus a "demigod . . . like the Greek heroes." Naming counterparts of Christ besides the pagan ones I'd met, Jung states that Christ symbolizes the inner self in every person. This gives me the key to understanding Christian texts.

His writings also support me by expressing scorn for literal belief, but with a twist. I learned from Jung that religious doctrines *never* are properly read as literal, rational facts, whatever religious people believe. He makes it seem so obvious, but I had not known this. For Jung, irrationality in myths is beside the point.

While he encouraged me to abandon literal belief, Jung took this stuff seriously. It was not just baloney to him, as it is to atheists. My intuition had told me the same, so this also encouraged me. Still, Jung puzzled me. Why did he counsel patients who dropped out of religion to go back to it? And why did he arrange to have himself buried in a

Christian ceremony when he died? It took me a while to know what to make of these apparent inconsistencies.

More study informed me that religious images have mysterious power that connects people with the invisible realm, which, Jung explains, presides in the vast unconscious of every person. This explains the warm feelings we get from myths like the Christmas story. They act as unconscious prompts to steer our conscious lives. Jung's writing contains many dream accounts, showing their role in guiding us while awake. I started to pay attention to my dreams. I started asking, "What is my interior trying to tell me?"

When I arrived at the School of Theology years later, I wished Carl Jung's concepts were in the curriculum. Teachers and students exposed to his work might stop treating doctrines as facts and see them as expressions of myths, as stories that reveal our mind-sets and guide us. Christian writers who know Jungian concepts interpret doctrines in a way that displays their expanded horizon.

I consider *Memories, Dreams, Reflections,* a kind of autobiography, the easiest way to enter Jung's thought. In this book he observes that his father, a Protestant minister, "suffered from religious doubts" (92). He watches his father wrestling with the Trinity and observes that his father is blocked by "lifeless theological answers," not "capable of understanding the direct experience of God" (93).

Jung complains that church ceremony "contained no trace of God." He writes, "My poor father did not dare to think, . . . hopelessly he was entrapped by the Church and its theological thinking. They had blocked all avenues by which he might have reached God directly" (73). His father didn't have a clue about "the vast despair, the overpowering elation and outpouring of grace [that] constituted the essence of God" (55). Jung himself experienced despair, elation, and grace in revelatory dreams.

Jung considered himself a scientist but one who does not ignore phenomena breaking common scientific assumptions. He took seriously dreams that foretell events and animals that sense earthquakes before they strike. His accounts of spiritual experiences in everyday life are dismissed by scientists as coincidence, but Jung saw meaning in clocks stopping precisely at the moment of death, in glasses shattering at a critical moment, in writings appearing just when we need them. These supposed coincidences are revealed in Jung's writings to be evidence of the spiritual realm. It became clear to me why religion kept drawing my attention when I tried to be an atheist. Spiritual reality independent of religion was beguiling me.

As a boy, Jung walked to and from school past the impressive cathedral of Basel. Once, he had a blasphemous thought that he fended off in agony for sleepless days, a sin he resisted with all his strength because he feared eternal damnation. Finally, he accepted it as God's will and allowed the image to come:

> I saw before me the cathedral, the blue sky. God sits on His golden throne, high above the world—and from under the throne an enormous turd falls upon the sparkling new roof, shatters it, and breaks the walls of the cathedral asunder. (39)

A precocious schoolboy summons the courage to watch God desecrate the church. This thrills me yet today. When I first met the account in *Memories, Dreams, Reflections*, I reread it several times, attracted to it and afraid to believe I read it right.

It reminds me of a novel I taught in high school—Mark Twain's *Huckleberry Finn*. It depicts the boy Huck floating down the Mississippi with loving and loyal Jim, a runaway slave. Huck has been taught that assisting runaway slaves is a sin. To avoid a certain fate in hell, he writes a letter to the slave's owner to tell her where Jim is. But as he thinks about Jim's goodness, Huck's conscience resists. Trembling, he decides to commit the sin of "stealing Jim out of slavery."

"All right, then, I'll go to hell," he says, and tears up the letter. While I was teaching, I never adequately conveyed to students the moral significance of Huck's soul-wrenching courage. The boys Huckleberry Finn and Carl Jung defied conventional morality, ready to accept society's punishment for acting with integrity.

7

JIM

Something Wrong

AFTER I REFUSED TO go along with buying a boat, Jim saved for a house by putting my whole paycheck into a separate account. We bought a lot in Avon and made plans to have a house built there. Part of my dream was coming true. Not until we were living in the house did I realize that I had admired the very maple we now owned while driving from St. Cloud past Avon to teach in Albany.

Our house was separated from I-94 by only one line of houses and trees. The diaper-changing table stood by a window facing it. Looking up while diapering my baby, my eyes fell on the freeway while thinking about precious baby, troubling husband. The interstate leading to the wider world lifted me from my personal challenges.

To save money, we wanted to do some of the construction work ourselves. I painted walls and stained woodwork. Jim said he would learn how to build the brick facade on the front of the house. That could be done after we moved in. Celia's husband got it started and showed Jim how. Evening after evening passed and all that happened was talking about doing it. The wall was not growing. "Why not?" Going out to look, I saw Jim standing in front of it, trowel in one hand, drink in the other. Progress moved by tiny increments. My brother-in-law came back and finished the facade.

I took a half-year off while baby and house entered our lives but went back to teach part time. Now I could no longer escape in schoolwork. Disappointment and discord were growing in our nest. After bowling waned in popularity, Jim escaped in racquetball and golf. I called myself a sports widow and said to myself that the one thing I could depend on was that I could depend on him for nothing. The word "alcoholic" surfaced in my mind from time to time.

Our evenings contained no togetherness. If he was not out, he watched sports on television, in the basement after we got a house. Like his dad who spent hours alone in their basement. Jim was absent, not only literally both days and nights, but absent as a partner in the life we should be living together. Home life was more peaceful when he was gone, but that was no marriage.

After we married, Jim stopped relating with me as an equal intimate. I heard other husbands and wives talking together as peers, husbands listening to their wives as partners. Jim didn't do anything like it. Our relationship seemed to be vertical instead of horizontal. He saw me as either up or down, on opposite ends of the vertical spectrum, either an opponent to be scorned and defeated, or a confidante. Sometimes he confided in me as if I were his mother.

There were no joint decisions. No discussions of plans. He seemed to have a need to thwart my wishes, springing to mind a two-year-old's "No. No." Ideas for home improvements or fun things to do had to come from him, and they came unpredictably. When I wanted to discuss decisions or plans, I carefully planned my words and rehearsed them. Too often they brought snarls in return. A few successes kept me hoping I could make it go right.

Pat was ten months old when he became fearfully ill. I arrived at the babysitter's after school on a Friday afternoon to find Maysie full of concern. An experienced mother of nine, Maysie told me to immediately take my baby to a doctor. Pat spent the weekend in the hospital, but beyond X-rays nothing was done. Over the course of the weekend, his little stomach swelled. On Monday morning, I was in a hospital phone booth to report my absence from work that day, when I overheard a doctor saying to another doctor, "Patrick Clancy is distended as hell."

Emergency surgery showed a bowel obstruction. Six inches were cut off baby Pat's intestine. Jim cried over the weekend. I remained stoic until after the surgery when I was in the room while doctors and nurses were working over my baby. Suddenly I leaned over his unconscious body and wailed in grief. They thought it best to get me out of the room.

Soon after Pat came home from the hospital, I landed in the hospital. Jim rose to the challenge by collecting Patrick from Maysie's after work and taking care of him during the evening. Doctors could find no physical cause for my illness. It was obviously a reaction to stress, like my bouts with laryngitis. Had our baby been reacting to emotions surrounding him? Not able to stomach them? Decades later, I would have bowel obstructions in reaction to significant happenings in my life.

Mollie, our second baby, was born with a cleft palate. While the doctor was describing it to me, I wondered why he didn't say "cleft palate." Later I learned he had used the term to inform Jim, and my husband had no idea what it meant. I wished I had said "cleft palate" to shatter the doctor's assumption that a woman would not know something if her husband doesn't.

Contrasting with Jim's testiness were his occasional warm behaviors with the kids. He is the one who started our family ritual of giving the kids a kiss and a hug at bedtime, a welcome correction of my cold family-of-origin habits. And there is the time he woke me after coming home, late as usual but all lovey dovey because the bartender rebuked him for leaving his wife alone night after night. Other times he surprised me with lavish gifts, a few times with roses. They didn't make up for his usual irritability.

Plans made didn't materialize. One time I tried to quiet our little boy by repeating a promise made by his father. Patrick knowingly said, "Dad just says that." Little Pat faced the fact of empty promises before I did.

Jim's verbal abuse escalated and its ferocity scared me. Clever with his tongue, he hit my vulnerable spots with cruel, cutting words. I was no match for his ability to fling insults. Today I can't recapture my fear of Jim's wrath, and I see how my own timidity then cowed me and cowed me in other relationships. Another reason I did not defend myself, much less respond in kind, is that I felt sorry for him. As his confidante, I observed his insecurities, his lack of self-esteem, his desperate attempts to fit in with successful men.

In school, laryngitis started interfering with my teaching. Now it had more serious effects than in college. In the 1960s and '70s, teachers did almost all the talking while students listened. I could play German tapes for German class, and the tape recorder had a microphone I could use to amplify my weak speaking voice for other classes. But I had to come up with creative ways to keep students learning while I did less talking, the best way to learn anyway, I now know.

Meanwhile, I could see the obvious message from my inner self. I was voiceless physically because I was voiceless emotionally. That much I knew, but lacking someone to listen to me and understand, I was helpless to mend things. When my high school principal said I was sick a lot, I heatedly denied it, a scene in my memory that still embarrasses me.

In one of his jobs Jim learned the art of cabinetmaking. I was not impressed when he invested in saws and furniture clamps and set out to make cabinets in our garage. But it cut back the hours he spent away from home and gave him new purpose. After some months, I grew to respect it. Cabinetry fed his artistic bent and raised his self-respect. He produced some nice pieces. I still use and treasure the grand hutch Jim made. Perhaps the most demanding order he filled was building kitchen cabinets for the new house my dad built on the "other farm" when he and Mother left the city and returned to the country.

Occasionally Jim enlisted my help to hold a large piece of wood as he guided it through a table saw. We were aware of possible accidents. A local cabinetmaker had lost fingers and there were stories of worse accidents. I had visions of hearing his desperate call from the garage and rushing down to see a disaster. That kind of disaster did not happen.

Jim's behavior continued to be unpredictable so that our home life wore on us as a family. Pat and Mollie grew warier as they grew older. Times I now know their father was having a hangover, we moved around him as if around a land mine, afraid of setting him off. Daily, my children listened to the way he insulted me in everyday exchanges—crabbily, in rude retorts, with sarcastic put-downs. In a letter to one of my children years later, I worried about the example he had set. "If this is not in your conscious memory, it is buried in you."

Any wish or plan I expressed could bring on angry retorts or snide digs. I tried to think of ways to say things that would not ignite a hostile response. A verse from Robert Frost's poem "The Death of the Hired Man," came to mind.

> I sympathize. I know just how it feels
> To think of the right thing to say too late.

Thinking of the right words too late occupied my days.

Jim let it be known that he hated holiday visits to my family. At first, I naïvely thought it meant my family were unsophisticated rubes, but I did note his complaint that my dad didn't offer drinks. Socializing without alcohol seemed abnormal to Jim. Years later, my brother-in-law Leroy told me that Jim expected him to join in complaining about the absence of alcoholic drinks at our family gatherings.

I do not wonder why women take beatings from husbands and cover it up. Although I was not physically abused—"only" verbally and psychologically—I acted out the same pattern of pretense for the outside world. The unhealthy side of Jim's personality was not known to others, as he behaved boorishly only to me. To others he was a helluva nice guy, gentle and harmless. I was the one who took all his belittling and hateful words.

"Because it was safe," said a perceptive friend many years later when I was talking about this. Like Jim, I wanted people to think well of him. It helped me to stay in denial.

Less in Denial

A pesky memory was surfacing—the doctor who knew the Clancy family. It was getting harder to ignore his warning that I was married to an alcoholic. I did not want to believe him because, if it was true, I had to do something. My denial persisted until Albany High School offered teachers a required drug-awareness course. It was interesting in an academic way, but then came the unit on alcoholism. Now it was personal. I learned about the anesthetizing effect of substance abuse. The reason Jim could not grow in maturity is that he was using a drug to deaden the normal pains of living.

One speaker gave us a surefire way to distinguish alcoholics from heavy drinkers: "If you need it, you're an alcoholic." *Oh.* I had suggested cutting down on drinks to save money and Jim had said, "Jeanie, I need it." Screwing up courage, I told Jim what I'd learned in the course, but, as expected, he didn't accept it. The disease of alcoholism in our marriage assumed sharper outlines in my mind.

Less in denial after the course, I still wanted proof. It helped to hear at an Al-Anon meeting, "Alcoholism is not about the amount of alcohol consumed; it's an emotional illness." This I could clearly see. There were times I said to myself that I had three children, not two, and Jim was the oldest, a contrary teenager.

When a storm threatened, I called the bar where I guessed he was and asked him to come home. He didn't. After the storm he did nothing to help clean debris from our yard. This was typical. When water flooded our basement in another incident, he was home and started cleaning up with me but soon quit and left me to finish the job alone. When I taught community education classes in the evening, I made sure I cleaned up after supper because I didn't want a repetition of what had happened before. I had left in a hurry and come home to dirty plates still on the table and food not put away.

One day we were sitting around a table with Jim's sister and he suddenly inserted into the conversation, "You have to admit you couldn't do what I do."

"No, I couldn't," I answered, nonplussed because it didn't fit what came before. Then I realized he was feeling inferior to me—not a secret to his sister. The same sister, whom I cherish as a friend, wondered years later why I married someone so ill-suited to me. I loved school and did well in academic pursuits but had no interest in sports. Although I have only a master's degree, I can talk the language of intellectuals and feel comfortable with them. Jim was nothing like an intellectual and he loved sports.

To his sister's question, however, I answered that we really did fit together, hand in glove. We both absorbed shame from our family situations. Shame was the reason I hung around with the Clancys more than my Blonigen family. I was trying to separate emotionally from my self. I had built the identity of married teacher—normal, respectable American—but had made myself a stranger to my farmer's-daughter self and my deepest self.

My habit of running from farm and family crumbled one day. We were in the car—Jim and I with Pat and Mollie—on our way to a Blonigen holiday gathering in the house my father had built. He and Mother were now "Grandpa and Grandma." There was a light blanket of snow. As usual on our way to a Blonigen gathering, Jim emoted sour feelings that I now explain as expecting to endure a day without alcohol. But joy bubbled up as I looked forward to being with my family, enlarged by many little ones. I turned toward the kids in the back seat and sang, "Over the river and through the woods, to Grandmother's house we go." My inner being's gladness over returning to my roots was spilling out.

Atheism to 12–Step

Al-Anon and Unity School of Christianity entered my life on the same evening. Maysie was not only Pat's babysitter but the person I call my kids' third and best grandma, a person I depended on almost as a mother. She also was my walking partner and an Al-Anon veteran who had been listening to my complaints during our walks. Maysie's alcoholic husband was not like mine. Lee took out his frustrations and anger in drinking, not on his wife. Every time Lee tried to stop drinking, he went back to it. It took Maysie separating from him and demanding he get hospital treatment before he got the tools to remain sober.

Lee was not mean to Maysie, just a drinker helpless to quit. My alcoholic husband did not drink tons but gave me tons of verbal abuse. I could not unburden myself to Maysie because she did not know domestic abuse, but she could see I needed Al-Anon, a program that grew out of AA for families of alcoholics, who also need healing. Maysie kept urging me to go to meetings, but I resisted. Finally, she got me to go by arranging for a schoolmate of mine to meet me there.

After the meeting, that schoolmate gave me a copy of *Daily Word* published by Unity School of Christianity. Its uplifting messages and Al-Anon's Twelve-Step spirituality reinforced each other. Both started me on the path to healing by assuring me and giving me hope. The inner guide had done it again, this time with Maysie's help.

In Twelve-Step meetings people bared their feelings and faults, their deepest selves. It soothed me as much as hearing how alcohol affected their family life. Gradually I learned from their example how to be real instead of trying to impress. I could do this best in meetings with people who were strangers. With them I could drop my mask. One familiar face, however, I was happy to see. Sue showed up in our meeting one evening. I told her, "We should have started coming here a long time ago."

Unity offered an idea new to me, that God wants for us what we want. Catholic preaching stressed humility, self-sacrifice, and self-debasement, training me to believe my deepest desires were anti-God. Unity writings encouraged me and began building a benign image of what's called "God," one aligning with my deepest desires. What a relief to think God is on my side! It was the beginning of admitting what I really craved—self-respect.

Unity writings interpreted scripture nondogmatically. Instead of encouraging worship of Jesus Christ or "the Father," they used scripture verses as positive affirmations. Most helpfully, they assured me that God wants us to be happy—a big switch from "Pride is the deadliest sin" and "Deny yourself for the Lord." Unity writings soothed me, while Al-Anon's Twelve-Step spirituality gave me the concept of a Higher Power. Together, these new sources of nourishment referred to God as an unseen force guiding us toward good, not a god demanding self-sacrifice. The new idea that my desires align with an exalted force did more to heal me than anything else.

Helping my transition from tension to tranquility was Al-Anon's "Let Go and Let God." I could lay my burden of daily anxieties into the lap of a Higher Power, whatever I imagined that power to be. It became a beacon guiding me through the rest of my life. In one of my Twelve-Step groups a self-identified atheist said this principle worked for him, too.

My attraction to Twelve-Step spirituality may be explained by Carl Jung having a role in it. A businessman from England, a rich and gifted entrepreneur, was destroying himself with drink. Desperate to stop, he went to Dr. Carl Jung in Switzerland. The doctor told him there was no medical cure for his condition. His only hope was to have an authentic conversion, a spiritual transformation. Jung explained that addicts long for spiritual solace and use a substance to fill the hole of yearning inside. *So that's why alcoholic drinks are called spirits!*

The businessman went back to England and joined a Christian evangelical group. In the group was Bill Wilson, an alcoholic. Inspired by the man's story, Bill had a powerful, ecstatic conversion in a hospital bed, after which he never took another drink. Bill and fellow alcoholic Dr. Bob co-founded Alcoholics Anonymous (AA). Twelve-Step principles outlined by them reflect Jung's thought and replace religion with what I call generic or secular spirituality.

Out flew atheism, which never had satisfied my spiritual yearnings. Jung explained my dissatisfaction with it. It does not stop with pointing out the foolishness of literal belief but denies that any spiritual reality exists at all. Many atheists and agnostics even deny that the man Jesus, in whose memory Christianity began, ever existed.

While I was trying to be an atheist, I really had been looking for authentic spirituality. This, I think, is true of other atheists. I never lost my liking for them. Conversations with an atheist about spiritual and philosophical matters stimulated me, while conversations with most Christians about the same matters were impossible. I thought about atheists a lot and devoured their opinions. They were offended by irrational beliefs and religious officials oozing corruption because, I think, they were disappointed in religion, as I was.

Religion should open to depth, but typical church-talk presents myths as facts instead of stories with symbolic imagery. Atheists reject the unbelievable myths and do not move to the symbolic truth behind them. I blame religious teaching for this, and I credit atheism for asking the questions that helped me to leap past Christian training to vast spiritual territory beyond it. As one Benedictine Sister put it, "Atheists can think!."

Marriage concerns did not stop me from educating myself. I continued my voracious reading, which tempered my foray into atheism while I learned Twelve-Step spirituality. I had yet to face my inner self as Jung advised, but I consumed readings in Jungian psychology, mythology, a smattering of Goddess literature, and science for non-scientists from Teilhard de Chardin. He added spiritual implications to science. Teilhard got me thinking about our mind's life, our consciousness. Before Teilhard, I had not thought of thought as spiritual reality.

As I write this memoir, I become curious about my spiritual evolution. This much I know: My new knowledge did not enter everyday conversations. I tried out a few insights on a few trusted friends, but never members of my biological family. It is impossible to track when I learned what and how much I knew at particular times, but an exchange I can date in the early 1980s reveals some of the chronology.

To a fellow Al-Anon member, a Benedictine, I scoffed at the idea that a father could have a son without a mother being involved. My friend gave the standard reply: "God can do anything." I persisted and confessed disbelief in the Father/Son myth. From reading Jung and Unity writings, I'd gained a new understanding, that Christ symbolizes our inner self, the divine part in us. After hearing this interpretation, my friend immediately got it and accepted it. She has accompanied me on my journey since then and remains a like-minded companion. For me, Christ, but not Jesus, became interchangeable with my Higher Power—divinity within.

Sometime during this period, a Unity writer impressed me deeply by writing, "What happens to us has less importance than our response to it." I remember being incredulous and resistant. *If something bad happens, I'm not going to think it's not bad.* But the idea of growing wiser from disappointments and failures lodged in my mind. Time and reflection matured it.

Unity, Twelve-Step, and raising children restored the habit of going to church. Reasoning that giving children a background with some religion is better than no religion, I returned to the Catholic Church. This brought our family life in tune with our cultural environment. For some years I shopped around for a better church, but everything I tried had the patriarchal base of literal belief in the Father/Son story, the belief that irked me. If I was going to stay Christian, staying Catholic made the most sense. My childhood religion had roots, majesty, and heft. Apart from the *magisterium* or teaching authority, I saw intellectual integrity in Catholic theology and glimmers of a larger perspective.

We joined the local parish and went to church regularly. Both Patrick and Mollie were baptized Catholic. I used my love of interpreting and declaiming to become a lector, but I didn't return to practices like confession, Mass on holy days, or Lenten observance. My expanding knowledge of religious myths accompanied me to church and kept my mind busy there. My husband simply followed my lead in going to church—religion was not a concern of his.

Diving Deeper into the Disease

Jim's alcoholism was not obvious because he did not make himself a spectacle in public. He did not consume a large amount, only needed a daily buzz. Even after I joined Al-Anon I continued a game of "Is he or isn't he?" I almost envied wives who complained about their husbands dead drunk on the floor. At least they knew the problem was alcoholism, and—this was important to me—others could see the evidence.

Al-Anon warns that the disease of alcoholism spills onto an entire family. My personality was a fine specimen. A bolt of realization hit me at an Al-Anon meeting when someone drew the picture of a typical wife. I'm on the floor while he wipes his feet on me, the floor mat. I work, work, work, save, save, save, do the house and yard chores alone, and instead of being appreciated, I get yelled at. He plays; I work. He wastes money; I deprive myself to save money. Always there's enough money for his indulgences and generosity to others but not for our family. My resentment and my training in penny-pinching deprivation contributed to our conflicts.

Something else rose to my awareness—the mother thing. Jim's mother was suffering from her own alcoholic marriage and denying it.

She started talking to me as one woman to another and gratified me by saying, "Jeanie, I like our conversations."

I thanked her for taking me into their family. "I love going to your house. I love Rosemary's kids." Continuing to enthuse about the Clancy family, I was interrupted.

"What about Jim?" she asked. I didn't answer.

On another day I gathered the guts to say, "We're both married to alcoholics."

"I never want to hear that again!" she said, and our woman-to-woman talks stopped.

Her son fought her by fighting me. Occasionally he said I nagged. I think he was internally hearing his mother. My own perception in retrospect is that I didn't "nag" or speak up enough. When he snapped at me, I pulled in my head like a turtle.

One day, Jim reported, "Bob is in treatment. He's admitting he mistreated Sue." I hoped Jim would apply it to himself. "Bob was an asshole," he said. I said nothing.

In a strange way, I became Jim's mother—arthritic and unhappy. On her recommendation and his, I went to her doctor. He prescribed Valium, which she had been taking for years. On the second visit with him, the pattern grew too obvious for me to ignore. I was not going to become my husband's mother. I stopped taking the drug and never went back to that doctor, a beginning step in escaping my husband's projected image of me. Later this drug's dangerous health effects became public and I congratulated myself for discontinuing it.

Jim had no model for a healthy marriage but learned to blame his mother for the family stresses, the common pattern in homes with an alcoholic father. An alcoholic man will call his wife's complaints senseless and lay all blame for his behavior on her—it's all "the wife's" fault. Al-Anon calls this "crazy-making." I observed it in marriages around me. In extreme cases, an alcoholic man gets his wife diagnosed as mentally ill. But at Twelve-Step meetings I was seeing AA and Al-Anon couples in successful recovery, and I was determined to make our marriage work.

In School

I tried escaping into teaching and my readings, tried to put marriage worries into a separate silo. The early days of teaching had been lovely.

We teachers enjoyed each other's company in the lounge, and students seemed to thrive in my classes. Former students remind me of those days, amazing me with their praise. "I loved your classes. You made class fun. You were my favorite teacher." Seeing my surprise, a former student encouraged me to bask in it.

I'd forgotten the feeling I had of myself in those days. I had confidence, liked myself, knew my students were understanding poetry, were speaking German after two years better than students with many years of classes. I remember teaching in heels and bounding up stairs, two at a time "like a gazelle," according to a fellow teacher, and after school running from curb to our apartment. Life was exhilarating.

That could last only so long before our disintegrating marriage took its toll at school, where I brought my feeling of being persecuted. My early confidence as a teacher was not strong enough to withstand the insults I took from Jim. Knowing that he picked on me because of his own low self-esteem was not enough to insulate me. My prior shame swelled.

When pregnant with Patrick, I had requested that my position be changed into a part-time job after he was born, and my request was granted. Continuing full time would have been impossible. Taking care of a baby plus full-time teaching with its planning and correcting papers left no quiet time to think. I needed time to ponder, to let buried thoughts rise to the surface without responsibilities in the outer world. My mother used to cry, "*Ich bin rappelig!*" (rattled, jumpy, crazy) when too much landed on her at once. *Ich bin rappelig!* sounded in me, as a jumble of emotional garbage plugged my pores. I had inner work to do.

A student of mine was identified by her friends as capable of palm reading. Her high-achieving group of friends wanted me to let her read my palm. Intrigued, I consented. At that time, our little Pat had no sibling and none on the way yet. My palm-reading student predicted he would have a sister and that I would be divorced. The first was exactly what I wanted and came true. The second was jarring, yet not surprising.

After I taught part time for many years, the principal and counselor asked me to go back to full time, warning that the demographic trend would force the school to let part-timers go in a few years. I knew I could not go full time. Another situation was unnerving me.

An older teacher I'll call Eleanor had earned respect, deservedly, for many years of competent teaching. When I started teaching, I related to her as to my superior. She maligned other teachers, and I accepted her assessments until I realized they were nothing but backbiting. She had many targets and wielded power. I feared becoming a target and became one. Not yet in the healing program of Al-Anon, I made the mistake of telling her I was on to her maligning of people. Unintentionally, I declared war. She became my persecutor and demanded loyalty from others. On top of the pommeling I was taking at home, I was tormented in school by her, by others I imagined she sicced on me, and mostly by my own fear of being persecuted.

Fellow teachers signaled compassion for me, although I confessed nothing of my marriage problems at school. One day a fellow English teacher struck up a friendly conversation with me while Eleanor was somewhere else. As soon as Eleanor was seen coming back, the friendly teacher's face turned cool and the conversation quickly came to an end. Similar scenes intensified my waning confidence. I was floundering from Eleanor's hostility on top of Jim's. One day, after mean words from Jim the night before, I could not finish a sentence in class. The students looked at me, waiting. Lamely, I switched topics and assigned them something, unable to think straight.

A feeling grew in school, a premonition that soon my life would turn from high school teaching to something else. This undefined something seemed big somehow, more significant than teaching teenagers, a barely-perceptible beam of intuition lying in the background of my consciousness. When I tried to give it words, I could think of nothing more than that it related to religion, spirituality, and psychology—the interior side of human life, the *within* of things in the language of Teilhard de Chardin.

Predictions of principal and counselor came true and I lost my job at the high school. Providentially, a representative from the languages department at St. Cloud State University had observed me teaching German in high school. Immediately after the Albany position, I was hired to teach German at the university. Leaving the high school faculty rescued me from Eleanor's hostility and power.

My compassion for her could not develop until I was booted out of that situation into college teaching. Taking the long view, I saw that Eleanor masked her own vulnerability by controlling others. Eventually I learned that she had divorced an alcoholic husband but never went to Al-Anon. She, like me, needed to heal from the illness of alcoholism. Taking her as an example of what to avoid, I resolved to do the work necessary to wrest free of it.

Religious writings kept preaching forgiveness. To prove it, we should pray for our imagined enemies. Thanks to readings in psychology, I knew

I should not minimize or deny the hurt done by Eleanor. Away from her, I saw what motivated her and could be kinder. I could sincerely pray for her highest good because it included becoming a better person. In this way, the experience lost its bitterness. I could stop obsessing, sincerely wish her well, and ask spiritual power to aid her. This manner of praying for hard-to-like people continues to serve me.

Years later I had the opportunity to talk to former colleagues about the atmosphere in the English department the last years I was there. We agreed it was "slimy." Teaching at a university suited me. Expecting my new career would be college professor, I promptly entered a graduate program in German at the University of Minnesota and enjoyed the one course I took there. But my Higher Power had other plans.

Do Something

For years I wrestled with the imperative coming from inside to do something—find a way to stop the pattern of our alcoholic marriage. A therapist at an Al-Anon event gave this graphic of an unhealthy relationship: "You are two cards leaning on each other. Each needs the other for the relationship to continue in the same way. If one of you moves, it can't go on."

I had to change something. I went to counseling. When an administrator at the high school noticed this fact in my record and gleefully mentioned it to me, I knew it was a disparaging comment on his own mental health, not mine.

Counselors were not always understanding, being as fallible as the rest of us. They know only as much about our situations as we are able to tell them, and I was not good at this. Having run away from emotions most of my life, I could not describe my corrosive marriage. I repeatedly told one counselor that my husband "put me down."

"How does he put you down? What does he say?"

I'd put up an internal shield to keep the venomous words from penetrating and couldn't reproduce them. All I could say was that his putdowns felt like daggers or arrows hitting me.

"And what did you say?" she asked.

"It did not go both ways!" I said emphatically. Then, "He probably sensed my disrespect for him, but I didn't say anything."

No counseling was entirely useless, because mulling over counselors' misunderstandings and paying attention to my gut feelings in time clarified our situation in my own mind. After a few years of counseling, I insisted that Jim go to some counseling with me and mentioned divorce.

He consented to counseling. While approaching the first appointment, I saw my husband almost trembling on the bed. He confessed that he feared what might lie in store for him during counseling. This gave me hope that he might look at himself honestly.

That did not happen. With his helluva nice guy mask he successfully conned counselors and led them to believe I had serious emotional problems, triggering my tendency to self-doubt. One counselor who had spent time only with Jim, never with me, challenged me. "When are you going to face yourself?"

That time I did not buckle. I knew Jim's ability to con. Evenly I said, "You don't know me, John." Silence, while John's surprised face admitted it.

Counselors recommended Jim go to AA. Apparently believing he would, they assigned another counselor only to me. They seemed to have fallen for the classic alcoholic subterfuge—the wife is *the* problem. One of them had been part of Jim's social circle before we married.

Feeling besieged, I struggled to say what was really going on and gradually got better at finding the words. After this a counselor detected Jim's deception and confronted him, and again Jim promised to attend AA meetings. He didn't then and never had.

The hope that this marriage could possibly work had been gradually fading for years but became more obvious as we followed counselors' recommendations to enjoy life together. "Play together," they said. Jim surprised me by trying to follow their suggestions.

We both truly enjoyed cribbage. One evening we were playing cribbage, and Patrick's friend Jason was at our house. The boys also were playing a game. Left alone and ignored, little Mollie declared loudly, "I'm not going to bed until I've been played with!"

"Good girl!" I said. Praising her lavishly for standing up for herself, I didn't add what I knew. I should do the same.

I loved walking, but Jim never walked unless it was on the golf course. Early in our marriage he had bought me golf clubs and took me to a course to learn golfing. I hated it. The golf course was beautiful and I wanted to enjoy it. Following that stupid little white ball interfered with walking on the lovely golf course.

We tried going for a walk in the neighborhood. Jim could not bring himself to walk beside me. He walked a little behind me or a little ahead; I had to either lead or follow. It was that vertical relationship I'd detected before. I was Mother or the dog.

I loved walking in the St. John's woods, usually to Stella Maris chapel. Pat was in the St. John's Boys Choir and learned to love the same thing, so I risked suggesting a walk in the woods as a family activity, even though a suggestion from me usually got an automatic dismissal. But we set out on our walk. We had barely begun when Jim stopped and headed back. The kids and I continued without him. Afterward, I asked him why he quit. "I had to go to the bathroom," he said angrily. *Why didn't you say so?*

Another time we were shopping together. I found the item and went into a checkout lane, the kids following. Jim came after us and deliberately went into a different lane. The kids left mine and went into his. I followed because he had the checkbook. Similar ways of asserting power over me were happening more often as we tried spending more time together.

For a brief period, Jim's behavior became bizarre. I struggled to read him until I realized he was trying to prove he could do without alcohol and was experiencing withdrawal. One Saturday he stayed home all day—this was unusual. He complained, "If you want me to stay home, have baked goods for me to eat." I was dumfounded. He rarely was home for a whole day, much less craving sweets. Puzzling over it, I recalled learning about a connection between alcohol and sugar, and I remembered his enthusiasm for ice-cream drinks years earlier after being told he had an ulcer.

Close to the end of our marriage, Jim enrolled us in a couples' bowling league. Men bowled on one side of the alley, women on the other. One evening I was angry, I was fed up and took it out on my bowling ball. Astoundingly—I am no fan of sports, either as player or spectator—I won a trophy for high women's score in the league! *Not bad for someone who disdains sports.*

Pat and Mollie did not talk about their dad's behavior or tension in the house. Talking about it was taboo; my uptight manner had made this a tacit family rule. But after a particularly caustic outburst from Jim, I overheard Mollie talking loudly to Monkey, her beloved stuffed companion. The word "angry" rang out repeatedly.

One Saturday morning I woke up and was startled by a voice inside saying clearly, "You are violating yourself." Sometime after that, we were together as a family in the living room of our home—it was a Sunday morning after church—when the realization hit again. I left, walked to the bedroom, and doubled over in pain at the thought of breaking up our family. The inner voice sounded again. "There will be no spring in your life unless you do this."

In church, ironically, the voice inside urging divorce grew louder, more insistent because it had less competition from outer voices saying, "What will people think?" My inner self's counsel bypassed religious rules. I had to get out of that marriage for my health. It was killing my spirit. But I wanted outer authority telling me to do it.

The familiar inability to speak for myself, a consequence of being unheard in childhood, frustrated me until I made an appointment with one last counselor. She listened, asked questions, listened to my answers, asked more questions, and I found our conversation turning toward the unavoidable decision—divorce. I think of that moment with some humor. One minute I was writhing in my chair under her implacable line of questioning, and the next she was saying in surprise, "You don't have to do it *now*!"

I am the one who produced the implacable line of reasoning because my inner being had worked it out, had already decided on divorce. I was just seeking endorsement from a counselor. The deed did have to be done "now." I was doing what my astute high school student had observed years before—taking it and taking it, before finally acting.

During summer break, I had a hysterectomy to remove a womb full of fibroids. Lying in bed at home to recuperate, my eye went to a crucifix hanging on the wall opposite me. It told me, "Do the difficult thing no matter how hard." I got up, went to the kitchen, scanned a list of attorneys in the yellow pages, put my finger on one, and called him.

That evening I told Jim. He had seen it coming and made immediate plans to move out. When we broke the news to the kids, Pat shredded a box of Kleenex. He had sat us down one day, his dad on one side and me on the other, and Patrick was going to fix our marriage. He was twelve years old. Days after Jim moved out, Pat said, "Dad was always gone anyway."

Even after we separated, I hoped the divorce would not happen. The hysterectomy was followed by diverticulitis, which dumped me back in the hospital. Jim visited and was kind. I yearned to take back what I had done. To my vulnerable self it looked like the easier path. My Benedictine

Al-Anon friend reminded me of things I had said when I was stronger. Without her support, I might have caved in.

If readers wonder, "What took you so long? What's the big deal?" they have no experience with a blanketing religious culture. Divorce was shameful, wrong, unthinkable. Good people and ordinary people did not get divorced. The hardest thing about the decision was knowing how others would respond to it. I knew it was good for my family, Jim included, but my religious siblings would not agree.

They were horrified. Two siblings phoned to denounce me. "Divorce is wrong. What will people say?" Catholic, Catholic, Catholic had been our life. Unlike some brothers and sisters, Mother and Father did not berate me for divorcing. I'm guessing they were stunned and sensed my vulnerability. I told them, "Jim's an alcoholic."

"There was alcoholism in my family," Mother said. Dad mumbled a disparaging comment about Jim. Today I wonder what other thoughts were swirling in their minds.

My husband's refusal to face himself became a blessing; his fear of inner work was fortunate for me. We were incompatible in many ways, making unlikely either marital harmony or healing for me. If he had had the courage to join AA—not only to attend meetings but to be honest— guilt would have prevented my following through. His refusal liberated me to leap free and grow to a level impossible while still coupled with him. It also prodded him to grow.

Therapists who work with alcoholics say that children in alcoholic families tend to have difficulty with intimate relationships. This description fit Jim perfectly and made him a perfect fit for me. By marrying a man who did not listen to me and gave me no physical affection, I met the psychological expectation formed in my family of origin.

Musing about it today, I am sure that my resentment, timidity, and lack of straight talk contributed to our toxic relationship. We were immature in the same way—both inheriting a shame base, both lacking self-respect, both anxious to prove our worth and make a good impression. The strange spark between Jim and me had not happened with any other guy. We were meant for each other. I did not say this to myself then, but I say it now. By living with each other, Jim and I were given the opportunity to grow emotionally and spiritually.

Having grown up as one of the "kits," I needed more resilience, resourcefulness, and belief in myself. After the divorce, I found chores in house and yard easier because I was no longer resenting Jim for not helping. Another blessing rose to my awareness when someone sympathized with me for being lonely as a divorced person. I realized I was *less* lonely. I was developing my own friendships.

For a short while after the divorce, Pat and Mollie came back from having spent time with their dad, treating me like an enemy. I knew why. At Catholic Charities divorce seminars, we were warned against the temptation of setting our kids against the divorced spouse. What I would have done without this admonition I don't know, but it prevented my retaliating in kind. The kids' hostility after Dad-visits soon stopped. They seemed to catch on and Jim apparently stopped it.

The divorce seminars also predicted that we'd fall in love on the rebound, another helpful warning. I had a string of infatuations that I don't call falling in love because "love" is too precious a word for it. I knew my yearnings were unrealistic and can't even remember all the men. My rational mind and fear of making a fool of myself kept me from succumbing to the emotions. In time, I decided to stop yearning for what might never happen and accept the single state. I got a Catholic annulment, though, because I wanted a public statement that mine had never been a true marriage of minds and hearts. Maybe at that time I also wanted to align with Catholic expectations.

Jim's unfortunate beginning in school and thwarted artistic bent had prevented him from getting a decent education. It drove him to rowdy drinking friends in high school and drove his escape in sports and drink. Being the son of an alcoholic made his own alcoholism almost inevitable.

8

Midlife Meltdown

Mid-life

If my goal
is to be whole

I cannot evade
the pain of your flame.

Before the remolding
Comes the meltdown.

Descending into Darkness

AFTER ONE YEAR OF teaching at St. Cloud State, the university had no need of my service for the following fall quarter. I needed a job now that I was on my own with the kids—child support fell far below expenses.

Desperately I applied for a job teaching ninth graders at St. John's Preparatory School, although teaching middle schoolers was not a good fit for me. The prep school had a superior German program built and led by a native Austrian with studies abroad in Melk, Austria. He had observed my teaching of German at Albany, which I am certain gave me the job at the prep school. While I was teaching there, St. Cloud State called and asked me to teach again during spring quarter. I couldn't take the position because I was under contract at St. John's Prep.

At the prep school I nearly fell apart. Supposedly I was teaching ninth graders, but my main job that year was the grueling, emotional work of getting divorced. One time I actually printed a test with answers and gave this to students instead of printing the test for them. At the end of that school year, the prep school director made the reasonable decision not to hire me for the next school year.

This propelled me into a depression that plagued me off and on for years. One career path after another led nowhere. A person looking at this from the outside might assume I should have gone full time at Albany to avoid unemployment, but I never regretted leaving Albany. I was glad of being free to do inner work.

Perhaps my orientation toward depression was fed in childhood by my mother's frequent, anguished laments, but even this I cannot regret. Without that impetus, I might not have had the inner journey. These are my thoughts after the period in life that has received many names, "dark night of the soul" and "midlife crisis" among them. I also call it my womb/tomb period, when I was being reborn.

I felt worthless, inadequate in every way. One thought moored me—I had accomplished my divorce. Propelled from inside, I had made the hardest decision of my life. Having lost my career as educator, I had no financial security, but I told a sister, "I have to do it even if I lose my house and land on the street with Pat and Mollie." Few women in my generation had the financial means to leave a marriage without taking a huge step out of physical comfort and safety. Fear kept them trapped. I know women who resisted their insides' push to divorce for fear of financial consequences and of defying public opinion. One told me years later that she envied me, saying, "I still feel trapped."

Once taken, the move out of marriage brought relief and conviction about its rightness. Financial panic set in at times, but always I was glad I got out. I thanked my Higher Power for helping me to pass the barrier of fear and move toward wherever I was headed.

Now, however, I had to face the awfulness of my situation. What would become of me? What was I to do? The university had found someone else to teach German classes and had no more need of me. High schools would not hire me because my years of experience made me too expensive. I dropped the plan to be a German professor and tried psychology by taking a graduate course leading to high school counseling.

I remember that class with sardonic humor because of how ridiculously wrong it was for me. Instead of psychological insights, various theories were taught. To me they seemed mechanistic, superficial facts irrelevant to the thoughts roiling my insides. Memorizing facts was required for the final. I got the lowest grade in the class, the opposite of my usual performance and a clear sign I did not belong there.

A few activities in that class, however, left memories of value. One was speaking to college freshmen unsure of their future. The group assigned me had low grade point averages. I drew from affirmations in Unity readings and told them that each of them had a set of skills suited to a worthwhile occupation, and they would be guided to it. As I spoke, I could feel their gratefulness. They might never before have heard an educator lifting them up in this way. In speaking to them, I was speaking to myself, I realized later. I had forgotten how rich with gifts I had begun teaching and how capably I had taught.

Now, stunned and grieving the losses of marriage and career, I felt incapable of coping with daily duties beyond ordinary demands of life like feeding myself and my children. The world and my kids said, "Get a job get a job get a job."

"Here's a night clerk position in a motel," someone reported, trying to help. I knew it would crush me more. Getting a job was all wrong. I wanted to shake off outer responsibilities to absorb the awful reality of losing my identity. I'd been teacher, wife, and respectable member of society. It was the end of my life as I'd known it. I wanted to belong somewhere.

Cheery Christmas greetings depressed me more. "Ryan made the hockey team." "Lyle's excited about his new position." "Janelle got honors at Holy Trinity School."

"How are you?" asked a friendly, unaware acquaintance. How could I possibly answer without lying? It was not the time or place to tell the truth. I have never stopped disliking that question and still look for ways to avoid conventional answers, which seem insincere until I realize that I *am* doing well. Whatever my answer today, I think, *you don't know how hurtful that question can be.*

Beginning to Rise

When in need, I look for answers in reading. Besides food for the mind, reading gives me comfort and counsel. Then, it was indispensable. It taught me stages of the grief process and how they applied to me. I had not lost anyone by death but had lost my former self, my position, my family, my friends. Friends? Before Al-Anon I had not had friends with whom I could be real. I had worn a mask to hide the feeling of inadequacy at my core. In Al-Anon I was building new and real friendships, connecting more deeply than ever before. We marveled that we didn't know each other's outer facts—where we lived, what we did for a living, who our parents and children were—but we knew each other's souls.

I did whatever I could find to do for recovery, propelled in part by the book *Inner Work: Using Dreams and Active Imagination for Personal Growth*, by Robert Johnson. A Jungian analyst and author, Johnson honored the tumult inside and helped me to cope actively with my grief. I meditated, prayed, journaled, attended workshops, seminars, and presentations. I read, reread, and reflected on the book of Job, feeling with him as he mourned his losses. Job's sorrows and complaints to God became consoling therapy because they validated mine. So did others' stories of sorrow.

Money worries dominated. What work was I to do in the second half of my life? Most urgent was the question of survival. How could I, responsible for Pat and Mollie, survive financially during the interim between careers? How were we going to live? The ill-suited path of high school counselor was one of five directions I considered while casting about for a new career.

The future seemed utterly bleak. In a desperate moment I was pacing around my dining room table, inwardly crying, *What's to become of me?* Suddenly a cup from high on my hutch shot out and into my hands. A plate propped upright for display had sat down and thrown the cup in front of it. Plate and cup had been positioned thus without incident for ten years before and have been there for thirty years since. Immediately I felt assured by the mysterious missive. I knew the cup falling into my hands had spiritual significance—don't ask me how I knew, I knew. A loving presence was walking with me.

This presence assured me also when unemployment insurance payments stopped. I had not paid attention to the termination date and needed $200 immediately for a mortgage payment. Out of the blue came a call from my parish priest to say that someone gave him $200 to pass on to someone in need. Did I need it?

In another moment, I'd come home from volunteering at a sexual assault center after the miserable year teaching ninth graders. There I heard young women outline their life plans. Amy was looking at college catalogs. Sherry was starting classes for an associate degree. Keenly I felt the absence of plans. I felt a failure, forgetting my nearly twenty successful years of teaching. Opening the Bible (still going there for help), I sought consolation. The words of John 15 rose from the page. "It was not you who chose me, it was I who chose you to go and bear fruit." Bleak hopelessness again was transformed into hope.

Religion still was my habitual source of soothing and succor. Catholic Charities offered seminars for persons in need of consolation and healing after divorce. I was not grieving divorce, but sessions on grieving seemed right for me. Others at the seminar bemoaned their single state. The Sister leading the seminars astutely observed that I seemed to be grieving, not the divorce, but something else. *Yes.* But I could not articulate my problem. It was loss of my station in life, my respectability, but more. Who was I?

We were told to deal with our feelings. Deal with them? I imagined dealing feelings like cards. Going past the bitter joke, I figured out that I should face them by letting myself feel them fully. I found it worked and have used the strategy since then. Cry. Hurt. Let it happen. Amazing, how the pain really can be felt out, pressed out (ex-pressed). It does not disappear, but it gets old and eventually fades. Getting to the other side of pain is not possible without sloshing through the muddy center of the feelings until they grow old and stop hurting as much.

A story in an American Literature text I taught from decades ago came to mind. John Colter joined the Lewis and Clark expedition. On the way back from the Pacific Coast, Colter left the expedition to have more adventures by himself. And did he! He was the first European to see the natural marvels in what would become Yellowstone Park (his stories were not believed), and he was the first to see the Grand Tetons.

Colter encountered the Blackfeet Indians. Stephen Ambrose, in *Undaunted Courage*, writes that the Blackfeet were the enemies most dreaded by American Indians and the Lewis and Clark expedition. The Blackfeet stripped Colter naked and forced him to run for his life. A fast runner, Colter left all but one far behind. Exhausted and bleeding from the nose, he suddenly stopped, turned around, and spread out his arms in surrender. His Blackfoot pursuer was so surprised that Colter quickly staked him to the ground, literally, and eventually escaped from the Blackfeet for good.

The image of Colter stopping to run from his pursuer, turning around to face him, and accepting his fate fortified me. Once I stopped running from the pain of my losses and feelings of inadequacy, once I met my hurting self, the pain stopped pursuing me and I could begin to heal. It took time and slogging through the swamp of unpleasantness, but I could not reach the mountain of serenity any other way. Going around the swamp does not work. To get past it, I had to go through it.

Al-Anon's Twelve Step spirituality and Unity School of Christianity continued to sustain me during this period. At an Al-Anon meeting someone responded to something I said with wide eyes and the words, "You are so hard on yourself!" *Huh? Isn't it good to criticize myself?* Unity publications reinforced the lesson that it's *not* good. Affirmations from Unity and Al-Anon members gave me permission to love myself and listen to myself. Loving and listening to others follows naturally.

Besides Al-Anon meetings, I went to ACOA for Adult Children of Alcoholics. My upbringing did not happen in an alcoholic home but a home where we did not acknowledge feelings. Catholic training reinforced this cover-up. At Twelve Step meetings I listened to others and recognized myself in their stories, gradually becoming aware of the turbulence inside. Squelched feelings were harming every aspect of my life. Until I recognized them, they wouldn't let me go.

But how to find those feelings and get past them? Mentors and counselors kept advising me to write them out in journaling. I finally stopped resisting and tried it. The first things I wrote seemed pointless but I kept at it. Then I let myself go, as pent-up emotions exploded. Some of what gushed out was unreadable, though eloquent. Deep gashes scratched on the page said nothing, but said everything. On one page I screamed that I felt more worthless than every other human being in the world.

The vehemence of the commotion inside shocked me. How worthless I felt! *This writing must not be seen by anyone else!* Some years later, I burned the journals from that period in my fireplace. I made a ritual of it, hoping to put an end to that chapter in my life. There are times I regret burning them, curious to see my emotional evolution.

Burning the journals did not erase from memory a certain passage that kept on burning. "Pay attention to me!" The feeling was roiling inside before I gave in to its demand to be written down. Ferociously I resisted while scratching out the words. They were embarrassing. I hated reading them. Why did I want attention? It seemed selfish.

Did I experience some trauma very early in life, before remembering begins? That seemed right. Was it sexual assault? Children who have been molested bury the memory where it can wreak havoc years later. I learned this when I volunteered at the sexual assault center and devoured the contents of files there. My journaling suggested I had buried a traumatic memory, and sexual assault often is the culprit. Those facts fit. But there was no plausible suspect in my life and sexual assault did not exactly fit my feelings. I decided that could not be it. The answer did not come until decades later.

Journaling was hard work, but it unleashed thoughts, feelings, and beliefs I did not know I had. This was spiritual work, and it was accomplishing more than going to Mass or confessing sins and hearing a priest say words of absolution. Religion had not led to authentic spiritual growth. All it said about relationships was to put others first. Psychology taught me to find and face the feelings that blight relationships.

I learned from Carl Jung that the Christian emphasis on sin and guilt encourages us to deny what we don't like in ourselves. He called this the shadow side of our personality. "You are so hard on yourself!" was a wake-up call. I had been taught that it's bad to think well of myself, bad to honor my desires, bad to want good things, and stupid to expect good things. Denying myself and being good to others resulted in kidding myself and not being much good to others. I was a "good Christian," out of touch with my inner, unknown self.

Actively I grieved my losses by doing inner work—long sessions in solitary quiet time that let in new light. Back I went to childhood memories and feelings, the emotional self I had ignored and covered over with intellectual pursuits. I'd been afraid of letting people know who I am because I didn't like myself and could not believe others would like me without the varnish of my smarts and talents. My real self, my genuine self, was hidden.

I found the lost lonely child who had no one to talk to while growing up on the farm. To hide her, I had put on outer faces to impress whomever. Shame afflicted our family, learned from Mother I think, coming from her childhood of being forced to put plow before school. I had absorbed her feelings of being victimized and shamed.

The lowest point in my life arrived when my unemployment insurance ran out. In desperation, I applied for a job at Sears peddling maintenance agreements. The first day was a few hours of training. I remember little of what happened that day and evening, because inside all was black. I do remember Mollie in the evening trying to cheer me up by asking me what she should wear to school the next day. *She thinks life will go on,* I thought, then realized with horror what it showed about my state of mind.

In the middle of the night I learned why it is said that people "burn in hell," because my body burned. If the only course possible was so completely wrong for me, so contrary to my nature, how could there be any goodness in the universe? Any harmony? Any purpose? A "good Christian" would accept this mortification to earn merit for "the kingdom of heaven," but I had come far enough in my spiritual journey to reject that nonsense. Why, though, should I be forced into work so repellent to me? How could it be that my natural interests and talents should remain so thwarted?

To get myself anchored in this life, I touched my cat at the foot of my bed, opened a drawer and sought relief in a Unity pamphlet. I don't remember the words that appeared that night, but the episode shows the saving difference for me of Unity teachings—their ability to heal me of my self-defeating patterns of thought. Unity literature teaches that we create our own reality with our thoughts, beliefs, attitudes, and feelings. My reaching out for hope led to hope, and that set me free of despair. I could go to sleep.

The next morning I returned to Sears, but the trainer released me. She had noticed my uninterested, distracted, and downright incompetent motions the day before. "Released" is the right word rather than "fired," because my heart sang on the way home. Goodness and Harmony exist! The universe does not run on random and nonsensical chance. Life has purpose and meaning! That I was set free from that dumb job affirmed my natural being. It told me I was not a mistake, and it said the same about all reality. I was perfectly aware the job was stupid only for me, not for someone suited to it.

In the evening, Jim came over to say he would pay the bills—the kids had told him the state I was in the evening before. Jim's action relieved me but did not surprise me. Before getting the guts to go through with the divorce, I knew he would treat me better if I stopped being his wife, if I stopped being the card that held up his card. I had seen him treat other women well. Now that I was not "the wife" anymore, he didn't need to fight me anymore. Jim showed more of this natural generosity in subsequent years.

Writers about the grief process tell us to deal with anger. A Sister in one of the many healing sessions I attended made anger less a menace when she gave us permission to get mad at God. "Let 'im have it!" she said. *What a relief!*

It was explained that anger resides in the body and must be worked out *physically* if we don't want it to show up at inconvenient times. I read that inanimate objects can't get hurt or hurt me back. From shouting out feelings in writing, I moved to beating out anger. Ever the educator, I knew all about assignments and pushing yourself to do them. Beating out anger became an assignment for times Pat and Mollie were in school and I was alone in the house. Deliberately I scoured rage and other crap out of my insides by pounding my mattress and the back of the couch. With them as my punching bags, I dug up buried anger and got rid of it. Did it work? My eventual transition from resenting Jim to appreciating the good in him shows that it did.

I tried not to do active grieving when the kids could see me, but during my plunge into the depth Mollie began to draw faces—always a woman, always sad. The drawings became more skilled, the woman sadder, sometimes with tears. Impressed by my daughter's artistic talent, I encouraged her to pursue it and bought art supplies for her. She never used them. The drawings stopped. The mood in her mother was changing.

Some questions were not answered yet. What was that thing between my mother and me? And wanting attention? Answers to these questions hadn't come yet, but I was getting at the cause of my depression and working on being real. I was starting to find the self who had been waiting to be discovered.

During my religious search I had tried a variety of non-Catholic churches, but none remotely satisfied me. My doubts applied to Christianity as a whole. No denomination had more intellectual power and validating history to wrestle with my questions than Catholicism. I was exploring the meaning of life—the mysterious inner center of life, the infinite realm, the *within* of Teilhard de Chardin. I had forgotten him, but his central message—his *within* merging psychology with religion, philosophy, and science—was still shaping my intellectual and emotional life.

Metaphysical musings did not put an end to anxiety over the course of my life. Among possible paths in pursuit of answers, I considered courses in theology and interviewed at St. John's, Collegeville. Weeks later, I received a letter telling me I had gotten a scholarship to attend the School of Theology at St. John's, brother monastery to St. Benedict's and even nearer to my home. Doubling over in surprise and relief, I wept tears of gratitude. The news felt like writing on the wall: "This is your path."

The School of Theology

At the School of Theology, the halls rang with an exhilarating melee of divergent accents, languages, and even religions, but Catholic culture overrode differences. Studying Christian theology seemed a homecoming. It was so familiar, but I recoiled in distaste when class content sounded like typical Christian piety. Repellent to me was worshipping a god named "Jesus Christ."

Unity writings treated "Christ" as the divine heart of humanity, distinct from the man Jesus in history but consistent with Paul's writing in Galatians 2:20, "Christ is living in me." During my midlife journey to the depth, I experienced this infinite Christ in myself, which is to say, in every person. It was my Higher Power.

The scholarship that sent me to the School of Theology surprised me so that I was unprepared to select a major area of study. From a list of possible majors, I hesitantly chose spirituality. At a session with fellow women grads, one told me she was majoring in systematics. I didn't know what that was. She and I have forgotten her description that day, but it felt right for me. I changed my major to systematics and kept spirituality as my minor.

Systematic theology, also called dogmatic theology, studies the system of beliefs or doctrines. Trinity and Christology occupy center stage by studying Jesus' place in divinity and humanity—precisely my question. I had been stretched beyond the boundary of Christian teachings and wanted to know how Jesus fares in the company of the Buddha, Isis, and other deities. Teilhard, Jung, mythologists, non-Christian authors, and my sojourn into atheism prepared me uniquely to study dogmatic theology for a master's degree.

I was used to sexism in the secular world, but its extreme form in theology made me aware of how much progress the secular culture had made in gender sensitivity by 1986, the year I entered the SOT. Patriarchal power pervaded religious texts and utterly excluded the feminine. God was always "He" and people were always "man." He/Him/His/Father/Lord hit me in the gut.

In texts on the history of spirituality, the contributions of outstanding women such as Hildegard of Bingen were recorded as the work of "laymen." Could women be any more effectively disappeared or demeaned? Males were assumed to be active, females passive. Some theologians decided that, in relation to God, every soul must be female, "she longing for her Beloved" and submitting to the divine "He." How could men stand this? How could people respect language so insulting to half the human race—no, insulting to both men and women?

Augustine believed and taught that a husband has authority over his wife's body. In wifely submission, she must accept his semen in the act of sex like soil for seed sown by her husband. My notes tell me that after a lecture on Augustine's Trinitarian theology, I erupted in fury after class. I don't remember the incident. According to my notes, I was embarrassed at the time but wrote, "I think they need such spontaneous displays of feminist anger."

In my private thoughts I railed against Christian gods and what I called "he-man" language. I struggled to reclaim the expanded perspective I had achieved before entering the SOT. Faculty, staff, and students surrounding me generally seemed oblivious of the sexist bias. But more than one male student told me that my insistence on inclusive language prodded him to greater awareness. No professor told me this, but I got the sense it was also true for some of them. In a few cases, however, I suspect my grades suffered because of unconscious bias in professors.

The contrast between the language that so offended me and the kindness at St. John's amazed me. Despite my distress over the male-centered system of thought, my stint there helped to restore me. The monks and theology staff were kind, and I needed kindness to soothe my battered self. I said I was a feminist. No matter. They accepted me kindly. It's not that they understood the feminist critique—they just knew they should be kind to everyone.

A woman instructor and I had a complicated relationship at the SOT—Sister Luella. The first paper I wrote at the School of Theology fulfilled a requirement for her class. It was a reflection on "The Cloud of Unknowing," a contemplative work highly esteemed and often quoted. It referred to the Cloud ("God") as "He," never "It" or "She," to which I objected because this exemplified male-dominant thought. My criticism of the treasured work did not sit well with her. When we met to discuss my paper, she disparaged my writing so harshly—not only the paper, but my writing—that tears sprang to my eyes.

Days later Luella told me that an acquaintance of hers raved over my inclusive interpretation of "Christ" in an article I wrote for *Sisters Today*, a magazine for monastics. She hoped, "This should make your day!" I appreciated her evident regret for having hurt me but also hoped she would seriously reflect on my challenge to patriarchal language.

In a later course I took from Luella, we had to present our papers orally to the class before turning in the final project. My paper surveyed the Christian tradition through the frame of a power shift. Using quotations from early to later writings, I tracked the shift from an adversarial relationship with God as a power over us ("the god out there and over us") to God as a power within each of us. My oral presentation garnered enthusiastic approval. Especially gratifying was affirmation from seminarians in the class. Their respect gave me a feeling of triumph. When I got the paper back and looked for the grade, I found no comments anywhere but a tiny penciled "A" on the last page.

Luella and I sparred intermittently throughout my time there and even after I graduated. Often I thought about our arguments. From Jung and Twelve-Step I'd learned that psychology is the study of spirituality and *psyche* is the Greek word for soul. Psychology and spirituality address the interior aspect of our selves—the truest, most important part. But Luella did not see emotional healing as spiritual healing, and she never budged from her position that, if it's not religious, it's not spiritual. I thought that if she would suffer trauma and probe her own feelings afterward, she would see its spiritual value.

While a student at the SOT, I was sorting through emotional baggage in addition to religious beliefs. Two fellow students, priests with experience in psychological counseling, gingerly and obliquely offered their help. "I see pain in your face," said one.

"That's no surprise. I'm close to the bottom of my life," I said, declining his offer. I didn't need any more divorce counseling. And I wasn't going to ask priests to reconcile the disjunction between Christian claims and facts coming from non-Christian religions. Today, I would love to have long talks with them because my awareness has matured since then.

Cancer

Money worries persisted. To attend the School of Theology, I depleted my teacher's retirement savings, which didn't cover the whole bill because I had taught more part time than full time. Worry led to cancer. The lump in my right breast was enormous, said the eyes of the doctor who examined me. He was less calm than I was. I had had lumps removed from my breasts before and knew breast cancer was not always fatal. I expected to survive this like everything else. It was just one more thing. Jim was getting married again, but that didn't upset me. He insisted on keeping me covered on his medical insurance.

I asked my oldest sister, Verna, to be there for me during my mastectomy. After the surgery, she told me with voice and face that the doctors reported serious concerns. I got the message that they expected the cancer would kill me. During the mastectomy they discovered it had metastasized into the lymph nodes. They cut out twelve nodes, those they could reach. Those not accessible by surgery would be attacked by radiation. First, I would get chemotherapy. I realized I might die, but it did not lead to panic.

I admire cancer patients who refuse chemotherapy and radiation to avoid their toxic effects on the body. Alternative therapists recommended meditation, visualization, relaxation, and yoga. I followed their suggestions for quieting my mind, but I knew I was not strong enough to defy the medical establishment by going the alternative path alone.

Carl Jung explained that cancer comes from unresolved emotional conflicts. His father, a Protestant minister, felt obligated to believe doctrines that didn't make sense to him. Jung tried to share his own felt experience of God, but his father could not understand. Jung "was seized with the most vehement pity" for his father, who became increasingly depressed, contracted cancer, and died.

In my first conversation with the oncologist who would be my primary doctor for seventeen years, I said that emotional stress brought on the cancer. He delivered the standard scientific dismissal at the time: "Emotions play no role in bodily health." He didn't convince me. I applied Jung's explanation to myself but didn't expect to die.

Money worries stressed me, but what occupied my thoughts more than cancer was the disparity between the man Jesus who lived in history and the god made of him by religion. Perceptive professionals had listened and helped me in the past but not with my unique issue. I could not think of anyone able to listen to my churning thoughts about religion. I could not die yet because I wanted to inform Christians that Jesus Christ resembled Greek heroes in pagan religions. I wanted Christians to *think*. In retrospect, I believe my determination to keep learning and inform others of my discoveries overcame the threat from cancer.

My experience with cancer told me there are things worse than death. I took federal financial help, at that time called AFDC (Aid for Families with Dependent Children), and this was much harder to bear, infinitely more painful, than physical ills. Being on public assistance was the most humiliating, mortifying, demeaning, embarrassing, shameful thing I have ever experienced. Cancer was a cakewalk by comparison. In fact, having cancer helped, because I could forgive myself for getting welfare while being treated for cancer.

Invitations to join cancer survivor groups didn't appeal to me. I had little in common with people "fighting" cancer. I wanted to address what was eating me. Continuing my inner work had to be done alone. Studies at the School of Theology fed my hunger for more information and took my mind off money worries.

I do not wish to have been spared the blows that gave me cancer. It allowed time to synthesize strands of life with metaphysical musings. Plunged beneath the surface of life, I learned to know myself and worked through garbage I didn't like, such as envy of others whose lives seemed easier. Cancer also became more blessing than curse because it brought badly needed attention and sympathy.

The years spent in self-reflection and despondency—I was never suicidal but understand the impulse—contained moments of sublime awareness, as an underworld of shadow and reflection revealed a mysterious world of beauty, full of meaning. A secret, hidden place opened inside as the darkest period in my life became the most glorious. Curse became blessing; suffering unleashed joy; misery led to ecstasy. In a state of uncertainty, I was certain I belonged there. Paradox and metaphor flooded me with inner truth. I knew I would never again descend to the depth of despair.

I call this my womb/tomb period because it felt like I went back to the womb to be reborn and spent time in a tomb to be transformed and resurrected. Slowly I died and slowly I rose. Returning to routine, everyday chores felt like returning above ground. Walking in my neighborhood past familiar houses, I felt as if I had been gone and come back, as if I had been on a journey. I marveled at how set apart I felt, how privileged to have seen precious wonders as I journeyed through my shadowed interior.

Gradually I climbed out of depression, but one question persisted. Why had the words "Pay attention to me!" burst out of me?

9

School of Theology Notes

Discovering Notes

I OPENED A DRAWER with the intention of cleaning it, that is, wade through stuff and throw out a lot of it. A cache of notes I'd saved from my School of Theology days came to light. So much writing! Mostly little slips on which I'd written thoughts, authors, and page numbers. I found packets of notes clipped together and newspaper clippings with items that pertained to Christian beliefs. Longer writings seemed early versions of papers for courses at the SOT. Some were full 8 1/2-by-11 sheets, typed. Computers were coming into use at the time but I didn't have one. It looked like I cut papers into parts, trying out ways to sequence paragraphs.

The cache reminds me of how I felt when I entered the SOT. On one of my half-page notes, I seethed over "a young inexperienced priest" being the only one allowed to preside and give homilies at Mass for "a community of religious women whose maturity and experience make them eminently more qualified." My stomach turns, I'd written, "when an older woman addresses a young priest as 'Father.'" I noted "a friend who is stuck in therapy with a male therapist because he seems afraid of her anger. He represents male power over her and it's not safe to be angry in his presence."

My notes recorded the struggle of Jackie, a friend who said, "God is foreign to me, a strength outside of me. How could that be in me? How could I be worthy?" It upset me that she took on Christianity's obsession with selflessness. To myself I wrote that the teaching to be totally selfless does not represent Jesus' teachings. "Your faith has saved you," says Jesus repeatedly in the gospels. To me this means that the historical Jesus directed people to respect themselves. His primary goal, making known the Reign of God within, reinforces this.

My notes recorded the confusion of another woman, who said, "Sometimes it's best to do what God doesn't want us to do." It startled me. She had shown herself to be fundamentally in harmony with her inner self. How could she say it's best to go against the will of God? She gave an example. "I know that it was best for me to divorce, but divorce is evil."

It was maddening. She confused Church teaching with God and split God from her own accurate perception of right and wrong. She did not doubt her inner voice as wise and true, but at the same time accepted religious officials' claim to represent God. Such conflation of Church teaching with God exasperated me also during a hospital stay when someone voiced the same confusion. My outraged answer may have carried to several rooms: "The Catholic Church is not God. The Catholic Church is not God!"

I was arguing with myself. The notes I found in my drawer both protested Church authority and showed my fear of it:

> Shoulds dominate my life.
> God is a bookkeeper who repays sin with suffering, tit for tat.
> It feels wrong to want good things for myself.
> Who I am is not good enough, no matter what I do.

In many notes I declared my determination to listen to my inner voice instead of giving priority to outer voices, showing my struggle to do just that. So simple to say, so hard to do.

Fear of crossing authority eventually made me mad at authority. I saw this in my indignant notes, where I likened piety to self-degradation.

> Sanctifying submissiveness does violence to victims.
> Sweet meekness keeps victims in their place.
> Guilt is necessary to make people dependent on religion.

My protestations against religious authority tell me how hard it was for me to cross that authority. The inability to calmly go my own way made me angry. I had forgotten how angry.

Mental disquiet throbbed out of my notes. I said that trying to believe what others told me to believe felt dishonest, like trying to hide my feelings. I had tried to convince myself I didn't feel hurt, angry, and resentful. But I did. Same with trying to believe what I'm "supposed to" believe. I argued, "I feel what I feel and believe what I believe, not what outer voices tell me to feel and believe."

My drawerful of notes contained reminders of tension during the era of John Paul II and Benedict XVI, formerly Josef Ratzinger, chief watchdog in the Congregation for the Doctrine of the Faith. During their combined thirty-four-year tenure, these popes squelched independence of conscience in opposition to the Second Vatican Council elevating the "whole people of God."

One note referred to the oath required of seminarians, priests, theologians, and teachers to swear allegiance to the teaching authority centered in Rome. I got a nice laugh from one quote by Ratzinger complaining there's "too much independent thinking" among the faithful. These words so obviously violated freedom of conscience that I imagined him looking chagrined when seeing his own words years later.

On one note I'd written,

> It is sad and funny to watch the Vatican trying to silence voices of dissent. Every time it creates a martyr like Raymond Hunthausen, Charles Curran, or Matthew Fox, it motivates more Catholics to be responsible for their own spirituality. A more liberal regime in the Vatican would not hasten the process as effectively.

My notes contained analysis of our tradition's moral theology:

> The disease of Christianity concentrates on external rules.

> Women and men yearn for a simpler time when all we had to do was follow the directions of "Father."

> I hear from Christian teachings that our first responsibility is to others. I learned the hard way that it's not so. If I'm not good to myself, I can't be good to others.

I saw my growing realization that religious admonitions to give up pride and practice obedience were written by men in charge giving orders, men at the top. Their emphasis on humility was fine counsel for themselves and others like them. Not good counsel for those taking orders and getting little respect. Not good for people-pleasing, afraid-to-disappoint personalities. In my notes I saw myself struggling to break free. I suspect now that I protested so much because a worm of guilt for divorcing and rejecting Christian doctrine kept crawling in me. Poring over the notes, I saw myself moving from confusion and anger to clarity and strength:

> I try not to submit anymore. My spiritual health depends on not taking too seriously people who try to should on me.

> Living for God and satisfying my desires is the same thing; they are not opposed.

> As I gain more courage to disobey human authority, I feel healthier, lighter, freer.

> What the hierarchy does concerns me less than it used to. Because I'm not in a religious community or working for the Church, I'm freer.

Official theology fought against the insights I'd gotten from Jung and Unity, but a voice within reminded me of my expanded perspective.

Godfrey Diekmann

One practice at the SOT impressed me with its wisdom—we were all on a first-name basis. The world-renowned Godfrey Diekmann, a great *peritus* (expert adviser) at Vatican II, was the beloved "Godfrey" to all of us. At the council, he persuaded the Church to institute liturgical reform by bringing people into active participation at Mass. For the first time, priests faced the people, Mass was said in English, and people answered in English.

These changes never were overturned by John Paul II and Benedict XVI (Ratzinger), although they would undo much of the spirit of Vatican II. Godfrey occasionally betrayed his concern with the culture they created when a provocative insight escaped his lips in class. He asked us, in effect, not to tattle on him.

Godfrey's mystical enthusiasm could move people to tears. One fan was my brother Al, who made a point of meeting Godfrey on one of his trips to Minnesota. While I was Godfrey's student, I did not know that he was born in Roscoe, a few miles from our farm. Early in the twentieth century his father, Conrad, taught our father in St. Martin. I am sure Godfrey did not know this. If I'd learned it, I doubt I would have told him because my father remembered Godfrey's father as the teacher who beat kids.

In my drawer's pile of papers, I found an article by Martin Marty, a Lutheran religious scholar who called Godfrey "a liturgical scholar unmatched in our time" for his role in the council's liturgy document—the "Magna Carta" for the laity. Marty directed his most effusive praise at what he called Godfrey's public *mea culpa*, in which Godfrey apologized for the change-making document he steered:

> It didn't really mean what it said about the basic equality of all members. . . . What we really meant, . . . was the basic equality of half the members—of those born male. . . .
>
> Neither in the preparatory committee . . . nor in the liturgy committee . . . nor the Implementing Committee was there one single woman—not as a member, not as a consultant, not as an observer. No women. . . .
>
> Worst of all, as far as I recall, no one of us who worked in these three successive groups adverted to this absence—this monstrous absence. . . .

So Godfrey Diekmann grew to understand the monumental injustice done by the Church to women! Great as were Godfrey's liturgical accomplishments for the Catholic world, nothing impresses me more than this confession. He said that the *periti* were ignorantly acting in "good faith" while oblivious to "the most urgent problem confronting the church today."

The "Problem of the Historical Jesus"

In my drawer I found a sheaf of papers on which I had written salient points in the thought of influential theologians. The history of Christian theology is studded with men breaking their heads over the question of why God would humiliate "himself" to become a man. They exclaim over the "vast chasm between God and man." They imagine divinity a distant, alien, unreachable entity "above man."

It disturbed me every time I met this so-called "problem of the historical Jesus" in readings or in class. I never said anything because I could not express what bothered me so much. I knew I was offended by the he-god and the use of "man" to mean all humans, but there was more. Today I know what disturbed me was the belief that a "vast chasm" separates us from divinity. I believe the man Jesus expressed divinity to an extraordinary degree, but we all are God-stuff.

Theologians conjured the "problem of the historical Jesus" because they had a low opinion of humanity. From Carl Jung, Teilhard de Chardin, Unity writings, Eastern spirituality, and my own experience, I became aware of depth in human beings, depth reaching into and participating in divinity. The official church preached the opposite. It said we are born with original sin, and we need a hierarchy of religious fathers to rule us and connect us with a father-god. The medieval ladder of worth and power placed children at the bottom, then women, then lay men without orders or power, then clerical men with power—deacon, priest, bishop, archbishop, cardinal, and at the top, the pope. Medieval church leaders expected kings, queens, princes, and all civil authorities to obey the pope.

Skimming my pages of notes, I stopped at my summary of a prominent theologian's thought. Anselm of Canterbury in the eleventh century interpreted salvation history in a way that struck me as outrageous and ridiculous. It was a nail I needed to hit.

To vent my scorn, I translated his ideas into a tragicomedy, a medieval drama with a cast of three: the feudal LORD-GOD who collects payments of honor, MAN who was created to give honor to LORD-GOD, and GOD-MAN JESUS. In the beginning, MAN dishonors LORD-GOD by sinning. He's in a fix—how to pay his debt to LORD-GOD? Negotiations between debtor and creditor arrive at an impasse because nothing MAN possesses equals the amount of debt he owes LORD-GOD. Poor MAN faces eternal damnation, an added insult to LORD-GOD, who demands payments of honor. Enter GOD-MAN JESUS, who as both MAN and GOD can meet the repayment amount. GOD-MAN JESUS takes care of the debt by dying.

This was Anselm's explanation of why Jesus had to come, his solution to "the problem of the historical Jesus." Reducing it to this dumb drama gave me some satisfaction for putting up with another male theologian preaching up-down thinking: We must obey and pay homage to those above us. We must feel unworthy because we owe a debt to a god outside of ourselves.

No female contaminated Anselm's theology, but in this he was not unique. Many theologians honored in our tradition believed women are defective. Some argued women have no souls. Thomas Aquinas elaborated on Augustine's belief that women's bodies are the soil for men's seed. Aquinas thought women are the defective result of defective semen planted by a man.

My cache of notes shouted outrage at the repellent beliefs. No one else seemed to have such strong feelings. Others seemed more able to slough off the misogyny in Church pronouncements. I could not. I had looked at religion as an atheist, had studied divergent religions, had imagined divinity feminine. My expanded perspective fought with the religious culture enveloping us at St. John's. In retrospect, I wonder whether others struggled in silence.

While I was there, I never overcame my fear of saying something that conflicted with prevailing beliefs. If I dared to say something unorthodox, I felt like scurrying into a corner and accepting rebukes. Now I see my study at the School of Theology as a chapter in learning to test my views against opposing ones without being disturbed by disagreement. I had to get over wanting others to agree with me.

Validation

A fellow student modeled the attitude I aspired to achieve. We were planning a liturgy and "Jesus, our savior," came up in the language. She said calmly but firmly, "Jesus is not my savior." I was impressed.

To be fair to the SOT, courses there did not teach the sentimental and saccharine idol of uninformed piety, although they taught a divinely exalted Jesus. Nothing I learned there overturned my prior convictions about Christian myth, and much supported it. Theologians use the terms "historical Jesus" and "Christ of faith" to distinguish between the man Jesus and the set of beliefs about him—the difference between man and myth. A group of scholars known as the Jesus Seminar came to my attention, notably Marcus Borg and J. D. Crossan. From them I learned to read the gospels with new eyes.

Jesus in history now came through as an illuminating sage and gutsy revolutionary, both compassionate and combative. This Jesus provoked people with wit, overturned common assumptions, and shattered certainties like a Zen mystic—"Happy are the poor." This Jesus mesmerized listeners and railed against religious officials, prompting his family to exclaim, "He's out of his mind" (Mark 3:21). This Jesus hung around with "the despised and rejected," a phrase from Isaiah 53:3 applied to Jesus after his death.

This traveling rabbi (teacher) kept reminding people of the spiritual reign beneath surface life. "Behold, the Reign of God is within" (Luke 17:21) and "The Reign of God is at hand" (Mark 1:15), meaning, to me, immediately available. Jesus kept pointing them to *the within*, to use the term Teilhard de Chardin used 1,900 years later. This was a man I could revere, not Jesus Christ on a throne at the right hand of God. My revised image of Jesus comes not from specific courses but from accumulated readings at the SOT. I am grateful for this.

Most valuable was the scripture class of Fr. Ivan Havener, who distinguished authentic sayings of Jesus from inauthentic sayings attributed to him. After Jesus' death, a natural process of myth-making ensued, producing inauthentic sayings not said by Jesus but put into his mouth by gospel writers. Ivan's book, *Q: The Sayings of Jesus*, put into stark relief the distinction between the man Jesus and the myth of Christ. It would inform my *God Is Not Three Guys in the Sky*. Ivan was fully aware that the official Church often teaches nonsense. One day in class he referred disparagingly to bishops in denial of facts. He wished religious officials would display more humility, and he stressed the need for changes in interpretation.

While I was studying there, Ivan died, stunning us all. No one on the faculty was more respected academically than Ivan, not even Godfrey. I was disappointed that I couldn't take another course from Ivan as I'd planned, but glad I'd gotten a critical signature from him. We grad students had to demonstrate proficiency in a language other than English by writing a test in it and using it in research. To demonstrate use of German in research, I cited a German article in a paper for Ivan. "Don't wait," warned a thought in me. I needed a signed statement from Ivan indicating I fulfilled the language requirement. Thanks to the warning, I got it before he died. My test result also gave me reason to smile. The faculty member who evaluated German language tests was surprised that a person named Clancy (obviously Irish) wrote well in German.

The paper I wrote for Ivan's class addressed a topic important to me—divorce. I intended to show that Church law conflicts with the man Jesus' statements. But after researching the subject I had to concede that the historical Jesus must have condemned divorce because this is attested in multiple passages. Matthew (5:32 and 19:9), Mark (10:11–12), Luke (16:18), and First Corinthians (7:10–11) all report Jesus speaking out against divorce. It is highly unlikely that all the accounts got it wrong. I was wrong in my expectation.

However, from information supplied by scripture scholars I concluded that Jesus condemned divorce for a reason. In his society, only men could initiate divorce—women were their property—and men could divorce for the flimsiest reasons such as burning food. Divorced women must have lived in exceedingly grim circumstances. I concluded, therefore, that Jesus of Nazareth opposed divorce out of compassion for women. After graduating I got the paper published in *Daughters of Sarah*, a Christian feminist magazine.

I suspect but cannot prove that a few grades given me at the SOT were influenced by the professor's unconscious bias. My feminism was graciously accepted by the monks and seminarians, but I riled some instructors with my edgy ideas. I cannot remember, though, ever daring to state my starkest dissent from Christian theology—not accepting Jesus as essentially superior to other human beings. I could not say, "I don't believe Jesus is God."

Times of unexpected pleasure and relief happened when fellow students shared my concern over the Church's treatment of women. One gratifying encounter happened in a bathroom where I met a woman who was as full of unsaid frustration as I was. We talked and talked and talked, sharing our reaction to experiences with oblivious males. In my experience, women at the SOT were aware of inherent sexism in Christian theology. That did not yet give me confidence to confess my belief that Christians and pagans had much in common.

The Saints

Theological writings enveloping us in the 1980s reeked of hierarchical views. I kept spirituality as my minor, and I'm glad, because the history of Christian spirituality exposed with damning clarity the damage done by patriarchal thought. Its most extreme form showed in Lives of the Saints, biographies meant to present models that the faithful were to emulate. They also were the most entertaining in their comic portrayals of humility and obedience spiced with gender prejudice.

The greatest saints were trained by the tradition to submit to authority above and to dominate subservient others below. A stronger woman than most, Teresa of Avila often apologized for being a woman. In her up-down universe, Teresa worries about the chain of command. Who is higher on the ladder of worth and power—the divine child Jesus or his human parent Joseph? Not even considering the possibility of Mary giving command, she decides that Jesus "was subject to Joseph . . . [so that] Joseph could give the Child command." The great Teresa of Avila caught in this trap of patriarchal authority!

Teresa's words come from her own autobiography, but most Lives of the saints were not history. They were hagiography—imaginative lives of saints, always adulatory and idealized. Hagiography, therefore, does not tell us much about the saints, but it tells us a great deal about the Christian mind-set at the time a life was written. One particularly entertaining for me was *The Little Flowers of St. Francis*. When Clare, Francis's feminine counterpart, is asked to bless loaves of bread, she answers, "I would deserve to be severely blamed if a vile little woman like myself should presume to give such a blessing in the presence of the Vicar of Christ." She consents to bless only "under holy obedience."

Francis, in *The Little Flowers*, gives "a wonderful sermon" about "the consuming fire of hell by which the damned have to be devoured for all eternity." He commands a monk to twirl around in "a childish way before all the lay people." It is the monk's duty to obey, even "if he should order you to throw stones." About the childish monks we read, "No one was heard telling stories or jokes . . . they wept over their own sins or those of their benefactors." The monks habitually think over their sins, do penance, consume only bread and water, go barefoot, and deprive themselves of sleep.

Hagiography about Antony, a prominent ascetic monk in the fourth century, also reveals the pathology of extreme asceticism. According to his hagiographer, Antony "mortified the body and kept it under subjection." He ate once a day at the most, often every fourth day. "His food was bread and salt, and for drinking he took only water." When he was about to eat, he would move away from others, "thinking he would blush if he were seen eating by others."

Benedict is considered the founder of Benedictines and of Western monasticism; his "Rule" continues to command respect. As with all great persons in history, myth attended his story. According to his hagiographer Pope Gregory ("the Great"), Benedict mortified his body. When the devil in the form of a woman beguiled him with "the softness of pleasure," Benedict resisted temptation by pondering the fire of judgment. On another occasion when the image of a woman rose to mind, Benedict fled sex by flinging himself naked "into sharp thorns and stinging nettles." He "had conquered pleasure through suffering."

So fanatically did the saints devote themselves to the doctrine of self-denial that they violated basic morality—love of self and others—by looking for ways to punish themselves. Antony refused to call his parents or relatives to memory. A brother in a life of Francis shocked his confreres when it seemed "he was grieving for his brother out of a natural and worldly affection."

Antony, Benedict, and the Franciscan monks were rendered foolish by hagiography. We would expect better from Teresa of Avila, but this is what she writes about her friendship with a monk: "His affection for me was not bad; but since it was too great, it came to no good." I read on, looking for how it came to no good but found only a chaste friendship focused on pleasing God. She castigates herself for being "grateful and loyal to anyone who loved me. Damned be such loyalty that goes against the law of God!" (Her exclamation mark, not mine.) In quoting Teresa, I do not deny her deserved reputation as a mystic; I criticize the deformed consciousness of the tradition.

Augustine of Hippo, Peter Brown's biography of Augustine, is copyrighted 1969. This balanced, informative study also reveals extremes in Christian thinking during Augustine's time. In the opinion of Augustine's mentor, absolute virginity was "the one thing that separates us from the beasts." Augustine himself wrote, "How sordid, filthy and horrible a woman's embraces seemed." When he preached on marriage, writes Brown, Augustine advised men to "love the sexuality of their wives and the physical bonds of their families only as a Christian must love his enemies." Augustine declared it was "Eve (the temptress) that we must beware of in any woman."

Before his conversion, Augustine had what we might call a common-law wife and a son by that union. His beloved's name is not mentioned in writings about the relationship he and the Christian community called "illicit." He did what the Christian world considered virtuous—abandoned her when he converted. But I react, *The Father's tyranny showing again!* I appreciate Augustine's contemplative writing but wish his patriarchal bias would not be overlooked.

My revulsion over religious patriarchy is amplified by its effects on my family. Grandma Thekla, *die Mädchen*, my parents, my whole family and I were influenced by the tradition's aversion to sex and its suppression of natural affection. Our lack of kisses and hugs, the emphasis on self-denial, and the sanctifying of prudery had Christian roots. As a St. Martin schoolgirl, I treasured pictures of saints given as prizes by the

Sisters who taught religion. At the School of Theology, the saints lost their idealized status in my eyes, but sanctity itself—plain goodness—became an attainable goal for everyone.

Wresting Free

In my drawerful of notes I found myself expressing surprise over my turmoil. Decades after being enlightened by mythology, philosophy, Goddess literature, and all the rest, I still was struggling to reconcile patriarchal Christianity with my pre-SOT revelations. I wrote that it felt "like going back and forth between camps." At the SOT I did not challenge Christianity's claim to having all the answers because "it was so uncomfortable disagreeing with everyone around me." They *apparently* did not question the Church's claim to sole authority. Is it possible some of them did?

When I was alone, I worked to regain the perspective that included the non-Christian world. Deliberately I shook off the conditioning on campus by reminding myself that rituals involving the Buddha, Isis, Persephone, and Mithra also immersed people in sacred space. I looked for universal ingredients in diverse traditions and found them.

Foolish questions and comments by a few seminarians propelled my efforts. Some fellow students betrayed their belief that Father, Son, and Holy Spirit were factual individuals—metaphor and symbol exceeded their grasp. One wondered, "How did the Son feel when his Father told him to go down to earth?" It reminded me of the gods on Mount Olympus responding to commands of Zeus. Another seminarian wondered how the Holy Spirit could be in two places at once. Amused, I watched instructors trying to grapple kindly with näive misunderstandings. I wanted to call out, "God is not three men!"

Witnessing literalist confusion in fellow students, I became determined to generate understanding that Father, Son, and Holy Spirit are figurative images rather than facts. Reflecting on this one day, the mantra "God is not three guys in the sky" burbled up in me. Surrounded by religious people earnestly preparing for church work, I did not dare say it, until I did. Beginning with individuals, then in classes and halls, I started saying, "God is not three guys in the sky!" No shocked looks. No reprimands. People around me seemed to understand. My courage grew. I thought, *It could be the title of a book: God is not three guys in the sky.*

Bright spots during my two years at the SOT came from beautiful people there. Caring and stimulating relationships brought me through the maddening content of patriarchal thought. I did not board on campus as it lies very close to my home. Other non-seminarian students boarded at Frank House and had liturgies in their communal living room, to which I was invited. With their inspiring contrast to most Masses, they converted my disdain for Christian liturgy to respect. Dan was the only ordained person in the house, so he presided, but what a presider! When people teased him by calling him "Father," he looked offended and said, "Nobody calls me 'Father.'"

For Eucharist, he sat cross-legged on the floor in front of a small, draped coffee table. The rest of us were comfortable on chairs, floor, or whatever. Tony competently led the singing with voice and guitar. "Led" misrepresents what this gentle man did. Neither he nor Dan wielded top-down power. The "homily" developed in reflections from whoever was inspired to speak, and prayer petitions likewise. We passed around the plate and cup, breaking off pieces of the bread for each other. Ritually we became bread broken for each other, as each of us received from one and gave to the next.

A potluck dinner followed, continuing the symbolism of sharing parts of ourselves. Frank House residents had to cooperate in preparing food because some had no kitchen facilities, only a room. Because I lived off campus it was understood that I brought nothing. At first I was unable to receive this generosity and brought something anyway. But they made sure I learned to just receive kindness from the community and let it happen.

It was in preparation for one of these Frank House liturgies that a fellow grad said firmly of Jesus, "He's not my savior." It was a memorable moment because Jesus is not my savior either, but I'd not had the courage to say it. I still try to emulate her unapologetic dissent.

The kiss of peace, more often hug of peace, was not perfunctory. It became necessary to limit ourselves to only the person on either side so that greetings did not interrupt the flow of the liturgy. I felt the genuine care of these people. The loving community healed and stretched me. In this ceremony I caught a glimpse of what motivated the spiritual explosion that was early Christianity. The most powerful and lasting images are of Dan sitting cross-legged on the floor in front of his low altar and of us sitting around him and breaking bread for each other. From these images I can receive some nourishment from my religion while putting up with patriarchal teachings in courses.

I am grateful to Elise for bringing me to the School of Theology before I knew I needed it. To Cyril for always using inclusive terms in reference to God and for sharing experiences in his native Ireland, making my dependence on AFDC bearable. To Godfrey for showing me the power and beauty hidden under the stale surface of Christian practice. To Ivan for communicating respect for scripture based on scholarship rather than authority. To Randy for trying and trying to reach me by phone to tell me that Ivan died suddenly. To Peter and Vivian for lugging my son's ghetto blaster to class to tape lectures for me while I was convalescing from my mastectomy. To Peter for calling me at the hospital to tell me he remembered me in the Mass he said that morning. To Joe for writing a birthday poem for me on a card he sent. It pictured a woman whose long, flowing hair sent life through her fingertips, adapted from Michelangelo's "Creation."

Studies in the School of Theology laid the foundation for my goal of escaping stale and oppressive religion, preparing me for a shift in perspective. It gave me tools for writing and speaking about religions and spirituality. It taught me to separate the intellectual probity of Catholic theology from the *magisterium*, which is defined as the teaching authority but manifests as the institution's meanest element, all-male officials intent on making rules.

10

After I Died, I Rose

I am a tree
budding into green,
bearing the brown
leaves of last season.

Cancer Struggle

I NEVER SOUGHT MEDICAL help to counter depression. My successful rebellion against Valium reinforced my determination to avoid psychotropic drugs for what I knew were emotional/spiritual challenges. Drugs might have made it harder to do the inner work necessary for recovery. But I wasn't up to defying my oncologists' prescriptions for treating cancer—chemotherapy and radiation. Today, I don't believe their assaults on my body made me well. I attribute my health to my persistent purpose for living.

I looked forward to doctor's visits and appointments for chemo or radiation because they provided interactions with adults who gave me caring attention. The kindness of medical attendants concerned for my health healed me more than their physical procedures.

When I was a child, lying sick in bed had been familiar and almost pleasant, but recovering from cancer alone was not pleasant. Hours spent in bed or dragging myself out of bed to meet physical needs were lonely. I was living this before stories of surviving cancer were common. Expecting to die of cancer was more common.

Radiation sapped my body of energy like nothing else. I wondered if broiling myself in hopes of tanning during college increased my sensitivity to radiation. Even today, I am frightened when exhaustion suddenly hits. It threatens me with a possible return of the complete physical wipeout after radiation. My head felt too heavy to lift off a pillow. Trying to make light of it later, I joked, "If you get cancer, don't tell the doctors. They'll try to kill you."

One time, weak from radiation, I asked for water and Mollie brought me water in her child's Disney cup. The too-small cup irritated me, though I tried not to show it. Later I realized the reason for it—she was trying to cheer me up. Her sympathy had shown in other ways, like hanging close to me when her father was verbally attacking me. But my children were too young to give me mature aid and support. And what hidden effects was all this having on them?

I didn't worry about dying of cancer. Was it because I'd been close to death before? Years before, we'd been floating down the Apple River on inner tubes and didn't heed the warning that rapids were coming. Jim and Pat were good swimmers and Jim would take care of Mollie. I couldn't swim but could hold my breath. The rapids threw me underwater, where I stayed so long that Jim assumed I was gone and focused on saving Mollie. Pat saw that my inner tube was on top of me and kicked it off. I surfaced, and the day proceeded with little more comment than Pat's, "Today I lost a ball game and almost lost my mom."

Terms like "impending death" or "terminal illness" did not occupy my thoughts, although fellow students and professors at the SOT were praying for me and doctors expected cancer to kill me. I wanted nothing to do with self-help groups fighting cancer. My focus was not avoiding death, it was life after death, life on the other side. I was working out what to think about the invisible domain and the meaning of existence.

During the months of chemotherapy and radiation I continued studies in theology. Having to miss some lectures, I asked fellow students to tape them on Patrick's boom box. By listening to taped lectures, reading fellow students' lecture notes, and asking for extended deadlines from instructors, I stayed on track and finished studies in two years along with students who started the master's program with me.

Why did I not ask for help at home? At the time it didn't occur to me. My siblings had enough burdens of their own and we were not in the habit of sharing troubles. More than help with cooking, cleaning, and so on, I needed caring and understanding ears. I expected no understanding from family. For them, being Catholic and divorcing was an impossible mixture.

Their denunciations hurt but didn't change my conviction that divorce was best for me and all concerned. Heaviest on my mind was wrestling with the gap between dawning religious awareness and the beliefs of almost everyone I knew, siblings most of all. Talking to them was out of the question. Or telling my parents. They were in their late eighties, and Dad was struggling to manage Mother's increasing infirmities.

What siblings could not give I got from grief ministers. During my womb/tomb period, the weight of negatives flattened me time after time. Someone always came along, scraped me off the floor, and put me together again. I'd be flattened again, and another angel would prop me up again.

Later I would draw from their example and try to be an angel for others, which benefited me as much as them. Somewhere in my reading I received the image of a cup as a cavity carved by sorrows. The more agonizing the pain, the deeper the cup formed to hold wisdom, joy, love, and compassion—the full range of human feelings. Patient listening with understanding given me during moments of anguish filled my cup. Now I could dip into it, gather its gifts, and pass them on to other lonely, hurting persons. This would not have been possible without the cup of suffering molded in me to make room for the pain of others.

While studying at the SOT and taking cancer treatments, I got almost daily phone calls from my Al-Anon friend Sylvia, who was dealing with her abusive husband. As usual, I was comfortable listening to another person's pain because it diminished mine. My role in our conversations amounted to counseling, but my Higher Self was really giving my conscious self the advice I heard coming out of my mouth. It usually ran along the lines of, "You don't have to take that. Stand up for yourself." This practice of mentoring self while mentoring others copies Bill Wilson, co-founder of Alcoholics Anonymous. When he had the burning desire for a drink, he looked for a drunk to help out of the same hole. I was following his model.

My body and spirit had their limits, however. While Sylvia was calling every morning and pouring out her problems, I was not telling her what was going on in my life. Chemotherapy was making me weak and sick in the morning. Unable to state my need directly, I took the phone off the hook.

Around the same time a certain dream kept waking me in the morning. In it I am teaching a class of students who refuse to be quiet and listen. I wake up in extreme frustration. Also at that time, I was taking a class at the School of Theology focused on emotional/spiritual matters. The instructor was recommended for her insights on this subject. But the class met in a room on the fourth floor. One day I was stalled by exhaustion while trying to climb stairs to the classroom. I was resting on a stair when someone came by who told me where to find the elevator. Of course, an elevator! I was so stressed I hadn't thought of it.

The instructor spoke about her experience with cancer, but she did not let me speak about my experience with cancer or any other matter. Why? Was I imagining that she avoided me? Had she heard about my unconventional religious views?

During a small group discussion of dreams, I related my recurring dream. A fellow student in the group told me the dream's obvious lesson—I wanted someone to listen to me. She noted that our instructor did not let me speak in class and avoided calling on me.

So I hadn't just imagined it. I'd been afraid to criticize an instructor recommended for her supposed understanding of emotions. The perceptive fellow student validated me when I really needed it—another angel. She shone light on a pattern in my life—not being listened to. I thought of Sylvia's phone calls. They should have been opportunities for me to open up, but when she called me for help I didn't reciprocate. Trained in being ignored during childhood, I thought I should help *her*, not talk about myself.

But that wasn't all of it. I didn't want to display my own vulnerability. If I had been honest, Sylvia would have respected my need, as I learned when I confessed what I'd done. Together she and I tried to make our conversations less one-sided. I credit my recovery, as much as anything else I did, to the hundreds of hours talking with Sylvia and others, vulnerably, honestly sharing my circumstances and fears with friends.

Toward the end of my stint in the SOT, some people told me I was called to be a prophet. Impossible, it seemed. I was sick from radiation, had no status, and was not strong or knowledgeable enough to challenge religious officials. But inside me the word "prophet" resonated. I was driven to challenge stale assumptions and expand horizons. I wanted to provoke Christians to deeper understanding of religious language and to see our tradition in the context of all traditions.

Jim

My husband never was unfaithful, unlike many alcoholic husbands. I knew in my bones that Jim was not running after women. He needed me. During the first days of our separation, Jim came over to talk to the kids. I went to the bedroom. Jim followed me, walked in, tenderly kissed me on the cheek and spoke a loving farewell. Passively I let it happen, frozen in astonishment. *Why were you so mean to me before?* How I had yearned for this instead of the cruel words he usually flung at me!

After our separation, Jim's behavior toward me changed drastically. Now I was no longer the wife to deny or dominate. Now I was someone to talk to, even weirdly confide in. No harsh words to me now—now he complained about his girlfriend. This surprised me less than the moment of tenderness. Jim was not sexist in the classic way. I had seen him treat Sue and other women with respect, and I had observed that only "the wife" had to be opposed. In his psyche I had been "the wife" modeled in his parents' marriage, and now I could get respect as a woman independent of that model. To this day it annoys me when I hear a man speak of "the wife" instead of "my wife" or saying her name.

While I was in the hospital after my mastectomy, Jim visited me. Silently he stood at the foot of my bed exuding feeling without saying anything. He stayed in our house with Pat and Mollie, saw my pile of bills and paid them, even the bill from my divorce lawyer. It made up for years of verbal abuse and wasting money on drinks. It made an eloquent statement of his generosity. If only he had faced what was pursuing him from childhood! Part of me wanted to take back my decision. Fortunately, I was past wavering.

Jim found another woman to marry, acting out the saying, "After divorce, women grieve and men replace." I was glad he found a wife, hoping it would relieve his shame from being rejected by me. I think he was trying to look normal and successful.

Meanwhile I was slogging through my meltdown and remolding. Pictures of myself during those years reveal my brokenness. People assumed Jim rejected me instead of me rejecting him. I grieved, but not the fact of divorce. Marriage had been lonely. After marriage, I made real friends and was free to be transformed. Having to live as a divorced woman in a Catholic culture challenged me to grow in self-knowledge and accomplishment. I was grateful for being led through the slough of my midlife meltdown.

After Jim married again, he wanted Pat and Mollie to spend Christmas Day with him and his new wife, who was eighteen years younger. The first year of this arrangement, he picked them up for Christmas and then sent Sherry to my house "to see the house." Did he want to hurt me or show off his new status to me or show off his old status to her or prepare her for building a house for themselves? She seemed as bewildered as I when she came, but I showed her the house, paying special attention to the hutch he'd built.

I hoped it would lessen anger that I imagined he had against me. I was afraid he would set the community against me. And there were unsettling incidents. One gave me a laugh. With a friend I went to a bowling alley to talk with someone there but met looks of bowlers that set me on my heels. They seemed to think I was out of place. I'd bowled there before, so what was this about? Was Jim spreading junk talk about me? After we left, it dawned on me, and I laughed as I told my friend that Jim was now managing the alleys. Odd looks from the bowlers didn't necessarily imply mean gossip. Even if it meant that, males naturally hang with males. Gradually I was learning to care less what others think.

My divorce lawyer did not really represent me. I learned later that he was an inexperienced rookie. I'd foolishly chosen a name randomly in the yellow pages instead of asking around for a good lawyer to represent a woman. The one I got asked no questions, learned nothing about my situation, seemed uninterested. He simply followed the lead of Jim's lawyer who, acquaintances warned me, was "dirty." He had just divorced his English-teacher wife and kept their house. Too heartsick to fight, I didn't inform my lawyer that during most years of our marriage I had been the major breadwinner while Jim struggled to find a career. My earnings made our assets possible, including our house and Jim's business. When we built the house, I liquidated my teachers' pension fund built up after eighteen years of teaching. Now my teaching career had come to an end.

In contrast to the lawyers, Jim was reasonable—no, generous. He left the house and nearly everything in it for me, including gifts from his parents, never contesting my right to stay there with Pat and Mollie. More than once he helped me out financially. Now I was no longer the mother and wife to fight but a woman in need. That brought out his best qualities and raised his self-esteem. In a conversation with me, he agreed to a higher figure for child support than had been decided by the lawyers. They were astonished. To Jim's lawyer I sent a silent *So there!*

The Clancy family never rejected me. Quite the opposite. They continued to enclose me in their fold and I continued visiting Grandma and Grandpa Clancy with Pat and Mollie. In the end, the divorce settlement didn't matter—I was the lucky one. I got the chance to heal and the money part worked out. It always does if I just stop worrying. But that was my problem.

Be Humble and Poor

During these years I had dreams of living in a new house—the welcome sign of making a new life. One dream, however, jarred me. I'm in a house and everything looks orderly until I go down to the basement, where I see a mess. Weeds and dirt are taking over. Upon waking up, I knew that housecleaning was needed below the surface. How could this be? I had scrupulously searched out my faults and knew what was wrong with me. What else needed to be rooted out?

Answers came, and one theme repeated itself—I needed to respect myself more, to stop being hard on myself. At an Al-Anon meeting someone's self-disclosure triggered an image of myself wearing a sign front and back that said, "Kick me. I'll keep smiling." This self-image manifested when I was my college class representative. For a reunion liturgy I was to lead the class in procession. I could not do it; another plan had to be worked out.

When my last school year at Albany was drawing to a close, one of my students, a cheerleader, asked me to attend their pep fest. I usually did attend them, but that time I'd planned not to go. Her request suggested that they planned to acknowledge my leaving. My suspicion proved correct. I was not there when nice words were said about me because I didn't feel worthy of respectful words about myself.

I was reminded of this when a male friend confessed that he said "No" in high school to a girl who asked him to a Sadie Hawkins dance. He could not believe she actually liked him. His emotional base at the time resembled mine, both of us distrusting the high regard others had for us. I used to divert compliments for the same reason. After getting a flurry of them one time, I asked a fellow teacher for help. "I don't know what to say."

She suggested, "Thank you." I thought I owed them more.

Feeling worthless and deprived governed that part of my life. In one divorce seminar, a facilitator responded to something I said by suggesting I had a victim attitude. She didn't mean, "Poor you!" She meant, "Get over it." I didn't understand it but also did not reject it. There had to be some truth in her observation, truth to come clear over time.

I tried to explain to an email friend that being poor suited me. I expected always to be poor. Her reply struck me forcefully: "Somewhere internally, you took a vow of poverty!! Hard one to break through." The way she put it, "vow of poverty," struck deep and spurred me to detect my unconscious belief: *Poverty is holier than wealth. Life should be hard. Be poor. Your solidarity with the poor is holy.* It was irrational. I don't help people in need by also being in need.

A dream was recurring. I'm at a feast serving delicious food. People are going through a buffet line and helping themselves, but my turn doesn't come. I'm not ready yet or others have to go first or I have to serve others or I have to finish some job. Or if I finally get to the buffet line, the good food is gone. I wake up frustrated with longing. The message is obvious.

My response to something my friend Faye said also poked me awake. She quoted a Buddhist saying and my insides recoiled in protest. Why? Buddhist psychology had appealed to me as an alternative to Christian gods. My surprising reaction alerted me to an aspect of Buddhism that reinforces Christian self-denial. Buddhism teaches: "Avoid desire." It echoed my Catholic training: *Be unselfish. Do not want what you want.* Now I flamed resistance to it. At the SOT, hagiography showed the absurdity of excessive selflessness.

A writing came to my notice that disputed the familiar preaching against pride. It argued with theological authority but from a feminine point of view—exactly what I needed. Valerie Saiving pointed out in the *Journal of Religion* that those who write theology are men in power. For them it's appropriate to tamp down pride and hold up the ideal of selflessness, but this is inappropriate for women and girls, who usually need to assert themselves more, not less. Men without power also need a stronger sense of self. Citing biological and cultural differences defined by psychology, sociology, and anthropology, Valerie Saiving provided the rationale I needed. It was one more piece in my growing arsenal to defeat self-defeating feelings.

Signs of Growth

I felt comfortable in Catholic surroundings despite my indignation at religious preaching. Catholic Charities offered more sessions on healing and growing. In one group, it became the pattern for me to voice a prayer at the end of meetings. My prayers reflected generic spirituality learned from Unity, free of religious doctrine. A woman in the group always added, "in Jesus' name." I felt like telling her to shut up and stop spoiling the prayer, but always I managed to quell the irritation stabbing me.

My prayers deliberately invoked a spiritual horizon larger than Christian, but she felt guilty praying to a spiritual force not distinctly Christian. Incidents like this magnified my opposition to He/Him/His church talk that creates belief in three gods, a belief no theologian would teach.

Unity readings had started the process of freeing me to feel worthy of good fortune. They encouraged me to hope for good things and enjoy them. They suggested that our deepest desires rise from our interior, the part reaching toward infinity. They assured me that God wants what we want. This felt unfamiliar but right.

Before, steeling myself to expect adversity had seemed realistic and rational. Now I was reading that hope alone is a worthy goal. We should aim for hope itself, not for specific results. How could I hope when circumstances predicted failure? Romans 8:24 had the answer: "Hope that is seen is not hope. For who hopes for what is seen?" Unity perfectly met my needs by grounding its counsel in scripture. Otherwise I could not have opposed Catholic training. In tiny stages I tried inserting hope into situations that seemed hopeless, and it worked. Incredibly. I tried it again and again when doldrums threatened. It really did work. This lifted an ugly burden of foreboding from my soul.

I read that someone who expects to be poor has low self-esteem. *Ouch! I have low self-esteem?* And anxiety about money, I read, produces money problems. Job 3:25 suggests this: "Truly the thing that I fear comes upon me, and what I dread befalls me." Worried about poverty and conditioned to accept it as my assigned lot, I brought it about. My own expectations created my reality. What a revelation!

At first it was hard to believe, but I read it in more spiritual-help texts, and over time I could see it happening in my life. I started breaking the "vow" and admitting my desires without guilt. Unity moderated the Buddhist teaching to stop desiring. It counseled letting go of attachment to *specific* results and trusting a wiser power to orchestrate good outcomes.

Pondering the fruits of my fear, I discovered other mental habits plaguing me. *They don't like me because I'm different. Their life is easier because they have two incomes. Physical comfort is not a good and holy goal.* On and on. I could not immediately erase them but recognizing these hidden beliefs—ridiculous, when uncovered—was a beginning.

I resolved to stop forecasting misfortune and steeling myself against failure. Imagining good fortune was hard, allowing it to happen to me, harder. Deliberately I practiced letting good things come without guilt, without expecting to pay for them. My readings suggested giving thanks to cure dark moods. This was hugely helpful, and easy. If I thought about it, I could be grateful for lots in my life. Things that could have ended in disaster didn't. I had enough of everything I really needed. "Thank you" became my trick to raise bad moods.

As self-critical mental habits faded, I took more notice of others. The more I liked myself and my situation, the kinder I could be to others. Small signs of change showed up in conversations. I got comments like, "You always put things in a different light." The teacher in me hoped they meant "put things in a deeper way."

Working on being honest with feelings, I practiced vulnerability and saw that it disarms aggression. With a priest one day, I tested this. I asked for a talk with him because he was sending barbs of anger. I have forgotten the subject of our conversation but remember the manner of it.

I made I-statements and talked about my feelings. He delivered accusatory you-statements ("You and this community. . . . They think you're . . .") with no admission that he was feeling hurt, rejected or angry. I stuck to my feelings and did not accept his shoulds ("You should be more. . . . You shouldn't feel that way . . ."). I persisted in I-statements, admitting hurt and anger. At one point I broke into tears, not deliberately, because it felt humiliating in the face of his hardness, but I did not accept guilt or shame from his you-statements. I stuck to saying how I felt.

Finally he melted, and we reconciled. I had not attacked him but had disarmed him with vulnerability. Paradoxically, it raised me in his estimation and my own. It was a sweet moral victory that came from honestly admitting my feelings in the face of his attempt to exert power over me. I was not always this successful, or even usually, but this time I dropped my mask and didn't pretend my feelings away.

As time went on I noticed that my intense earnestness turned off people who dislike heavy subjects. Gradually I climbed out from underground to live more on the surface, but I did not stop looking for below-surface meaning and trying to strengthen my intuitive powers.

A party I attended one afternoon clarified the contrast between the under-the-surface habitat familiar to me and everyday culture above ground. I had looked forward to the party because I knew that people in a helping profession would be there. They worked for justice. During the party I became uncomfortable, and toward the end of it I was sitting in the bathroom feeling phony and out of touch with my center. I didn't know why. Rejoining the party, I determined to overcome my discomfort but it persisted to the end. Coming home, I thought, "Thank God, tomorrow night I have my Al-Anon meeting."

I didn't have to wait for Twelve-Step relief because my Al-Anon friend Faye called. She happened to know the party guests well and could tell me, "They're accustomed to speaking publicly and agitating for justice, but they don't talk about personal feelings." They had nothing like the Twelve-Step experience of uncovering and sharing pain. Yes, they were addressing structures of oppression, but their work was external. I was used to heartfelt conversations full of self-revelation.

To me their main goal seemed to be the acquisition of material goods. One woman was dissatisfied that she was working only four days a week instead of five. Her work was demanding and exhausting. It required a high degree of skill and left little energy for family life. With her husband's salary they had an adequate income. I asked why she wanted to work more hours. "Money," she said as if it were obvious.

"You and your whole family would probably be less happy if you worked full time instead of part time." It seemed a novel idea to her. My remark violated the religion of our dominant culture, that material wealth trumps everything else.

But there was more to my feeling of discomfort. My response to the party reminded me of what I value in conversations—honest admission of doubts, needs, fears, difficulties. The partygoers did not live in this habitat familiar to me, making their talk seem inauthentic. After life in the nether world, I was still somewhat a stranger on the surface.

My Mother

An adult choral group based at St. Ben's was founded. Immediately I joined Minnesota Center Chorale and for years enjoyed singing with them. Driving to rehearsals, I carpooled with a woman from Avon. One day she mentioned having missed a phone call from her mother. I learned she had many phone conversations with her mother and enjoyed them. What could she have found to say to her mother? I could not imagine doing the same. The contrast seemed a rebuke. I had told a friend, "I love my mother, but I don't like her." It felt nasty but spoke truth, and it rose not only from snobbery or embarrassment over her accent and clothes.

My troubled relationship with my mother nagged me. I could not blame her and tried not to blame myself. *But well-adjusted women are close to their mothers, aren't they?* I tried to do better. Visiting her in the hospital one time, I watched nurses struggling with her. Apparently forgetting that the patient's daughter was there, one of the nurses said angrily, "She's gonna screw this up too!"

Heatedly I sputtered a defense of my mother that made little sense but communicated indignation. My loyalty to her that time relieved me somewhat when guilt pestered me other times. I grew up understanding that Mama was emotionally fragile. Even during my youth, I understood that she needed help and didn't get it. Wrapped in grief from emotional wounds, she had no compassionate adult to help her work through them.

As I write this memoir, Mother's deep connection with the inner domain, her psychic sensitivity, becomes apparent. When Celia was working in Mexico for PAVLA (Papal Volunteers for Latin America, a Catholic counterpart to the Peace Corps), she contracted Hepatitis A, known as "yellow jaundice," usually transmitted by food handlers with poor hygiene. She was misdiagnosed at first, complicating her recovery. We in Minnesota did not yet know Celia had hepatitis, but my mother experienced strange distress unlike anything felt before. She emerged from her bedroom, walking unsteadily and clutching her breast while struggling to describe her anguish.

Mother also had a near-death experience. I heard her talking about it when I was very young but rely on Al's book, *Discovering My Inner Child*, for a fuller description. When my mother was a teenager, she was forced to work in the fields alongside men. During a painful menstrual period, she begged off and asked her mother to intercede. "Get that lazy thing out of the house and working," answered her father.

Her pains increased. The following Sunday she fainted in church and experienced her soul leaving her body. Bright light, celestial singing, and a hill with flowers surrounded a deceased aunt coming to meet her, her godmother. The rapturous scene was interrupted by her older sister Louise calling, "Leni, Leni, Leni!" It brought Mom back into her body. I recall hearing her enraptured account of the beautiful flowers. Mom was always cultivating her beloved *Blumen*, her flowers.

She loved talking about the past. That and my own love of history led me to the idea of interviewing her. Bringing a tape recorder to their house on "the other farm," I taped my parents. Mom did almost all the talking, as I knew she would. In this interview she told the story of great Grampa Weymann and his oxen in the blizzard.

The interview gave me some understanding of why Mom did not refer to her father with bitterness.

> He was liked all over. You know what everybody—my cousins—say? *Vater Arnold ist der zweite Grampa Fuchs.* [She called her son "Father Arnold" and said he's the second Grampa Fuchs, meaning her father.]
>
> And I say it too. Right away, his acts and everything. He wants to lead, get everybody in ah. . . . He likes to please people, and not anybody sitting around that is left or so and so.
>
> He wants to help everybody. *Ja*, he always has parties. Oh, he often played with the. . . . We danced.

Mom was conflating her father with her son, prefacing a trick of her mind that bloomed elaborately after she spent some years in Koronis Manor. In her mind, her children became brothers or sisters of her younger years. I liked being her sister Rosie.

Father Al

After Arnold left to become a priest we did not see much of him, even less after ordination. As Father Al he continued to surround himself with music, and when his superior sent him to New York to study music he was ecstatic. A professor listened to him sing scales and said, "You can sing two octaves effortlessly. Have you ever thought of becoming an opera singer?"

It would have been his dream come true, but Al answered, "I just got ordained so I don't think that would get the approval of my leadership."

Al was different from many clerics and religious; he spent more time with lay people than with his religious community. His ministerial passion went into marriage counseling, charismatic prayer groups, youth retreats, and inner healing retreats for adults. Revealing his own spiritual journey in *Discovering My Inner Child*, he invited others to discover and communicate with their inner selves.

For some of his emotional-healing work, he was accompanied by Shirley, a bereavement counselor. They took occasional car trips together, traveling through rural areas to appointments in various cities. Al liked to show off his farm knowledge to Shirley, who grew up in Chicago. While driving through the country, they would encounter the smell of manure. He would sniff and then identify its source—cow, pig, or horse. He assumed she knew what he was identifying. Until the time they were driving past a field and Shirley saw the manure close to the road.

"It's . . . it's . . . !" she sputtered.

Seeing her sudden comprehension, Al asked, "What did you think it was?"

Al's musical ability and accomplishments far surpassed mine, and he was eight years older than me, but today I recall ways we resonated already on the farm when he was Arnold. Looking back now, I appreciate this more. As a little girl once, I was captured by a scene of trees and stream in our pasture. "This should be in a movie!" I exclaimed. Arnold reacted with pleasure.

Another cherished memory recalls us listening to opera as adults. Whenever he was around, MPR Classical was on. We were in a car, Al driving and I lying on the back seat, weak from radiation. An opera singer was showing off his voice by roaring out a high note. I interrupted with the observation, "He's flat," afraid of offending Al but fed up with the stupid singing. Al responded with a gratifying "Yes!" that said, "Good for you!"

Our emotional journeys had similarities, too. A cousin to whom I revealed my vulnerabilities said I sounded like Arnold. When Al was active in Marriage Encounter ministry, he asked me to help heal the family. Apparently, he was frustrated that he had success as a healing minister to others but was unable to help his own family. Marriage Encounter, like all helpful healing programs, guides people toward honest expression of feelings. I was flattered that he asked me but could not think of anything to do that would not raise more hurt feelings in our family. Strong, un-voiced emotions suddenly expressed could explode a family session. I said it was best to let things develop organically. He did not push it, apparently agreeing with me.

Al was not a person with whom I could discuss my evolving views on religion, although he did not judge me when I was going through my trying-to-be-atheist phase. Without comment, he observed the changes in my relationship with religion and could see atheism was no longer my home long before I entered the School of Theology. But he was not privy to my deepest reflections. I rejected literal belief but grew in a kind of faith that encompassed more than religion.

Father and Mother

Dad's penchant for hard work never left him, but he made the transition typical of men in their elder years by mellowing and valuing relation-ships. When Jim remarried and I was alone on Christmas Day, I used the opportunity to visit Mom and Dad on that day. Otherwise they would spend it alone because their married children were spending the day with their own children. On the Sunday after Christmas we all would celebrate with Grandpa and Grandma.

As I was ready to set out one year, I noticed that my gas gauge was low. Not sure I could get to a gas station open on Christmas Day, I called to say I wasn't coming. Dad answered, and his voice expressed disap-pointment. It surprised me. I was not used to Dad wanting my company. I hadn't known my visit would mean that much.

My siblings and I didn't pay enough attention to our parents' strug-gles, absorbed in our own. I pieced together our parents' story years later. It became evident that Dad was the one in charge of the house as they aged. He was the only one capable of cleaning. In winter a kind neighbor took care of snow removal. Mom gradually sank into dementia during her last ten years of life while Dad did his best to care for her, feeding her and helping her to bathe.

He had never been a cook. For the noon meal, the main one, he typically drove the three miles to Paynesville to eat at a café and bought a sandwich to bring home to Mom. Knowing she was not getting a bal-anced diet, he drove to my house for vitamins he had me procure for her. That's when he told me about her slipping memory. During sponge baths, she kept telling him to wash her back when he had just done it. Much later I learned that the only time she left the house was on Sundays, to go to church. Two steps separated their main floor from ground level. To get her back into the house, he stood below her and nudged her up with his body while she used the banister to pull herself up.

When I became more aware of their plight, I arranged a day with Celia for the two of us to meet at Mom and Dad's to clean their house, ending with washing the kitchen floor. Celia had to leave and I stayed longer to wax it. That's when I realized my mistake of not looking ahead and bringing them a meal.

The one who rescued them was Al. Always the doer and mover, Al. On one of his visits, he saw Dad's inability to meet Mom's needs. Noting the progress in her dementia, Al overcame Dad's objections—it wasn't easy—and got on the phone with Koronis Manor, the nursing home in Paynesville. They happened to have room and he moved her in on the same day.

The move was necessary, but Mom's confusion was exacerbated by activities in Koronis Manor. I hated the photo of her smiling too hard with Santa Claus, an American icon that had no place in her life. Taking a picture of her with Santa Claus robbed her of dignity. When I visited her and identified myself as her daughter, she couldn't imagine that she was old enough to have children. With more wisdom than she realized, she said soon after entering the manor, "*Allein mit Fremden kennt man sich selber nett*" (Alone with strangers, one doesn't know oneself).

I wish I had done more to help them. Those were the years I was reeling from loss of marriage and career, had cancer, and was studying theology. I had little knowledge of dementia and elderly needs. But I wish I had been less absorbed in my own problems and more aware of theirs. I blame my siblings, too. We adult children of this family were not emotionally close but should have been more attentive to our parents' needs.

Al lived farther away, but his visits home for days at a time allowed him more insight into their situation. In *Discovering My Inner Child*, he relates his slow, painful journey of healing from his anger toward Dad and reconciling with Dad. Al and I had talks about healing, a subject engrossing both of us. I described how Mom's complaints seared me when I was growing up. He detected my belief that there was no love between Mom and Dad. But he had seen them more intimately while home on visits and could correct my perception by saying, "I saw their love for each other when I stayed there."

"Really?" Surprised and pleased, I imagined scenes he might have observed that showed their caring. As I grew in maturity, I increased my efforts to overcome negative feelings for my mother. My educator self knew that unresolved problems with Mother mean an unresolved life for Daughter.

11

Post School of Theology

The Goddess in Christianity

At the School of Theology I strove mightily to agree with things said in classes, and often I could, but those darn guys in the sky kept annoying me—Father, Son, and Holy Spirit treated as facts instead of symbols. God-talk pronouns never veered from He/Him/His. I started untangling my knot of disagreements with Christian doctrine there and forming my own interpretations. My concept of God was expanding.

By writing papers, I found what I believed, what I rejected, and what I accepted as mystery. In my papers I tried to bring Jesus down to human size, gently. I did not dare say I don't believe he's God, surrounded by students and professors who apparently believed it. In retrospect, I wonder if all of them did. Was I the only doubter? How many professors and students avoided confessing their true beliefs for fear of the Vatican led by John Paul II? I was less afraid of the Vatican than of people around me.

While researching a paper for Trinity class, I came upon a pleasant surprise that validated my rejection of father and son gods pretending to be God. I found an article in the *Bible Translator* by Rodney Venberg, a Bible translator for people in southwestern Chad, Africa. He wrote in "The Problem of a Female Deity in Translation" that their word for the Great Spirit—*Ifray*—was related to their word for "mother." It meant that every time they referred to God, they said "Mother." They could not fathom the idea of a male creator. Venberg wrote,

> To speak of God (*Ifray*) with such terms as "he" and "Father" was totally inconsistent with their grammar and went against their whole notion of the creation (after all had a man ever given birth to a child?).

From my perspective today, I solve the translator's challenge by changing pronouns to fit the people's grammar. Genesis 1:31 could read: "God looked at everything She had made and, behold, it was very good."

During my last months at the SOT, I had gotten so fed up with male-only God-talk that I started saying to individuals and then in classes, "God is not three guys in the sky." I didn't know what effect this had on instructors and fellow classmates, many of them seminarians and priests. One day a man called my name. We were in a press of people after class and I was on my way home. I looked over and he handed me a little pamphlet. Without even reading the title I took it and went on. When I had time to read and absorb it at home, amazed gratefulness to the unknown man washed over me. "El Shaddai: A Feminine Aspect of God," introduced me to a fascinating subject.

The pamphlet explained that *El Shaddai* was the name of God known to Abraham, Isaac, and Jacob. According to Exodus 6:2–3, Abraham (and Sarai) brought *Shaddai* with them to Canaan from Sumaria. She established the covenant with Abraham and his progeny in Genesis 17:1–22. We don't see *El Shaddai* in our Bibles, although it appears forty-eight times. Bible translations render *El Shaddai* as "God Almighty," which makes Her sound masculine. But "God Almighty" subverts the original meaning, as this pamphlet and subsequent research showed.

The best source I found was David Biale's writing in the journal *History of Religions*. He states that *El Shaddai* is correctly translated, "God, the Breasted One." The Hebrew word *shad* means "breast." In ancient Akkad north of Babylonia, *shadu* meant both "breast" and "mountain," a link easy to see. The Egyptian word *shdi* meant "to suckle." And *Shaddai* ends with an Ugaritic feminine ending—*ai*—which also is the name of Abraham's wife in Genesis 17:15—*Sarai*.

This feminine meaning shows in the context of *El Shaddai* in biblical passages. Genesis 49:25–26 asks that She bring blessings of breasts [*shadayim*] and womb [*rehem*], then blessings of the everlasting mountains and delights of the eternal hills—just one verse of seven in Genesis indicating that "God, the Breasted One" inhabits the book of Genesis. *Shaddai* again is God's name in the book of Job where it again is mistranslated,

"God Almighty," incorrectly suggesting masculinity. Our Bibles always refer to Her with male pronouns—He/Him/His.

I wish I could thank the fellow student (or faculty member?) who led me to *Shaddai*. When he handed it to me I had no idea of the pamphlet's significance. If I saw him later, I did not recognize him. Only after I graduated from the SOT did I absorb the information and fully appreciate his gift. I muse about him and others in the SOT who might have been thinking independently. Did my seething presence make a dent in others' awareness? I hope so.

What to Do?

As graduation from the School of Theology approached, I wondered how the degree I was earning could lead to a job. Church work looked more than doubtful, considering my beliefs. I mentioned my bleak prospects in the SOT lounge one day when another student, a priest, said that his situation was comparable to mine because he doubted he would be able to use his master's degree in any church position.

Overhearing this, a member of the faculty who had a wife and children inserted himself into the conversation. Quickly he quashed the priest's claim that his worries for the future resembled mine. A Catholic priest would never have to worry about feeding himself or family; the Church would take care of him. I was happy for the intervention but didn't mention my bigger worry about beliefs. Any parish or diocesan office would avoid hiring a person with my views. John Paul II and Cardinal Ratzinger were keeping a tight grip on Catholic expression. Was I right in feeling I had been steered toward a master's in theology? My confidence wavered.

A position opened at Newman Center, a hotbed of liberal ideas according to some, but my questioning moved far beyond liberal. After applying for the position, I sat up suddenly one night in the middle of a deep sleep with the thought, *I don't belong there.* But what was I to do with my degree? What had I accomplished besides feeding my own curiosity about metaphysical matters? That I could not regret, whatever else would come of it.

I had to survive financially. No school would hire me to teach English or German because my years of experience made me too expensive. Substitute teaching in schools seemed my only option, but when I began subbing it seemed degrading. I felt that substitutes are disrespected just for being subs, and some experiences confirmed this. They involved students with little acquaintance of me, far as I knew. I was walking through a hall one day and a student passing by said something derogatory about subs meant for my ears.

Another day in the same school, a few students tested their strength against the substitute teacher, me. At the beginning of a class period, before I introduced any activity, students deliberately instigated a rebellion. It took all my psychic strength to quell the swelling riot, and without appealing for help from the central office. It felt like a triumph, but I'm sure that substitute teaching and money worries caused my second case of cancer.

This time my oncologist told me, "The American Cancer Society has found that stress can cause cancer." He was kindly correcting his response during our first conversation, when he dismissed my belief that stress caused my cancer. At that time the medical establishment was still denying the role of emotions in disease. Now my doctor accepted my explanation, but he warned that my bones were probably full of cancer and ordered a bone scan. It showed no trace of cancer. This amazed the doctor more than me. I was glad, of course, but numb from the long stream of challenges coming at me. Without more comment, my oncologist prescribed another round of radiation.

Writing

My first writings for publication had the simple purpose of educating. They appeared in an Albany newspaper while I was still teaching German and English, a series about German-Americans in Stearns County. I signed the series using my first family name because "Blonigen" is known here. And what would a Clancy know about German-Americans? For consistency in writings after that, "Jeanette Blonigen Clancy" became my name as a writer. I never bothered to change my legal name.

After graduating from the SOT, I was fortunate to land a writing assignment probing my dissatisfaction with traditional Christian beliefs. My monthly column appeared in a publication based in Roseville, Minnesota. The *Phoenix* was devoted to recovery, renewal, and growth, and my column, "Christian Rebirth," presented new interpretations of Christian teaching.

The column lasted only a year, and there was no pay—often the case for writers and typical of work that challenges accepted narratives laid down by authority. But for me it was a satisfying exercise. Writing for the *Phoenix* was my first experience of working with an editor. His revisions made sense and tempered my English-teacher focus on correctness.

I was driving a Phoenix. The significance escaped me until a former classmate rode in my car and saw its name on the dashboard. "This is a Phoenix!" exclaimed Jane. What was so big about that? Its fittingness in my life right then, its theme of rising. I had missed the personal significance while writing my column for the *Phoenix*. Jane also is the one who introduced me to the great mythologist Joseph Campbell. She heard themes of Campbell in my words and knew I would resonate with his works.

The phoenix is a mythological bird that lives five hundred years, burns itself to ashes in a pyre, then rises from the ashes to live another five hundred years. It has become a well-known symbol of resurrection. At the School of Theology, we read about the phoenix in the *First Letter of Clement*, an esteemed early Christian writing, part of the scriptural canon in Egypt and Syria. But Godfrey Diekmann, my patristics professor, seemed embarrassed by this pagan symbol in Christian literature, as if it polluted the resurrection theme.

During the year my column appeared, I went to my first writers' group meeting at North Star Press in St. Cloud. That night I had a dream altogether different from my usual dream of being paralyzed when I want to move. In this dream I am striding triumphantly, leaping over distances and covering outrageous spans of ground.

Another dream ended with a voice saying, "It's time to sing again." I should go back to Minnesota Center Chorale? I'd loved singing in the chorale because its members were accomplished musicians whom I could lean on for reading music. But when emotional stresses and cancer hounded me, I left it. Then radiation to fight cancer damaged my respiratory system, which added a cough to accompany every deep breath. Surely the dream could not refer to singing.

It had to mean writing. Already, writing was satisfying my need for self-expression more fully than singing had done. My appetite for being published had been whetted by the German-American series in the local paper, SOT papers I'd gotten published, and the *Phoenix* column. It felt good to be read and get feedback. I wanted more. But seeing myself as a writer surprised me. I'd never aspired to it because writing is slow, strenuous work for me.

A minister started to attend my writers' group. He responded enthusiastically to my writings on historical-critical studies of the Bible. Then, one writing gave him pause and my answers to his questions seemed to stun him. They revealed my disbelief in Jesus' exclusive divinity. He quoted the Fourth Gospel where Jesus says, "I am the way and the truth and the life."

I was reluctant to unsettle him but said, "The historical Jesus did not make the I AM statements in the Fourth Gospel. They bear the marks of a literary creation." I could say it with confidence because I'd read it in a text used in scripture study at the SOT. The minister never came back to our writers' group.

I did not decide to be a writer—it happened to me. Confronting beliefs of people in front of me was daunting because it set off my fear of displeasing others. At the School of Theology, I could not gather the guts to say, "I don't believe Jesus is God." In writing I have more courage. Perhaps this is the reason my inner self led me to writing. I wrote because I could not *not* write. I had a lot to say and couldn't shut up about it.

In writing I could pass on subversive facts. *This should be known*, I thought frequently in an unrelenting campaign to inform. Not satisfied with learning something for myself, I wanted others, too, to learn the fascinating facts. Today I tend to toss a critical eye at any view "everybody knows." When an opinion dominates, I am inclined to think, *Wait. What's the other side of this?* I like to awaken minds asleep, to poke holes in calcified assumptions, to subvert oppressive systems.

Writing also revealed my unconscious feelings and beliefs. The journaling urged on me by mentors during my dark days broke open my interior and released a flood of memories and thoughts wanting words. Seeing my self-defeating patterns on a page, I could start letting go of them.

My first writers' group led me to my first book, a centennial history of Albany. The historical society there had been gathering information for a book to celebrate their history, but when centennial year loomed, they realized they needed someone to organize and write a book. Appealing to North Star Press, they were directed to me. I had to set aside my passion for probing religious questions and turn to local history. It provided pleasant relief from the hard work of writing about abstractions, and I enjoyed working with older persons.

We were all German-Catholics and I had taught kids in their families. Socializing after one meeting, we talked about changes after Vatican II. One getting attention was the Vatican Council demoting the Blessed Virgin Mary. We were advised to pay less attention to Mary and not pray to her during Mass. Sister Luella at the SOT used to disparage devotion to "the BVM," as she jokingly referred to Mary. But Anna in the Albany group moaned, "She was my favorite." Official Christian theology said that Jesus is divine, but his mother is not. This is absurd from the perspective of pre-Christian religions whose Great Mother reigned supreme. But I could not say this to the Albany group.

Writing and getting some of it published led to self-respect. As I liked myself better, students liked me better and substitute teaching grew more pleasant. In one school, a teacher who taught English and German asked for me as a sub when she had to be out for several days at a time. I planned learning activities so that she could rest peacefully without having to plan lessons during her absence.

I remember one English lesson fondly. In my writers' group were three talented poets, some of whose poems I was sure would appeal to high school students. I read them in class and enjoyed the students' enjoyment of the poems. The next day almost all of them aced the "quiz" I gave, an exercise intended for review rather than assessment. Later I overheard this teacher telling fellow teachers, "When Jeanette subs for me, about all I have say is 'Teach 'em.'" My ability to teach was returning because my confidence was returning.

I noticed that teen behavior in high schools contrasted sharply with my Catholic-boarding-school background. The sexes were mixing with ease in public schools, which I admired, but my prudish background triggered a negative reaction to changing fashions. More reflection does not change my dislike of girls wearing form-fitting leggings in contrast to boys' loose-fitting jeans. One girl wore a top with a conspicuous line down the back pointing to her bottom. Such deliberately provocative displays were rare. More commonly, girls innocently went along with fashion, and fashion calls attention to female bodies.

I remain indignant. Why do necklines plunge for women but not for men? Why do women wear clinging fabric but not men? Our fashions teach us that sexy is the female way to look attractive, that women are the objects of sex and men are the consumers.

It's hard to imagine TV programs showing women covered up to neck, wrists, and ankles while men wear partially-open, see-through shirts. Hard to imagine an ad displaying a man's genital area scantily clad in a flashy, clinging fabric. In animal life, females choose mates and males strut their plumage, prowess, or dance steps to attract the ladies. I'd like to see some of this role reversal in humans to validate women as agents—doers and deciders—rather than objects.

Church

I continued going to church but not to follow the Lord or save my soul. My faith was informed by scientists, atheists, agnostics, Hindus, Buddhists, and the Goddess. Churchgoing was more than habit, however. Without shedding what I knew about the Father/Son myth, I found in church a spiritual atmosphere that somehow fed me. Living a Catholic life, I had pagan facts tucked in recesses of my mind, ready to show up when summoned. I was connecting dots between diverse sacred traditions and paradoxically feeling more at home in Christianity. My perspective was expanding and maturing.

Declaiming scripture as a lector in church became interesting. I did my best to change Jesus from an idol to a revered spiritual master, to soften oppressive depictions of God, and to make these changes inconspicuously. Often "He" could be replaced with "the One." And "Lord" could easily be changed to "God," which does not offend me because I can say "Mother God" and "God . . . She," but I can't say "Mother Lord" or "Lord . . . She." As a lector, I could not replace "Father" with "Mother." And I could not replace "He/Him/His" with "She" and "Her."

Some texts with patriarchal bias severely challenged me. One Saturday evening I arrived at church to lector and discovered the reading was from Ephesians 5, including verses 22 to 23:

> Wives should be submissive to their husbands as if to the Lord
> because the husband is head of his wife just as Christ is head of
> his body the Church. As the church submits to Christ, so wives
> should submit to their husbands in everything.

Not having time before Mass to prepare language inoffensive to women, I did it on the fly, while reading. What I said I forgot as soon as it was out of my mouth. Did it convey the spirit of the original? I tried but don't know if I succeeded. No one, including the priest, challenged me on it. They knew my marital status.

CSB/SJU

After some years of subbing, I got a job that felt perfect for me, teaching symposium at the College of St. Benedict and St. John's University. First-year students take symposium to improve their reading, writing, speaking, and listening abilities—skills I had taught before. Being a college professor suited me, and during the first semester things went beautifully. The students seemed to like and respect me and each other. But during spring semester some students became indignant at the content of the course.

We could teach communication skills using a theme of our choice. I chose religious myth, which let me introduce works that indirectly challenged literal Christian beliefs. I played tapes of Bill Moyers interviewing Joseph Campbell on *The Power of Myth.* This PBS series had captivated millions with mythic images and commentary that evoked the deepest dimensions of human experience. It ennobled all myth systems, which raised doubts that one alone has authority.

This shook first-year college students who had never looked at their religion from outside of it. Their distress was predictable. I had repeated a familiar teaching mistake—forgetting to consider the level of my students.

Second semester I followed the mythology of Joseph Campbell—already hard to take for some students—with writings about quantum physics. I had discovered its intriguing connection to spirituality. The outcome of every quantum experiment depends on the decision of the experimenter, a fact that baffles physicists because it demonstrates the power of consciousness, the nonphysical or spiritual part of human beings.

Too late I realized that such heady, abstract content was inappropriate for teaching communication skills to first-year college students. I had been following my own inquiring curiosity, the same mistake I made when teaching German history in high school—forgetting the students' perspective.

My self-confidence slumped, and after one year of teaching my stint ended. I worried that my subject matter was the reason, but maybe not. Apparently St. Ben's and St. John's were terminating adjunct faculty without a doctorate. A faculty member who had taught there for many years with credentials similar to mine also was terminated.

The loss of this job devastated me again and brought on my third bout with breast cancer. The first had been expected to kill me. Here I was, contracting cancer a third time. My primary oncologist said little, only prescribed a third round of radiation. I imagined him thinking, "What is it about her?" The radiation oncologist predicted I had about four years to live. This was in 1994. I went back to the only reliable means of survival I knew—subbing in high schools.

Mother

My dear Irish Aunt Margaret did the most to improve my attitude toward my mother. I was puzzled, awed, and reproached by the extraordinarily respectful way Margaret helped Mom with a toileting issue. Puzzled that is, until she told this story, which must have happened shortly after Mom entered Koronis Manor.

Margaret's husband, Mike Fuchs, was dying in the manor, the same nursing home where his sisters, Aggie and my mother, Lena, were residing. Margaret's son Edward says he remembers Mom during that time with her younger siblings in the Manor. "She seemed to fall back into her big sister place, sure she knew what was best for them." Edward added, "And I guess she did."

Uncle Mike seemed afraid of death. He was thrashing around the day before he died, unresponsive to Margaret's and the nurses' efforts to settle him down. Margaret was desperate for some way to relieve him. Mom came into the room in her wheelchair to visit her brother. Seeing Mike's distress, Mom wheeled herself up to the bed, quietly spoke into his ear, then proceeded to pray the rosary in German. He listened, settled down peacefully, and remained peaceful until his death the next day.

Why did I not know this precious story before? I asked my cousins for the date of Mike's death. Their answer made my mind sway. It happened when I was taking a full load of courses at the School of Theology while being treated for what my oncologists assumed was terminal cancer. It is good that my mother didn't know this. She could not have helped me; she could help her younger brother. Mom's dementia abated enough to carry out that assignment from her Higher Power.

Her dementia had progressed a few years later, when my oldest sister, Verna, was found to have a brain tumor. Neurosurgeons assured Verna's husband, Leroy, that it was not malignant and could safely be removed. But during surgery her brain swelled, indicating a stroke. Quickly they closed her up and fought to keep Verna alive, an outcome in doubt. Weeks in hospital and nursing home ensued while we visited her.

One time we picked up Mom from her nursing home and Dad from his retirement home and drove them to the hospital in St. Paul to visit Verna. Some days after this, I got a phone call from Koronis Manor asking me to talk to my mother.

> She's agitated and it's hard to restrain her. She's talking about a baby that she thinks she lost. We can't calm her down. She talks about a baby and east and west and hayland and her folks, and we can't orient her to reality.

Mom kept trying to leave any room she was in. They tied her to a chair and she dragged the chair across the room, frantic with worry about her baby.

They put her on the phone to me. "Jeanette, where's my baby?" she asked. She made no more sense to me than to the nurses, telling me she left her baby by the hayland in the east and some people came and tore everything apart. "Where's my baby?" She repeated. "Somebody should tell the folks."

I tried to straighten her out, but she left the phone grumbling, "You don't know anything." At the end of that call, she was somewhat calmer, but it was the first of four that day. One of the nurses said that just hearing a familiar voice calmed her and that the day before had been the worst. I'd visited often enough that my voice was familiar to her, although I doubt that she knew I was her daughter.

One nurse told Mom that the Blonigen sisters were taking care of her baby. Knowing what *die Mädchen* meant to my mother, I expressed doubt about the wisdom of that approach, but the nurse said it had worked until now. On another day a nurse asked me to come or they would have to give her a shot to calm her.

Pressured by preparations for my Symposium class, I felt I could not take off right then, and I could think of no sister or brother who might be able to drop everything and visit Mom immediately. Guilt gnawed at me for refusing to go to her, though I doubted my presence would relieve her anxiety. They gave her the injection and came up with the idea that the baby was in the hospital. I decided that sometimes lying is justified.

Too late I realized who Mom's baby was. I might have soothed her by giving her good news about Verna. Hospital and nursing home staffs had warned Leroy that Verna would have little mental capacity after the calamitous surgery. They predicted she would have the mind of a child. Against their firm recommendations, Leroy insisted on bringing her home.

It was most fortunate that he prevailed because Leroy got Verna moving. Starting with exercises, he eventually had her taking walks in malls and years later even dancing. Exercises woke up functions in her brain that the neurosurgeons thought were gone for good. Years later, neuroscience would conclude that, when parts of the brain are removed, other parts take over their functions.

Koronis Manor was no longer calling me. Mother's agitation subsided.

12

Defying Patriarchy

Early Christian Belief

Substitute teaching allowed time and freedom to return to my spiritual quest. Following my curious nose again, I discovered revisionist Christian history. It turned out that Christians right from the beginning disagreed fiercely with each other. *Orthodoxy and Heresy in Earliest Christianity*, by Walter Bauer, identifies vast geographical areas of "heretics." This indicated that most early Christians did not believe Jesus is God—a stunning fact! I'd thought Christians always believed approximately what we were taught.

Bishops who won the contest for "right thinking" or orthodoxy could easily have lost the contest. What if "heresy" had won? What if Christians revered Jesus as spiritual master and prophet instead of the only son of a father-god? Did my theology instructors ponder these questions? Today I observe that theologians elevate Jesus above other humans—the phrase I hear is "uniquely divine"—but I don't hear them saying he is God. *Hmmm.*

Richard Rubenstein, in *When Jesus Became God: The Epic Fight over Christ's Divinity in the Last Days of Rome*, tells the story of orthodoxy defeating Arianism. This widespread theological controversy raged during the third to fourth centuries and beyond. Arianism argued that the Son was created by the Father. This made Jesus less than God. No heresy, I was taught, ever threatened Christianity like the heresy of Arianism. All over the Roman Empire people heatedly disputed the question of Jesus' divinity.

Rubenstein's book reads like a thriller novel, full of suspense and violence, surprising plot twists, murders, and at least one massacre. They were not imaginatively contrived for a novel but historical facts showing that Arianism could have become Christian doctrine. Rubenstein's history shows the orthodox leader, Bishop Athanasius, behaving at least as brutally as the Arians. Some Catholics today call him "St. Athanasius."

Constantine called the Council of Nicea to settle the matter, wanting unity in his empire. The Nicene Creed resulted, but large swaths of the empire went on distinguishing the divinity of Jesus from the transcendent source—God. Allowing for differences evolving over centuries, I conclude that Arian belief comes closer to my belief about Jesus and, I believe, Catholic theology today. I agree with theologians who warn against "Christolatry."

My research continued while subbing. I took notes and wrote content intended for *God Is Not Three Guys in the Sky*. Always grabbing my attention were facts that usurp patriarchal power. Among these nuggets were findings from archaeological sites dating back to 25,000 BCE—naked figurines with heavy breasts, buttocks, and thighs, some with belly extended in pregnancy.

Archaeologists speculated about their meaning. Men conditioned to think of woman's body as sex object called them "Venus figures." Mythologists interpret the archaeological finds as evidence that God was Mother for tens of thousands of years before God turned into Father. Some suspect that the earliest humans were not even aware of the male role in reproduction. Besides the figurines, a vast number of artifacts present woman personifying the Creator. The Goddess Hera, later portrayed as the shrewish and jealous wife of Lord Zeus, earlier reigned supreme over heaven and earth.

Archaeologist Marija Gimbutas is known for her research into the Neolithic and Bronze Age cultures of what she called "Old Europe." Gimbutas writes in *The Goddesses and Gods of Old Europe* that Hera occupies the central position in artifacts unearthed at archaeological sites. Zeus does not sit on the throne. Hera sits on the throne, and Zeus stands at her side.

Evidence from prehistoric cultures aligns with the people of Chad who made a Bible translator's job difficult by praying to *Ifray*, a feminine image of God. To them, woman is Creator. With Her body She generates new life, She gives birth, She suckles. At Mass, priests and fellow congregants might have been aghast had they seen my imagined picture of the Creator based on the figurines—a woman heavy with child.

My image of a pregnant woman presiding at the altar neatly reverses the indignity of a Church practice going back to medieval times and inherited from Judaism. Based on Leviticus 12:1–5, it acts on the belief that giving birth made a woman "unclean." A girl baby made her more unclean.

> When a woman has conceived and gives birth to a boy, she shall be unclean for seven days, with the same uncleanness as at her menstrual period....
> If she gives birth to a girl, for fourteen days she shall be unclean.

As late as the 1970s, Catholic women were "churched" or purified after they gave birth. It was called "blessing" but retained the smell of sanitizing after the dirtiness of birth. I was spared from undergoing this ceremony when Pat was born. It was not done at Newman Center, where Jim and I were going to church.

Imagining the Source/Creator female instead of male makes an enormous difference. In prehistoric art, She is represented as Lifegiver, Earth Mother, close to nature, because the female body's generative power in childbirth reflects the earth's regeneration in spring. Before becoming a fervent feminist, I had read Rachel Carson's *Silent Spring* and started worrying about humans degrading the earth.

The environmental movement seeded by Carson marks a return in mythic consciousness to the Great Mother. Rachel Carson along with Jane Goodall, who noted the similarity of chimpanzee behavior to human behavior, drove the paradigm shift from seeing nature as alien to seeing ourselves as part of nature.

While studying theology, I took note of allusions to the Goddess. After graduating I found more. Feminist authors taught me to find feminine imagery everywhere. Attributing feminine traits to what is called "God" is so instinctive that patriarchal religions like Christianity could not avoid it. Church "fathers" advised people to drink the milk of Father and Son. Irenaeus of Lyons wrote,

> [Christ], who was the perfect bread of the Father, offered Himself to us as milk....

> The Spirit of holiness opened [the Father's] bosom and mixed the milk of the two breasts of the Father. (quoted by Berger, *Gender Differences*, 77)

Clement of Alexandria wrote,

> By loving, the Father has become woman.
> . . . only those who suck at this breast are truly happy . . .
> . . . the Father's loving breasts supply milk. (Reid, *She Changes Everything*, 12)

The same "fathers" who wrote such things banned the Goddess. They stole Her properties, then cast Her out. Theological research during graduate studies and continuing afterward intensified my outrage at the patriarchy. My midlife meltdown contributed by opening to illuminating intimacy with infinity beyond. Its fruits continued to appear and ripen. I could not talk about these things with many people, but a few were ready and gave me moments of release.

Demeter and Persephone

Continuing my search for context to the Christian story, I became a fan of mythologist Joseph Campbell. From him I learned of innumerable myths around the world telling stories of Christ-figures whose lives resemble the Jesus story. The myths tell of transformation—dying and rising—often through the death and resurrection of a god or goddess. Campbell called this ubiquitous theme "the monomyth" of ancient civilizations.

The Aztec god Quetzalcoatl evokes Christ on the cross by sacrificing himself and descending to the Underworld—in the Apostles' Creed, Christ "descended to the dead." Quetzalcoatl's heart then rises to the heavens—"He ascended into heaven"—to become the star Venus.

The ubiquity of this religious motif seemed to demote our Christian story by converting it from history to myth, until I realized it was not a demotion. In popular culture myths are despised lies, but the factually-false images of religious myths pitch people into awareness of the spiritual source beneath or within physical things. I started seeing Quetzalcoatl, Mithra, Venus, the Buddha, or whoever, as enriching the myth of Christ. Alternative Christ-figures accompanied me during Mass.

Book after book, example after example, revealed pagans prefiguring the Christian story. In Egypt, the Great Mother was Isis and her child Horus. When Christianity displaced other religions in the third and fourth centuries, figurines of Isis with Horus on her lap were conveniently renamed "Mary with Jesus." No religious or political figure deliberately or intentionally changed the names. The renaming evolved in the way of all myths, which emerge naturally out of the collective consciousness. The popular Mother with Child motif evokes strong chords of sympathy in every human culture.

One myth gradually assumed a prominent position in my mind after I realized that it balances the Father/Son myth of Christianity—a Mother/Daughter myth of dying and rising. Persephone, the daughter, is seized by Hades, ruler of the underworld where the dead live. She descends to the dead. Her mother Demeter becomes enraged by Hades' abduction of Persephone and withers the earth into a wintry death. Demeter and Hades come to an agreement. He lets Persephone ascend to earth and live there for two-thirds of the year. And Demeter allows the earth to reawaken when Persephone rises. The earth bursts into the fertile growth of spring at Easter, named after the goddess Eostre.

During my attendance at Mass, the priest would disapprove if he knew that, along with Christ hanging on the cross and rising from the tomb, I imagine Persephone being abducted into Hades and rising to spring freshening the earth. On the other hand, as someone reminded me, the level of depth in priests varies greatly. There was, for example, the man at the SOT who handed me the pamphlet about *El Shaddai*.

As the Father/Son story is commemorated in Christian liturgies, the Mother/Daughter story was commemorated in the Eleusinian Mysteries, religious rites revered by Greeks—later Romans, too—for nearly two thousand years. In Greek, *mysterion* means "secret." Under penalty of death, participants were forbidden to reveal what happened in the Mysteries. The elusive final ceremony themed by Persephone's ascension and reunion with her mother sparks the greatest curiosity in me. It hints at the origin of some Christian rituals. George E. Mylonas scrutinized ancient writings and unveiled some of their secrets in *Eleusis and the Eleusinian Mysteries*. His studies and others that detect common elements in religions excite me more than detective crime stories.

The Mysteries were celebrated yearly at Eleusis and Athens. They lasted about fifteen days and included fasting in addition to a great fourteen-mile procession between the two cities. This outer journey stood for an inner one. Participants in the Mysteries traveled with their divine beings through grief, as Christians do when observing Lent—Ash Wednesday to Palm Sunday, Holy Thursday and Good Friday.

For Christians, grief turns to elation on Holy Saturday night and Easter morning. The Eleusinian journey ended at Athens with a spectacular drama, during which participants beheld a sacred mystery that left them jubilant. Something like Easter. During the culminating event, participants drank a brew that I associate with wine at Mass. Because of the sublime impact attested by ancient writers such as Sophocles, Cicero, Pindar, and Plutarch, modern scholars think the brew at Eleusis contained ergot, which can cause hallucinations.

Whatever the secret agency, the rites at Eleusis and Athens parallel Lent and Holy Week. I got my first inkling that the Eleusinian Mysteries inspired rites in the Jesus movement when I read a passage in my scripture text for Ivan Havener's class. Intrigued, I did more research, found the subject in many books, and finally came upon the book by Mylonas. He wrote that the mysteries

> satisfied the most sincere yearnings and the deepest longings of the human heart. The initiates returned from their pilgrimages to Eleusis full of joy and happiness, with the fear of death diminished and the strengthened hope of a better life in the world of shadows. (284)

Cicero wrote,

> "Athens has given nothing to the world more excellent or divine than the Eleusinian Mysteries." (Mylonas, *Eleusis*, 285)

I can't think the Mysteries stirred pagans any less strongly than Christian rites stir Christians. Devotees of all religions are refreshed and uplifted by walking with their respective divine beings through travails and on to resurrection.

The ancient parallels did not diminish the story of Christ for me but enhanced it, especially during Holy Week. Helping me to make the connection was *The Goddess Within: A Guide to the Eternal Myths That Shape Women's Lives*, by Jungian psychologists Jennifer and Roger Woolger. I read it while traversing womb and tomb at midlife. Persephone's descent to the dead, they suggest, symbolizes a descent into the unconscious, where she is transformed. The Woolgers imbued with nobility my own drop into the depth. Like Persephone, I had gone underground, there to be ground up and transformed.

Few people heard me talking about pagan parallels to the Christian story. I certainly didn't talk to priests, not even my brother. In our world, Christian belief held a monopoly—it was truth while other religions had weird fables. Facts debunking this accepted interpretation marinated in my secret thoughts.

Women and Spirituality Conference

Sandy, the feminist in my first writers' group, introduced me to the annual Women and Spirituality Conference at Minnesota State University, Mankato. This conference hugely influenced my life by reducing my fear of rejecting Christian claims. This was in the 1990s, when challenging Christian doctrine was still rare in my world. The Mankato conference shaped me as a writer. After attending the first year, I returned for twenty years to give presentations, year after year. It was immensely satisfying because I found people ready and eager to receive my out-of-the-box interpretations of Christian teachings.

Pieces that would become chapters of my book were gobbled up, my challenges to traditional belief received with enthusiasm. Men were rarely seen at the conference, but a few showed up in my presentations. One listener begged me to give her the copy of my talk and I foolishly gave in to her, forgetting I needed it for my second presentation. That one I had to deliver from memory. In one session, participants organized a way to pay for copies of my text. They signed names and addresses on a list, trusting me to send it. One woman unable to attend my presentations begged me to have conference organizers schedule another one.

Sometimes my high from a weekend at the conference lasted more than a week, and it boosted my writing confidence much longer. Freed from the fear of offending traditional believers, I could say what I truly believed, which I had not been able to admit at the School of Theology. In answer to a listener's question, I said I did not believe Jesus is God or that his death saved the world. After this spontaneous declaration, I knew where I stood and hung on to it.

The Mankato Women and Spirituality conference showed non-Christian spirituality in action. Returning yearly, I was weaned from the breastmilk of Catholicism. There, psychics and mediums unashamedly believed in the paranormal and encouraged personal healing by non-ordinary means. I inhaled the atmosphere and pushed myself to accept spiritual currents many in our culture consider flaky. Struggling to un-learn prejudices trained in me, I attended one workshop that turned into a neo-pagan rite resembling communion. Gamely I participated, all the while wrestling with guilt.

The conference program alone exposed me to a new world: "God-dess Symbols in Rural Minnesota Churches," "Taoist Meditation," "The Power of Crystals and Gemstones," "Channeling Loved Ones," "Intuition 101," "Sacred Circle Dance" "Care for the Earth as Spiritual Practice." There were presentations about crones, Tarot, faeries and ghosts, Shakti, Aphrodite, Gaia, Isis, and the Black Madonna, Sufis, mandalas, drum-ming, and smudging. Speakers presented suggestions for spiritual heal-ing: "Exploring the Un-known Self," "Transforming Anger to Power," "The Sacred in You," "Strengthening Your Intuitive Muscle." Presenters taught Tai Chi and Qigong, how to see auras, how to work with chakras. I interacted with believers in reincarnation and channeling loved ones who died. Many sessions were experiential workshops, but I preferred presentations with intellectual content.

Jung and Teilhard de Chardin had given me respect for psycho-spiritual phenomena, and at Mankato I saw their power. The cumulative effect from experiences at the conference year after year made apparent the difference between religion and spirituality. I could see that confer-ence participants rejected traditional religion but had healthy spiritual practices. These visits with non-Christian spirituality reduced its foreign-ness and my fear of talking about it.

My presentations bridged Christian beliefs with new spiritual cur-rents, repudiating the Christian claim, "We own the truth and you don't." In my presentations I spoke about Catholic sin-talk, the Goddess in the Bible, "Pagan Christians," science and spirituality, atheist spirituality, sexist God-talk, and other provocative topics. I related what I'd learned about myth, parallels between Christian and pagan beliefs, and paral-lels between the Buddha and Jesus. I gave scriptural evidence to show that Jesus intended to raise awareness of the inner realm, not to promote himself. His Aramaic words for the realm were translated "kingdom of God," which creates the misleading image of a male monarch ruling over his subjects.

One listener asserted that Jesus was made up, purely the product of human imagination. She believed there was no Jesus in history. It's a common belief among debunkers of the Christian myth. There was a time when I considered the possibility, but I told her study of the gospels and church history changed my mind.

The god of popular piety worshipped in churches never walked the earth, indeed, but a real man shines out of the gospels of Mark, Luke, Matthew and the gnostic Gospel of Thomas. Jesus is no one-dimensional, copycat idol made up by myth. He is too distinctive, too unique, too singular in his manner of teaching, and too scornful of religion to have been invented by religion. Ivan Havener taught ways of recognizing which Jesus-sayings in the gospels probably came from the man and which were put into Jesus' mouth after he died.

Moments at the Mankato conference that affected me most addressed mental blocks to my emotional health. I was cruising through the vendors one time, not interested in buying anything, just seeing the offerings. Book stores attracted me most. A woman diverted my attention by offering to demonstrate the service her group offered. They sold sessions designed to mend some emotional snag, and she offered a free session for a minute.

I took it, knowing I needed healing from my vow of poverty. She asked which hand she should hold. While holding it, she put her thumb between my thumb and pointer finger. Without saying anything, she invoked healing power. I closed my eyes and invited healing to come, letting peace permeate my being despite the hubbub around us. When it was over, I noticed a lessening of obsessive money worries. It continued in the weeks, months, even years after this.

A similar healing came more remarkably some years later. The main conference building was being refurbished, leaving less room for visiting before sessions began. My companion and I found room at a table, and when space opened we invited two women seeking a place to join us. They were there to give a workshop on angels, not a subject that appealed to me because angels seemed a fad, too New Agey. But we enjoyed talking politics, about which we agreed.

After I gave my own presentation and was walking down the hall, undecided on which session to attend next, I saw the pair getting ready to begin their angel presentation. I walked in just because my friend and I had gotten to know and like them. In the workshop they described ways that angel cards guided their days and suggested they could do the same for us. Each of us was invited to pick an angel card. From the outstretched hand I chose mine with the thought that it would be just right for me. It said,

I am Serena, the Angel of Abundance.
The money you need will come to you,
and God is in charge of how that will happen.
Have faith.

As I read Serena's words to people in the room, they came out in sobs. I was embarrassed, thinking this revealed money problems, but wonder and joy won over embarrassment.

Effects showed up almost immediately. Back at home, I found in my mailbox a check for my first allocation of Teacher's Retirement. Before I left for the weekend I had received notice that it was on the way, but it was about twice what I expected. Days later, more funds arrived, a regular check for work and back pay. I could stop worrying about a huge property tax bill due soon. Of course, mundane forces had sent the money into my mailbox, but reducing it to that distorts the experience.

What hit me was not mundane chance. It felt unearthly, the work of an unseen power orchestrating events—the two women sitting at our table and befriending us, their session after mine and in the same hall beckoning me to their session, Serena's words with their profound effect on me, and the checks in my mailbox at home. Scientific materialists would pooh-pooh my interpretation, but I believe they were the result of my trust in transcendent power, not an accident or chance. Carl Jung coined the word *Synchronizität* to describe such coincidences manifesting numinous power.

When I need a faith boost, I recall the moment of reaching for the card and being overwhelmed by the words. They always halt the train of worry that wants to take off on its well-worn track. Years later I recounted the incident and Serena's words to a walking friend. Her emotive sounds as she walked beside me told me that the words also assured her.

13

Father Al and Europe

In Africa

AL WENT TO SOUTH Africa to visit Mariannhill missions there and to give retreats. After six months he took over a mission station, which required learning the Zulu language. He continued marriage counseling in South Africa and gave inner healing weekends. After a month in Zimbabwe missions, he returned to the United States to resume work as vocations director for Mariannhill and to earn a master of divinity degree.

Then he went back to missionary work in Africa, where he had to learn another African language—Xhosa, a language requiring tongue-clicking sounds. That he learned two African languages well enough to communicate amazes me. He also continued Marriage Encounter and inner healing work.

Knowing my interest in justice for women, he told me that he met Rosemary Radford Ruether in Africa. She is a renowned Catholic theologian, feminist, and author of more than a dozen books. Her *Sexism and God-Talk* informed me, motivated me, and became the model for my term "sexist God-talk" to describe exclusively male references to the transcendent mystery called "God."

Al suggested that we send each other speaking tapes to communicate while he was in Africa. I was living through trying times, mustering the courage to divorce. In one cassette sent to him, I talked out my realization that the word "victim" fit me. Al never told me directly how he responded to this new information, but I sensed a change after this.

Al was devoted to Jesus in a way I never was. The worm gnawing at my insides did not live in him. He was perfectly happy praying to Lord Jesus and never questioned its rightness. He did not think about metaphysical distinctions or trying to fit religion with science. But he did not blow off my ideas and was not a slave to church doctrine. His professor of dogmatic theology at St. Meinrad had introduced him to new concepts coming out of Vatican II.

Reincarnation

In a conversation memorable for me, I declared one of the most daring ideas I was trying out. Al was home from Africa, and we were in a car. As usual, he drove. Something in the conversation made it possible for me to say (but not brashly), "I believe in reincarnation."

"So you don't believe in the resurrection?"

"Reincarnation could be the resurrection."

"What did you say?"

"Maybe reincarnation is the resurrection."

"What?"

"Reincarnation *is* the resurrection." We were quiet after I said it the third time. He'd understood my words the first two times but thought he couldn't have. Now, apparently, he was considering how reincarnation could be the rising after death. I didn't belabor the point, just hoped that his silence signaled openness to the possibility.

I had less of a leap to jump in accepting reincarnation. Both of us believed that life continues after physical death, but I learned from Jung and Unity authors that doctrines are symbols, which allowed resurrection and reincarnation to melt together and become one in my mind. This led me to imagine living other lives. Teilhard's *within* helped by opening to a mysterious, unknown, inner sphere of vast infinity.

Strains of reincarnation sound in many stories of child prodigies. One on *60 Minutes* resembled Mozart's. Alma Deutscher became a pianist and violinist at three, composed at four, wrote an opera at ten. Alma's father quoted her piano teacher: "It's difficult to teach her because one always has the sense she'd been there before." A professor of music at

Northwestern University in Chicago sent her some assignments when she was six or seven. He said,

> I expected her to crash and burn, because they were very dif-
> ficult. . . . It was like listening to a mid-18th century composer.
> She was a native speaker . . . she speaks the Mozart-style. She
> speaks the style of Mendelssohn. . . .
>
> She's batting in the big leagues. And if you win the pennant,
> there's immortality.

Ah, immortality. For my purpose, it was good to hear him say "immortality."

I hear strains of reincarnation in many less celebrated lives. While listening to an *On Being* interview by Krista Tippett one Sunday morning, I jerked alert when mathematician Margaret Wertheim spoke of being born with scientific curiosity mixed with love of math. Wertheim said,

> As a little child, I was obsessed with the question of how math-
> ematical concepts seem to appear in nature. So I can remember,
> when I was maybe 6 or 7, lying on the grass and staring up at the
> sun. And we'd just had a lesson at school about Pi, the number
> embedded in circles. Circles, in some sense, as defined by the
> concept of Pi.
>
> And I thought, "Is Pi real? What does it mean that there
> is this sort of mystical number at the heart of the sun or in a
> hubcap or any circular thing that you see?"

It is clear that Wertheim always "got" math, that she was captured by it from birth in the same way that musical genius accompanied Mozart's birth.

To a typical Christian today, reincarnation is a foreign concept, but a 2016 survey found that 51 percent of the world believes in it. Early Christian theologians accepted it too, showing its compatibility with Christian doctrine. I think reincarnation is the counterpart of belief in heaven, hell, and purgatory but better satisfies our need for moral justice. By living lives other than our current earthly one, we may all get many chances, not only a second chance.

I used to protect myself against scorn by saying I was *open* to the idea of reincarnation. Now my belief in it guides my personal journey. It eliminates fear of and abhorrence of death. It enlarges Christian hope with hope of growing in spiritual maturity beyond our current lifetime.

Al's talent was addressing emotional needs, and this he continued in Africa by ministering at Marriage Encounter weekends. But the parish role he had to play in Africa grew as distasteful as the farm work forced on him by our father in Minnesota. Africans at his mission expected the white father to supply them with "mealies" or feed for their cows. Such practical matters in running farms were not the way Al wanted to spend his energy. Finally, he persuaded his superior to let him come back to the United States.

Back in Michigan, he became ecclesial chaplain for Worldwide Marriage Encounter of Metro-Detroit. He began to present at Retrouvaille weekends for troubled marriages, while continuing inner healing work. To encourage others on their spiritual journey, he wrote *Discovering My Inner Child*, revealing his bedeviling frustrations over working for our farmer father, his rage, and finally reconciling with Dad. Al never imaged God as Mother. He relieved his theological problem with God as Father by relating to a gentler Jesus.

Al's zest for travel was fed by a wealth of international experiences. He served two terms as provincial superior of Mariannhill in the United States / Canada province. During that time he visited Mariannhill missionaries in South Africa, Zimbabwe, and Papua New Guinea. In Europe he made the acquaintance of Blonigen and Fuchs relatives. I shared his interest in our roots.

In Europe

It started with a phone call. "Can you afford it?" asked Al.

"No," I answered. He knew it was financially impossible for me.

"You won't have to pay for anything." He obviously enjoyed my reaction. The word "unbelievable" does not express the immensity of this gift from him. Al took me to the German-speaking countries of Germany, Austria, Switzerland, and the Netherlands. In every country, we stayed in Mariannhill houses. He presumed on their hospitality because as provincial of Mariannhill in North America he had hosted a conference and extended generosity to European houses.

A vivid moment told me, "Appreciate and do not forget." After I was shown to my room in one house, an open window beckoned. Walking to the window with shutters splayed to each side, I looked down onto tops of trees and heard a real burbling brook. A fairy-tale sound and view.

Then I caught sight of the brook. Never, I resolved, would I let this privileged moment leave my memory.

I liked staying in religious houses; they felt more comfortable than hotels or motels. One house invited us to have our laundry done by the Sisters who did their laundry. Male religious houses in the United States also used to employ religious Sisters to do domestic chores. I felt uncomfortable turning my underwear over for someone else to wash, but it would have been harder had I thought a man would do it. The next day I saw a Sister hanging my panties on a line.

In Stearns County, I had enjoyed listening to German-born families. The child of Austrian immigrants enchanted me when he said, "*Nicht?*" his pronunciation evoking a culture unlike ours. Now I was getting lots of the real thing—*echt Deutsch*. It was delightful but also disappointing. I have difficulty processing the spoken word in any language, English included. My oral proficiency lagged far behind Al's, although he said he was astonished by how well I spoke German. In locales with a dialect unfamiliar to me, I gave up trying to understand his conversations, and I understood little of German news reports on television, which I could have understood in writing.

The first Mariannhill house we stayed in was near the magnificent cathedral of Cologne. Father Adalbert ruled the house with formidable presence, but his female housekeeper's welcome made me comfortable. I knew that during my absence, Mollie had come home from Colorado, where she had lived for about two years. I called her, using a house phone. This was before cell phones.

Mollie was despondent from having broken a relationship and moving back to Minnesota. She had moved to Colorado right after graduating from high school. I supplied a listening ear but felt Adalbert's disapproval as the conversation went on. He objected to the length of the call, even after I offered to pay. The relationship between mother and daughter elicited no sympathy from him.

Adalbert made intelligent observations about social and political events—just what I wanted to hear from a European—but I had difficulty keeping up with his rapid-fire delivery. One time I asked him to speak more slowly. Immediately he switched to English, just what I did not want. Fortunately, he soon reverted to German. Speaking about World War II, he said that when the United States entered the war, Germans knew it would soon spell the end of Nazism. I got the impression that Germans eagerly awaited America's entry into the war.

The mountains of southern Germany, Austria, and Switzerland enthralled me. I love walking and had time to do it but was still suffering the effects of radiation "therapy" for cancer. Walking up hills was hard. One time I gave in to the temptation to walk down a steep hill, knowing that climbing back up would be a challenge. At the bottom it seemed impossible. The possibility of having to be rescued entered my mind with dread. Slowly, taking enough time, I made it back up the hill.

When we arrived in Würzburg, it was dark and after bedtime. Al had lived and studied there almost four decades earlier. Evidently, he'd gotten instructions on how to get into the Mariannhill seminary where we were to stay. But how to find our rooms? I will never forget Al leading me through dark rooms and halls as he recalled the layout of the building.

Feeling his way, he brought us along more than one path that led to failure. He held my hand while descending stairs in pitch dark, but in the basement we came to a locked door. I worried—we needed help. The locked door did not deter him. Finally he found a way to the floor with our rooms. I was in wonder at his boldness, as if this were his home and he had a perfect right to walk through a European building whose inhabitants were in bed.

German people close doors between rooms. A house with open doors signals a house abandoned. In one of the Mariannhill houses, I found a library and better yet, a biography of Jung, which I happily dove into and enjoyed for a while. When I left the library to join everybody downstairs, I faced a phalanx of closed doors. Which one led to the stairs? Utterly confused, I stood in the hallway for long minutes, unable to detect what was behind the doors surrounding me. Opening the wrong door could invade someone's privacy. A door opened, and it was Al. Was I relieved!

In Austria, we stayed in an abandoned castle that had an earth and stone ramp built up to the second story. In earlier centuries, knights had ridden their steeds up the ramp to their residences. The castle was actually a ruin, only part of which was fit for occupancy. Closed doors again became a challenge.

During the day I rehearsed the way I would have to take for potty breaks in the middle of the night. I had to open and close five doors on my way to the toilet and five doors back, fortunately not without lighting. A short part of the way went through a public hall that I took the chance of walking in my nightgown. Shower and bath during the day required a long trip down that public hall, not in my nightgown.

At Saas Fee high in the Swiss Alps, Fr. Pirnen hosted us in what is now a tourist town. He had grown up there and skied everywhere in his youth, learning to climb up hills with skis on his back. When he drove us from the train to his Mariannhill house, he raced up the mountain at heart-stopping speed, whizzing around hairpin curves. Breathtaking and heart-stopping also were the craggy cliffs and towering peaks we passed. In the journal I was keeping, I mourned my inability to find words more adequate than overused phrases to describe it all.

Unique features of particular locales charmed me: The bewitching streets and buildings of Rothenburg ob der Tauber; Viennese carriage rides; a boat ride down the Danube; *Sound of Music* sites in Salzburg; many architectural wonders destroyed during the war and rebuilt; the Roman edifices of Germany's oldest city, Trier, with a basilica that had been Constantine's imperial palace; flowers, flowers, flowers everywhere; the canals of Amsterdam; near the Danube an exquisite baroque church with fantastic sculptures of angels and saints dropping from heaven; the magnificent *Residenz* in Würzburg built for prince-bishops. Its foremost message was showing off power.

Near Salzburg, Austria, farmers grow pumpkins only for pumpkin seed oil. They throw away the meat we use to bake pumpkin pies. In Switzerland's Saas Fee, granaries are built on stilts, the bottom part of each leg a stone slab to keep mice from reaching the grain. In Würzburg, a fresco in one church depicted the Annunciation (Mary learning she would give birth to the son of God). A long tube trailed from God's mouth to Mary's ear, with baby Jesus visible in the middle of the tube. This and other art works made real the challenge of communicating in an illiterate world.

A monk in Austria demonstrated emotional sensitivity that contrasted with the absence of it in Adalbert of Cologne. Most of our male hosts did not include me in conversations. Conrad probed, but I did not feel violated. It was a treat to meet a man who listened to me and cared about feelings. Other men interacted only with Al, as if I couldn't think about serious subjects. Ironically, their political and philosophical interests were more my thing than Al's. I yearned to engage in the conversations, but limited proficiency in oral German prevented it.

Conrad had been with Al in South Africa where Al vented about his upbringing. Conrad wanted to know if Al got the worst of it in our family. No, I said, we all were seriously affected. He didn't think I was. Having come through my midlife meltdown, I loved hearing this but corrected his misimpression. I said I was divorced, knowing that in his mind that alone would indicate a problem. It did.

Conrad showed his sensitivity again when he accompanied us to a concentration camp in the area. He was more affected than I was. I had taught a unit on the Holocaust as a high school teacher. Perhaps Conrad felt some responsibility as a citizen of Austria.

I told him I did not believe everything our religion teaches. He was shocked, saying sadly, "*Man soll es glauben*" (One should believe it). I had come too far to feel guilt. The familiar "should" part of believing had confined me for years and saddled Jung's father. I am sure dear Conrad prayed for me. I longed to explain my theology to this lovable European monk, but limited German vocabulary frustrated that desire.

In the Rheinland we stayed in Steffeln, near Prüm, which lies near Belgium in the Eifel region. From Steffeln our great-grandfather Johann Blönnigen emigrated to avoid conscription into Bismarck's army. Steffeln has two Blönnigen houses bearing the name of their traditional owners, although no Blönnigens live there anymore. The mother in the family we stayed with is a Blönnigen descendant. Their house and barn were one structure, typical of homes on German farms. A large manure pile in front mysteriously did not stink.

Al officiated at the marriage of youngest son, Mark. Wedding revelries lasted late into the night and began again early the next day, but I did not observe drunkenness. It challenges the belief that German culture brought alcohol abuse to America.

I asked our distant relatives about the Nazi era. Mark said he felt overwhelmed by the enormity of his country's descent into madness. His father described the oppressive atmosphere and suspicious signs they observed during the early days of Nazi persecution. My brother later confessed he was initially horrified when I asked sensitive questions of Germans we visited, but he grew to appreciate it. He had studied in Germany in the 1950s, when it was best to avoid the subject of Nazi atrocities because feelings were still raw.

We were scheduled to fly back home from Schiphol, the airport in Amsterdam. On the train to the Netherlands an elderly Dutch woman shared our compartment. Eagerly I asked questions. A native of Amsterdam, she bemoaned the loss of her Holland. Angrily she complained that foreigners were spoiling her city. Turks bring big families and live off the most generous welfare system in Europe, she said, but the system does not do enough for senior citizens who built the country.

She pointed out dikes. I knew little more about them than the children's story about the boy who kept his finger in the dike. The dikes we saw in Holland were impressive affairs, huge earthen mounds in a system that cleverly drains land to steal it from the sea. At one point we saw a barge floating high above us in a canal directing water back to the sea. The woman boasted, "God made the world, but the Dutch made Holland."

Dutch is close to Deutsch, less close to English, but close enough to make the language in Holland seem like a comical imitation of both. I entertained myself by figuring out meaning in printed matter, although I could not understand spoken Dutch. Written Dutch words seemed to lampoon both German and English.

The trip brought me out of myself by reigniting my curiosity in people and places. It brought to my notice fascinating facts that sparked joy and passion. Europe deepened my understanding of Christianity by showing its history, especially its medieval phase. So many great experiences and stupendous sights exhausted me—rapturous beauty, historic information, interesting people, and cultural curiosities packed into three weeks—so that when it was time to come home, I was ready. I had been brought out of myself to find the world bigger and more fascinating than I remembered.

When Al called me a week later, I told him the trip boosted me out of the depression I was in before the trip. I felt lighter.

"Was it really the trip?"

"Yes, being in Europe made me feel different." The trip changed me, moved me out of the emotional state that had exploded in my journal years earlier. The answer Al fished for also was the truth. Following my answer, his gladness traveled over the phone, silently.

14

Passing Over

Dad

After Mom was moved to Koronis Manor, Dad continued driving the three miles to a Paynesville restaurant to eat a sandwich, usually a hamburger—always a California burger, his concession to nutrition. Then he visited Mom in the nursing home. He was living alone, but his faculties were failing too. We moved him out of their house and into an apartment in Paynesville.

Adelbert, our oldest brother, handled their financial matters, but Dad called me one time to come and help him with something. I wondered what it could be. It turned out that he had worked out a sum he wanted to give each of his children for Christmas, but the job of writing all the checks was hard for his hands and that became my job. The amount, though considerable, does not stick in my memory. What sticks is my happiness that I'd done a little cleaning for him so that he called on me to help him. I felt privileged.

A few years later, Dad entered Good Samaritan, an assisted-living facility. At Good Sam I asked him, "Do you like it here?"

"There's nothing to do."

"What would you like to do?"

"Work."

It was understandable. Work had been his life, but I couldn't help him with that. Residents at Good Sam could use a car, allowing him to drive back to the house he and Mother still owned. He puttered around and then spent an occasional night there. The staff at Good Sam told me this could not go on. I asked for his car keys and he handed them over, one of the unforgettable moments in my life. I, one of "da kits," had actually pulled this off. After this, I drove him to medical appointments.

In his waning years, Dad told me more than once—in rare self-reflection—that he was good at making plans in life and making them happen, but he could not control the big happenings in his life. This seemed less a frustration to him than a mystery. I think chagrin over the plans he had made for his sons was at the bottom of his insight. Dad had acquired farms to pass on to his sons, but farming was not their vocation. It was his. Only one of his four sons farmed and Jerry would not stay in farming. Dad's reflection reinforced my feeling at significant turns in my life that unseen forces direct me and they direct all of us.

My parents and I had never talked about religion. It took no effort to avoid the topic with them. Normally, that was the case with siblings, too, but with them I was wary. Sometimes I imagined hostility, feeling rejected and defensive. I did not bring up my beliefs with them, and they didn't, but I feared their disapproval. On rare occasions, a brother or sister accosted me about a religious matter, but we didn't go deeply into interpretations of doctrine or probing the depths.

Jim and I had hosted family Christmas gatherings in the past, but more recently we had gathered in the house Dad built near Paynesville. Now our parents no longer lived there. Whatever divisions existed, I wanted to keep our family together. For that purpose, I offered to host Christmas gatherings at my house. It was centrally located between family members living in the metro and those around Glenwood.

My siblings apparently agreed it's good to stay together as a family and accepted my invitation. I hoped they also wanted to reconcile after my divorce. I was proud of being able to host the gatherings after the difficult journey I'd taken, unknown to them. Siblings brought our parents, and for a few Christmases Jerry and Dianne brought *die Mädchen* to our Christmas gathering.

Die Mädchen

The aunts' land had been taken over by Jerry and Dianne, who were crop farming. No animals. Jerry had had too much of manuring barns for Dad and *die Mädchen*. The aunts relied on him as they had relied on their brother Herman.

Jerry and Dianne had a good relationship with them. "They were always very gracious to me," says Dianne. "They would invite us at Christmastime and treat us to a feast with dandelion wine and sweets. They sent food home with us."

In summer *die Mädchen* gave them surplus from their garden—lettuce, tomatoes, sweet corn, and cucumbers. They helped Dianne prepare mailings and stuff envelopes for an NFO newsletter she wrote. In articles she wrote for the *Paynesville Press*, Dianne featured their gardening skill. "I wondered who lived on that beautiful farm," said a reader. "When I drive by I admire their attractive yard and the garden with gorgeous flowers." *Die Mädchen* grew the flowers for bouquets they arranged to adorn the altar in the St. Martin Church.

Occasionally, Jerry and Dianne spent days at a time at national NFO conventions. *Die Mädchen* then babysat their son Darrin. The school bus route conveniently passed their farm, where he could be picked up for school in Paynesville. He liked staying there and they enjoyed having him. After being in their garden, Darrin persuaded his parents to plant a garden at home.

Die Mädchen generously donated to Catholic missions. A priest from India came to stay with them for a week. They had funded his education in preparation for ordination and he came to meet his benefactors. But years later some of their money must have gone to unscrupulous operators. The president of St. Martin Bank intervened when he noticed an enormous sum about to go out. He detected a scam, stopped payment, contacted the intended receiver, and told the party he would report them to authorities if they ever again contacted the Blonigen sisters.

Jerry observed that, with time, *die Mädchen* grew less shy and more accepting of strangers. And more thoughtful. Earlier they were still sure that anyone not Catholic would go to hell. After Vatican II, Rose said the priest "did not follow the rubric. He did not say the right words." In later years, Rose was pondering moral dilemmas when she asked Jerry, "How do we know we're doing the right thing?"

Regina, the oldest, had multiple sclerosis and was the first to die. By that time, they had brought modern plumbing into their house. The surviving four aunts led a serene life centered around church. Every day began with morning Mass in the church they decorated with flowers.

One Monday morning, their Blonigen cousin Sophie missed them at Mass. It bothered her; they *always* went to Mass. After church Sophie started doing her wash, but an inside voice insisted, "Call them." She did. No answer. Rose or Froni should have answered.

Finally, Agnes's voice came on: "I don't know what's wrong. They're all lying on the floor." Alarmed, Sophie called our farm. Dianne flew over, assessed the scene, called 911, and opened doors and windows. Soon a swarm of emergency vehicles appeared in their yard.

A Stearns County sheriff's deputy saw the breakfast table's contents, looked down at the four inert forms, and said, "I don't think these ladies died from food poisoning. They've been canning all their lives." Dianne's suspicion proved correct. Carbon monoxide rose up through an open laundry chute into the kitchen. Something had gone wrong during chimney repair.

This episode started a gradual decline. They were never the same. Rose and Froni, the youngest and most active ones, were hardest hit. Emergency responders told Dianne it was because they breathed more deeply than the less active Monika and Agnes. Rose had been the one who made decisions, asserted religious views, and wrote letters. She, the strongest and head of the household, was "almost a goner," said Jerry.

He was at an NFO board meeting, about to begin a presentation, when Dianne's call interrupted him. He never gave the board that presentation, which morphed into his book explaining why family farms were dying. Now Jerry took over the aunts' financial matters. Their deterioration began to show in personal appearance as well as in house and yard.

Monika, the second oldest, died in her sleep. Froni fell down the stairs and was taken to the Paynesville hospital, connected to Koronis Manor, the nursing home. Then Agnes broke her hip on the basement stairs. She had been the one who did the cooking.

Dianne, Jerry, and others who provided services in their home noticed that they kept using a gas burner that leaked gas, despite warnings to stop turning it on. Someone even had placed a note on the burner, but Rose ignored it. Clearly, the aunts were not safe. In the case of any crisis, they would not know how to call for help or even that they needed to call for help.

By this time Jerry and Dianne were giving up crop farming. While visiting Froni, the idea rose that the aunts should move into Koronis Manor. Learning that the Manor had room for them, Jerry and Dianne knew they had to persuade the aunts to leave the farm. "We're getting jobs in St. Cloud and won't be here in case you need help," said Jerry. "There's room for you in Koronis Manor."

Rose turned to Agnes. "What should we do?" To Jerry and Dianne she said, "We talk it over."

"Froni is doing better since she went to Koronis Care Center." Jerry pointed out to encourage the move.

"We think about it," said Rose. Within the hour she called back to say, "We will go." Later, she told Jerry, "I am glad you're taking care of everything. I always wondered how things would be taken care of."

Physical affection had not been part of their lives, but in the Manor Jerry saw Rose tenderly touching Froni's cheek. The youngest four aunts passed away between 1997 and 2002. Rose had rallied enough to be the last to go.

Jerry asked his siblings to help clean the house in preparation for the estate sale. This became a nostalgic journey into the past. The basement of the house still had the opening to the yard with stairs over which, years before, coal and root vegetables had traveled. Canned vegetables still stood on shelves. The main floor held valuable antiques in pristine condition. Upstairs, I found gallon pails full of yellow chamomile they had picked in the yard to make chamomile tea.

Jerry contracted an auctioneer who specialized in estate sales. Their beautiful antiques were snatched up by St. Martin parishioners and others who knew that elderly sisters living in a house with no children were certain to have valuable items well preserved. In the months and years following the auction, we heard from acquaintances who treasure the elegant pieces they were able to buy. Jerry observed that valuable antiques were sold for less than their worth, but Dianne noted that odd items we might consider junk brought surprising sums.

Mother and Father

Al had left Africa and was residing in his seminary at Dearborn again. Every winter he arranged with the Catholic pastor of St. Louis Parish in Paynesville to take over duties while the parish priest enjoyed a vacation. This brought Al home to spend time with Mom and Dad, as well as siblings and extended family. He would schedule a Sunday for us to attend Mass and afterward we'd all go out to eat at the Hilltop Restaurant. I thoroughly enjoyed these family gatherings.

While I was visiting Dad toward the end of his life, I blurted out something that still stabs me with regret. He brought up his considerable accumulation of wealth relative to other farmers in our region. Without thinking, I said his money "all went to the nursing homes." Even before my mouth finished saying it, I was sorry. Lamely I said something to soften the blow, but the damage was done. His deflated look stays with me.

I knew I would feel better for the rest of my life if I got closer to Mom and Dad as they advanced in age. Proximity made me able to visit them more often than my siblings. I became the main contact and took pride in it. Dad and I fell into a pattern. I would pick him up at his apartment, later at Good Sam, and we'd drive together to the Manor to see Mom.

During my visits I made efforts to overcome my distance from her. She often talked nonsense, but the three of us enjoyed amiable togetherness. Sometimes I combed her hair and even cut it once or twice. She had a natural curl that I enhanced with a wet comb. My fussing brought a pleased look on her face, and I could see that Dad enjoyed it, too.

Deliberately I changed the family habit of no hugs. It was hard at first—the cells of my body resisted fiercely—but both Mama and Daddy returned the hugs eagerly, with no hesitation at all. Daddy's hug was astonishing—accompanied by a great wet kiss. *Oh joy! He really did this!* And he did it thereafter. It gratifies and moves me still. The results of cold family conditioning have not left me. It still is harder for me to hug siblings than acquaintances.

Mom had a moment of lucidity a few weeks before her death, when she was ninety-four years old. It began with her usual ramblings in rooms of the past when she was a child. This time, when I told her she was old and had lived a long life, she understood. Her eyes, clear with understanding, surprised me. She was "normal."

Then she berated herself for being "so dumb" that she had been confused. I corrected her, gave her reasons for respecting herself—raising eight children, cooking, cleaning, gardening, and . . . I searched for more details to raise her self-respect. Later, I thought of more ways to seize the opportunity, but this moment helps to assuage my guilt for less-considerate times. Since then I have learned that such moments of lucidity shortly before death are not uncommon among patients with dementia.

Most painful is regret that I did not heed signs of Mom's impending death, nor the warning from nurses at the manor that her end was near. Not one of us was with her when she died. Celia and I had planned to visit in a few days. She said she was "maxed out" with duties for her kids, teaching CCD, cleaning the aunts' house, and more. I cannot remember what kept me away but remember thinking I'd been too absorbed in my own activities to be attentive. We all should have been visiting more often while our mother was dying. We pitied her when we were growing up but were not there for her at the end.

A nurse thought she knew when it happened. She described the sounds coming from the room while she was walking past it. I was horrified imagining the sounds and the scene. Taking her words as a reproach, I laughed artificially to cover up guilt and shame. Then I was embarrassed that she saw me react so inappropriately.

Dad had bought a plot in the St. Martin cemetery for himself and Mother. The pastor at St. Martin was not going to allow it because they had lived away from the parish in their elder years. Al had intervened. He pointed out their extensive ties to St. Martin. "On the roster of the St. Martin cemetery," Al said, "the name 'Blonigen' appears more often than any other family name." The pastor gave in.

Flying in from Detroit, Al was too late to see Mother before death but in time to preside over the visitation and funeral. I drove Dad to her graveside and left him in the car during the ceremony because of his difficulty walking. Dad would not be deterred. He insisted on being helped to her grave. His sons, one on each side, supported him as he hobbled over to her casket to sprinkle holy water in blessing. This touched and surprised me. I had not seen the love between them that Al had.

After Mom died, Dad followed the pattern in many elderly couples. When one dies, the other, bereft, soon joins the departed one. Dad was moved from Good Samaritan to Koronis Manor, where almost daily he had visited Mom. He had cancer, and the nursing staff at Koronis Manor told him he should have his bone marrow tested to see if it had spread. "No," he said, "I'm old and if I have cancer, I will die of cancer." I admire him for turning down expensive treatment at the end of his life.

By the time his death arrived a year and a half after Mom's, he also had sunk into dementia. Celia and I regretted our neglect of Mom when she was approaching death and resolved to do a better job with Dad. We were with him when he was in a coma and uncommunicative. I had read that people in a coma can hear sounds. "A prayer in German might soothe him," I said, and Celia agreed. But the words of *Vater unser* ("Our Father") did not come. Lamely I told Celia, "My way of saying it would not sound right to him." It wasn't true. The German words just refused to come to me right then.

My sadness that we didn't do more for our parents in their elder years sharpens when I learn about hospice care for the dying and services to keep elderly persons in their homes. And when I recall Aunt Margaret's story of Mother easing the passage to death for her brother Mike.

When she had been moved into a nursing home and Dad was moving into an apartment, we cleaned out their house. I found a tiny piece of newspaper she had cut out—my letter in the diocesan paper explaining that "Mother" is an appropriate name for God because of what mothers do. It warms me still that she apparently treasured my letter. After Dad moved from his apartment to Good Sam, I found an envelope on which he had written the names of his children, apparently noticing that his memory was failing and not wanting to forget. I, the seventh of eight, was at the top of the list. I wish I had kept those scraps of paper.

Grandma Thekla

In midlife, when I was casting about for a new direction in life, I had volunteered at a sexual assault center. Consuming the files there, I learned the facts surrounding sexual assault. I read the profile of a victim, stopped, and read it again. She often develops the attitude that sex is dirty, yucky, icky, ugh. Bingo—Grandma Thekla. Was she sexually assaulted or molested? Was this the reason for her excessive prudery and not letting her daughters live normal lives?

After Mom and Dad passed away, I told my siblings what I suspected. Immediately they could see it, especially Fr. Al, always quick to understand psychological dynamics. Adelbert had a nose for genealogy and connected with more Blonigen relatives than the rest of us. In this way he learned something that corroborated our suspicion. Grandma Thekla's brother told Bert that Thekla came home after one job as live-in maid behaving strangely. Whatever had happened to her, she was changed.

I had the opportunity of sharing these facts with Bill Cofell, the sociologist who had observed the behavior in Grandma's house when he conducted his survey in the 1950s. "I think she was sexually assaulted," I added. He agreed before I'd finished telling him why I thought so.

As I gaze at the photo in my living room of the young woman in her wedding dress surrounded by the golden frame, I wonder, "What did she endure?"

It took my stint in a sexual assault center to reveal why Grandma Thekla wanted to protect her family from others and shield her girls from lecherous men. She took refuge in rigid religion that taught repugnance of sex. This form of religion gave her a measure of solace but left toxic fallout for her descendants. It devastated our mother, who never wavered in her conviction that Thekla Blonigen caused her babies' deaths. Mom never stopped feeling badgered by her in-laws.

When our aunts died and their estate was settled, we living children of their brother Herman inherited some money. Mom would have rejoiced.

15

BENEDICTINES

I HAVE A LIFETIME history with Benedictines beginning with my birth in the St. Cloud Hospital, founded by the Sisters of St. Benedict. Our parish in St. Martin was pastored by priests from their brother monastery, St. John's Abbey. Benedictine Sisters gave us religious education on Saturdays and in summer, and then they taught us full time when our public school became a parochial school.

This led to Sister Bethany steering me toward the scholarship that brought me to St. Benedict's High School. Growing up at St. Ben's, I saw women being leaders. They did everything on that campus except maintenance work, for which local men were hired. All positions requiring mental acumen were held by women. Senior year in high school, we were invited to fill out the matriculation form for the College of St. Benedict. There it sat, in front of me. Something inside whispered, *Just do it and see what happens.* Filling it out went quickly, easily, and defying my father's authority seemed less fearsome on a familiar campus.

Decades later, after venturing into atheism and finding it lacking, I searched desperately for a path to the second half of my life. Casting about for some postgraduate study, I landed a scholarship to St. John's School of Theology. Back to the Benedictines.

While I was studying theology, Faye, a fellow alumna of the College of St. Benedict, told me she attended Mass with the Sisters in their chapel at St. Ben's. I tried it, and it felt like going home. I had come there as a child and spent eight formative years there. Sunday mornings found me driving to the campus after Pat and Mollie became independent and moved away from home. Gradually I stopped going to my home parish in Avon, also called St. Benedict's. Now I claim St. Benedict's Monastery as a second mother besides my biological mother. I continued my religious dissent with its frustration and anger, but the Sisters softened it, tempered it.

Shortly after graduating from the School of Theology, I exchanged letters with an editor at Harper & Row, to whom I sent chapters planned for a book. I was sure of only one thing, its title *God Is Not Three Guys in the Sky*. Editor Thomas Grady expected my "work in progress" to be that of a recovering Catholic, an idea sweeping the country in the late 1980s and early '90s. This project fizzled. I could not go on writing what I thought he expected me to write. Without realizing it, when I began writing about theology I was debating theologians I met and read at the School of Theology. My relationship with religion had complications that would take years of reading and reflection to unfold.

While I was arguing with Christianity, Benedictines decided for me whether to stay in Catholicism or leave it. They kept me in the fold by being in my life. They showed me goodness in Catholicism and depth in religion. I follow the example of Catholic feminists like Rosemary Radford Ruether, who chose to stay and critique our religious system from the inside, reasoning they would have greater weight inside than outside. But friendships with Benedictine Sisters did more to hold me in, showing relationship to be the heart of spirituality. Besides feeding my reflections, they led me to interaction with nuns and priests elsewhere.

Professed religious people seem more enlightened and thoughtful than most churchgoers. Their theological understandings come closer to mine than Catholics in typical parishes because many studied theology academically. I like being on a college campus with people who take spiritual life seriously and ask deep questions about life's meaning. But the Sisters seem to be inspired by Christian imagery and I am not.

I love Sacred Heart Chapel's ambience and architectural beauty. It had gone through two renovations since my school days, altering its exterior a little and its interior a lot, also altering my feeling of going home. I joked that they should have consulted me before making changes. It tells me how much I am attached to the place.

After my divorce, when I yearned for security and belonging, I imagined joining their community, but reality always intruded. It would have been much easier than life as a single woman on the outside, but the monastery could not have accepted me because of my independent spiritual perspective, and I could not have accepted life there. It was not where I belonged.

Still, St. Ben's is an anchor in my life. The Sisters welcome everyone, whatever their brand of faith, no questions asked. While differing in belief, we are united by faith, which I define as trust in the invisible domain. When I get the chance, I let the Sisters know my beliefs, but they do not stop welcoming me into full participation in their liturgy and much else. As a boon to living near St. Ben's and St. John's, I enjoy concerts, lectures, plays, and a wide variety of activities on their campuses. For years I participated in peace demonstrations in St. Cloud started after 9/11 by Benedictine activist Merle Nolde.

Beliefs in religious communities range from literalist to nearly as progressive as mine. I enjoy interacting with the progressives, those with fierce and keen awareness. Sisters have called me to support my writings and Sisters have suggested I write to the pope. They seriously chew over my ideas while, understandably, remaining loyal to the Catholic Church. To my observation, their unwavering loyalty to their community surpasses their loyalty to the institutional church. Nuns are great thinkers, but direct argumentation is not their style. For them, dissent from traditional belief would have more negative consequences than it has for me.

If St. Martin had not gotten a parochial school, I would not have entered the catechetical contest and won the scholarship that placed me in St. Benedict's High School. If I had attended a public high school, I would not have had the audacity to enroll in college. Without college, I could not have had my lifelong career in education. If I had studied in a state college, I would not have become attached to St. Ben's. And without my closeness to the Sisters, I might have failed to develop a balanced view of religion. This order of events seems arranged by an inner power.

I explained to a self-described "secular humanist" that I see more goodness in Catholicism than he does because I have friendships with religious people.

"You see the trees, I see the forest?" he suggested.

"I wouldn't say that at all," I replied. "I see the forest, but I also have lived and continue to live in the trees."

I see both. If I didn't see the forest, I couldn't write what I do about Christianity in the context of science and all religions. My mission is to encourage the trees around me to grow taller and see a larger perspective.

Here I am, landing back in the lap of Catholicism and Benedictines, where I started. Having come back to Catholicism after leaving, I know it better now; I know it "for the first time," to quote T. S. Eliot. My life is a closed circle, poetically connected to Father Pierz inviting European Catholics to Minnesota, to my forebears in whose log cabin he said Mass, and to Benedictines answering his request for a religious community to minister to Catholic immigrants.

But Robert Frost's poem "The Road Not Taken" comes to mind.

> I took the one less traveled by
> And that has made all the difference.

Following the less traveled path, I move beyond religion alone to weave in science. It leads me to reject literal religious belief, but I remain immersed in spiritual reality, anchored by my Catholic heritage.

My pet villain being the patriarchy, I appreciate the story of Benedictines planting a base in Minnesota, led by a heroic woman who managed to subvert patriarchy. In 1846 the first Benedictine monastery was established in the United States—St. Vincent Abbey in Latrobe, Pennsylvania. There, Boniface Wimmer ruled as abbot and sought German nuns to staff schools for German immigrant children. Benedicta Riepp, OSB, volunteered and was sent to Pennsylvania as the superior of Benedictine nuns.

She arrived with two companions, but immediately developed a tense relationship with the autocratic Wimmer. In 1857 she led some of her nuns, allegedly without his consent, to St. Cloud, Minnesota, where monks from Wimmer's abbey had begun ministering to German immigrants. They answered a call initiated by Fr. Pierz.

Irritated by Mother Benedicta's resistance to his rule over their internal matters, Wimmer declared he was head of all Benedictines in America. He called Benedicta Riepp and her companions a renegade band of women, deposed her, installed his own superior, and tried to have the plucky Riepp banished. But Riepp returned to Europe and at the Vatican sought independence for Benedictine women in America. Eventually she succeeded.

The mission society of King Ludwig of Bavaria, famous builder of Neuschwanstein Castle (the outlines of which Disneyland evoked), sent a gift of three thousand florins to the Sisters. But the money went through St. Vincent's, where Wimmer diverted it to the Benedictine monks in St. Cloud. Upon receiving from a representative of King Ludwig a letter of censure for misapplying the fund, Wimmer apologized, but argued the Sisters would use it "to no good purpose." The money was used by the Benedictine men to buy more than 2,500 acres of Indian Bush at Collegeville.

Wimmer named the new location *Sankt Ludwig am See*—the word "ingratiating" comes to mind. But the monks had dedicated their first chapel in St. Cloud to St. John the Baptist and brought this name to the new locale. Wimmer's sexism is not shared by today's monks at St. John's. The two monasteries cooperate, as do the colleges they founded.

Mother Benedicta Riepp remains a hero in my eyes, an intrepid woman who had the foresight and courage to resist male domination. She was doing this while Elizabeth Cady Stanton, Susan B. Anthony, and Lucretia Mott were founding the secular women's rights movement. In my personal list of feminist founders appears the name of Mother Benedicta Riepp.

16

AFTER 2000

Avon History

THE ALBANY HISTORY LED to my next book, the centennial history of
Avon. Like the Albany book, it entailed working with seniors. This time
there had been no advance working group, but I had three years to work
and liked doing all the research myself. It gave me more intimate and
substantial knowledge of the history, because I had time to see connections and could dig deeper with informed questions. This produced a
longer book—more than twice that of my history of Albany, a much
larger town.

In addition to poring over historical records, I spent many hours
listening to seniors telling their stories and corroborating stories of their
peers. Telling me whom to interview was an excellent source—my neighbor Lee Schmid. He was related to the founders and prominent builders,
knew "everybody," and had lived in Avon all his life except for a stint in
the US Army Air Corps during World War II.

When information from an interviewee left questions, I often called
Irene, an older relative of Lee. She was born about 1911, lived in Avon her
entire life, was about ninety years old, and still had a sharp mind. She said
she looked forward to my calls. Conversations with her and other oral
informants led me to realize something—interviewers perform a kind
of ministry. I sensed that my interviewees felt appreciated as I listened,

entered totally into their reality, and asked questions to make sure I had their stories right.

A centennial celebration was planned that would include the unveiling of my book, *Nestled between Lakes and Wooded Hills: The Centennial History of the Avon Area*. I fell into a familiar train of thought: *Don't count on appreciation. People won't recognize its quality.* This time the observer in me detected the self-defeating pattern and prodded me to correct it. I practiced saying, "It's OK for good things to happen to me." Expecting respect and appreciation was new.

At the festive opening, I was placed beside piles of my book to greet people entering the display building. Effusive compliments came, the beginning of many to come. I kept reminding myself to accept and bask in them instead of deflecting them or finding reasons to devalue them. Garrison Keillor co-owned a restaurant in Avon, which brought *A Prairie Home Companion* to Avon for the show's thirty-fifth anniversary, performed in the culture of Garrison's imaginative Lake Wobegon. When he asked a co-owner of the restaurant for local background information, she recommended my history. That is how I got on the show. It produced more recognition and sold more books. My change in attitude had paid off.

Supervising

While substitute teaching, I had time to read, digest, and take notes of books feeding my perennial passion—the Christian brand in relation to other belief systems. I wrote text intended for the book I hoped eventually to have published. My drafts included information mined during years of study and flashes of enlightenment that struck while wandering in midlife depth.

The research and writing built up to about four times the amount of text that could fit into one book. When I looked for a publisher by sending outlines and sample chapters, kind editors replied that my contents addressed too wide a scope and contained many times the amount of material for my type of book. Their comments echoed a dawning realization in my own mind.

In schools, the easiest days of substitute teaching happened when a student teacher took over and my only role was to be the credentialed person in the room. On one such occasion, the student teacher's university supervisor showed up. She was not a tenured faculty member—her credentials equaled mine—and she supervised while also subbing in high schools. She said more supervisors were needed and encouraged me to apply.

This is how I became an adjunct supervisor of student teachers for St. Cloud State University. It gifted me with affirmation of my own powers, satisfaction from guiding others, and welcome income. I continued supervising for seventeen years with many teacher candidates in some semesters, few in others, and occasionally none. Cooperating teachers in schools told me they would like to do this after retiring, a perfect part-time way to finish a career in education. I knew they would be at least as skilled as I, but rarely do opportunities like mine pop up. I interpret my good fortune as another sign of invisible strings pulling us through our lives.

While communicating with student teachers, I used the failures and triumphs of my own teaching experiences. Failures seemed most useful as examples. "This is what I did wrong," motivated them to improve more than, "This is what you need to correct." One habit frequently needing correction was giving more attention and encouragement to boys than to girls in their classes. I did it as a young teacher and saw student teachers doing it.

Another fact of my life guided me in guiding them. I used to flounder during my school day if I had taken cutting words from my husband or met someone's disapproval. My performance also suffered when I felt unrespectable for being a substitute teacher. On the other hand, compliments and confidence could turn me into a good teacher. I tried to apply this lesson in mentoring, considering it my job to build up student teachers' confidence, and I regretted it when I forgot. Besides continual affirmation, the most valuable help I could offer my students seemed to be my listening ear. Their comments at the ends of semesters indicate this.

Immigrants

Like subbing, supervising as an adjunct for St. Cloud State gave me the flexibility for other pursuits. As enrollment fluctuated, the position brought widely varying numbers of students, and I could limit the number I took. This flexibility allowed me to take an immensely gratifying position—teaching English to adult immigrants in the Adult Basic

Education program (ABE) of St. Cloud. In my lifelong career as an educator, nothing has given me more satisfaction.

I have always had an affinity for immigrants. I suppose it started with feeling like an outsider in my youth. But more reasons developed while teaching adult immigrants. I observed them easily grasping mind-stretching ideas less available to native-born Americans with a smaller horizon of experience. Immigrants have seen life from perspectives that broaden them. My adult students seemed wise, grown up, and adaptive, having to absorb a startling American culture. One Somali said that when he arrived at the airport in New York, he assumed that a scantily-clad woman was insane and other Americans were just being nice when they treated her as normal.

The adult immigrants I taught—Africans, mostly Somalis, Latinos from Latin America, Chinese, Pakistanis, South Koreans, and other Asians—poured lavish respect on teachers that contrasted with teenage attitudes in American schools. I was not allowed to pay for my meal in a Chinese restaurant only because I taught at ABE. It did not matter whether I taught students they knew. My still-insecure soul hardly knew how to take in so much respect. Dignity renewed by the position assuaged wounds from past abuse.

The position gifted me with more evidence that Christians do not have a monopoly on spiritual wisdom. A Buddhist from South Korea impressed me with her Zen-like demeanor and calm willingness to answer my questions about Buddhism. She corrected me when I referred to it as a religion. "It's a philosophy," she said.

I was aware of the question, "Is Buddhism a religion or a philosophy?" and decided it's both. Like religions, Buddhist sects have developed mythologies and Buddhism teaches a system of belief, but not belief in a deity, making it a non-theistic or a-theistic system, thus a philosophy. Its focus on wise living rather than worshipping a deity appeals to me.

I began to educate myself on Islam and Muslims because Somalis comprised the largest portion of my students. Little-known facts learned then stay with me: Indonesia is the largest Muslim nation. During Christian Europe's Dark Ages, Islam excelled in science, mathematics, medicine, and culture. Not Islam, but Middle East tribalism imposes female genital mutilation and the dress code on Muslim women. Islam reveres Jesus as a prophet and Mohammed as the last prophet. From lectures by imams I learned that Muslims believe Jesus will return at the end of time to build the kingdom of heaven. This last floored me. If only right-wing Christians knew!

One day a Somali man whom I hadn't seen before tried to correct me when I referred to the Shia. "They're not Muslims," he said. Aware of the lethal rivalry between Sunni and Shia, I began to explain the origin of the split dividing them after Mohammed's death, but my words would have carried no weight in his eyes had not his fellow Muslims in class communicated respect for them.

A few Somalis expressed their soul experiences in writing assignments. The way they related to God—it was not about theology—resembled Christian relationships with divinity. Most of them wrote "God" instead of "Allah," recognizing the universal intimacy of soul with spiritual power. I felt honored that they entrusted me, a non-Muslim, with their precious thoughts.

I addressed controversial topics in class, something I could not recommend to my student teachers facing American teenagers. Knowing that the bulk of my immigrants were Muslims, I freely exposed my bias for Palestinians in their conflict with the state of Israel. Consistent with my habit of siding with the underdog, I side with Palestinians, who are powerless while the state of Israel keeps stealing their land for Jewish settlements and imprisoning Palestinians for resisting. My preference pleased more of my adult international students, not only the Somalis.

When I discussed the restricted role of Somali women in public life, Abdi, one of the Somali men, said that Somali women don't mind the expectations of their culture. "I don't like it," piped up a Somali woman. The same woman stopped us when we were posing for a class photo at the end of a term. "Wait!" she cried. Stepping into a nearby hall, she took off her hijab and came back for the photo.

Abdi did not hold my feminism against me. He became a cultural navigator in St. Cloud schools and asked me for help when he wanted to communicate in written English. I invited him to my home so that I could work on my computer while he told me what he wanted to say. He used to bring a large Somali meal that would take me days to consume, until I persuaded him to stop. "I am passing on kindnesses given me by others," I explained. Abdi has been in my home many times, has brought his wife and children, has prayed in my home, and has become my friend.

Due to budget cuts, I lost the position at ABE. There had been many warnings that staff would be cut and I was last hired, but I hadn't prepared myself. When the blow came it surprised me. Somali students at

ABE sent a letter of protest to the director. They wanted me back. One Pakistani student was angry at *me* before she learned I had not intentionally abandoned them but had been terminated.

After losing the position, I sank into depression again. Increased income from the job had enabled repairs and improvements on my home. I'd depended on it, expected it would ensure my financial stability until social security payments arrived. This time depression manifested in my body as a systemic infection of poison ivy that put me in the hospital again.

But I had more experience now, more tools to handle depression. A phone conversation with Al years earlier came to mind. When my teaching stint at Albany High School ended, he told me I was kicked in the butt for a reason. He was right. Another relevant memory rose. Years earlier, in a phone conversation with my Al-Anon mentor, I was in distress about something that, significantly, I can't recall. The part I vividly recall is the concern in her voice because I clung to my own idea of what was best for me. I could not surrender to my Higher Power.

Now I decided to let go of specific plans for my future and started chanting to myself, "Accept, surrender, and trust." It opened possibilities for plans better than I could envision. Al-Anon and Unity taught me that I could choose hope in circumstances that previously would have induced hopelessness. "Accept, surrender, and trust" joined "Let God and let God" to open doors of infinite possibility. They released me from attachment to specific results so that invisible power could work out solutions beyond my ability to imagine.

They prompted gratefulness for gifts given by the opportunity to teach adult immigrants. To a former colleague at ABE I wrote, "I loved it there because it infused me with dignity sorely needed after years of verbal and psychological abuse." I also admitted that the director "actually did me a service by depriving me of that job."

Accepting, trusting, and letting go prompted gratefulness for my new knowledge. When I see bias against immigrants, I can counter it with stories of my experience with them. I frequently cite my admiration for their determination to make a successful life in America. After working all night in a manufacturing plant, some showed up at ABE the next morning to learn English before they went home to bed. I am learning to use facts like this to counter hatred and invective against immigrants based on ignorance. My new knowledge broadened my own outlook. I expect that after my generation dies, the nations of South America,

Africa, and Asia will play a more respectable role in world affairs than they do at this time.

I was still supervising student teachers for St. Cloud State and now—trusting invisible power—I realized that the end of teaching at ABE gave me time to work on the book I had in mind. My brief depression's end was hurried by a poem I wrote and got published in *Sacred Journey* (August/September 2005). It shows me learning the lesson that my Al-Anon mentor years earlier had wanted me to learn:

SURRENDER

Buffeted by blow after blow
I cower in confusion,
let misfortunes take over,
stop thinking, planning,
    reasoning,
questioning,
        and wait.
    Empty.

Holy Power holds me.
I wait, empty.

Tiny glimmers invade.
A child smiles.
Sun glistens on wet leaves.
A bird chirps.
I take note,
    unbend,
    open,
    and accept hope.

Health Turn

My main oncologist moved from oncology to internal medicine and continued treating me as an internist. In 2004 he announced he would stop practicing at the clinic in St. Cloud and a woman internist would be my doctor. I no longer needed an oncologist. I liked him, but having a woman doctor suited me. It had been ten years since my third cancer episode. I was embarrassed as he looked at the rolls of fat on my body but relieved when he told me I no longer needed Megace, the anti-cancer drug he'd prescribed ten years earlier. I'd like to think he saw in me the power to heal myself. This new concept was seeping into the medical establishment.

Megace came with a warning that it caused weight gain. I had taken half the dose he prescribed, and after a while that is the amount he prescribed. Nevertheless, Megace blimped me out. I was glad to be liberated from taking the drug but gladder at the result—losing 25 pounds, more strength, my middle shrinking, and a conspicuous turn toward general health. With amazement, I watched my body slim down and noticed I was not puffing as much after going up a flight of stairs. I could do yard work for hours without collapsing.

Friends worried that I was losing weight fast, but I assured them I was healthier than before. Despite a permanently weakened lung, I could with minimal help keep up a house, a car, a garage, and a large, maintenance-greedy yard. And keep on writing. It increased my doubts about the wisdom of some conventional medicine. I believe "Accept, surrender, and trust" did more for my healing than radiation.

My former oncologist began practicing internal medicine in another town, where it happened that he treated my sister-in-law. To her he expressed amazed delight at my recovery. And, she said, he liked my writings. This last detail pleased me as much as his gift of releasing me from cancer "therapy."

My brothers and sisters never learned about cancer's repeated onslaughts, nor did they suspect its severity. This I suddenly realized years later when Celia was telling me about someone's miraculous recovery.

"There was a miraculous recovery right in your own family," I said.

A pause. "Who?" She seemed incredulous until I told her of my oncologist's surprise over my recovery.

Gradually, family blood sweetened our interactions. Time and cooperating with each other in dealing with family struggles softened frictions. I told myself, *If they disapprove, it's not my problem.* I stopped wanting siblings to understand and they stopped trying to convert me. A nephew argued against my views, but his disagreement did not disturb me. It was easy to avoid religious views at family gatherings. In time, differences in religious beliefs stopped mattering. It is enough that we get along. We are not close but care about each other.

I found support elsewhere and writing helped. It released my inner voice and gave it the stage in my thoughts, which built confidence in my convictions.

17

Closure

Pay Attention

YEARS AFTER MOTHER AND Father died, I uncovered the reason for
the words that burst from me while doing inner work: "Pay attention
to me!" It seemed a selfish demand, and puzzling, until Al and I were
walking together in the St. Martin cemetery after visiting our parents'
grave. We reminisced while looking at familiar names and came upon
the gravestone of Albert Mandernach, who had died of appendicitis as a
child. By the time a second doctor correctly diagnosed it and operated,
Albert was full of infection. Al told me that Albert's death helped to
save his own life. I had known of Arnold's attack. He tells the story in
Discovering My Inner Child.

Mama suspected her boy was having an appendicitis attack in the
middle of the night because she recognized the symptoms. As she couldn't
drive, she pleaded with Daddy to take him to the hospital in Paynesville,
but Daddy refused, "because of his fear of doctors," wrote Al. Daddy gave
Arnold medicine for a stomach ache, which aggravated the condition.
The morning after that, wrote Al,

> I was in worse pain and so I did not go to school. But my fa-
> ther refused to take me to the doctor. All day long my agony
> increased. When the older kids returned home from school,
> Mother sent my older brother to the field to get my father. . . .
> However, he waited until it was too dark to plow any more be-
> fore he returned from the fields. (35–36)

Finally, after more arguments and pleading, Daddy drove them to a chiropractor, who told him to rush his boy to the hospital immediately. There they learned that Arnold's appendix was ready to burst. It was already poisoning his body and he was slipping into a coma. After the surgery, Arnold was delirious and in danger of dying. Following twelve days in the hospital, he was brought home for Mama to nurse. She had him sleep in bed with her, and Daddy slept upstairs with the other boys.

Here's the thing. I looked at the date on the gravestone—the year I was born. I was an infant when this happened. Now I knew why I felt abandoned as a very young child and related to Mama as to a stranger. I am sure she had cherished Baby Jeanette, but her loving attention stopped while she frantically saved the life of her eight-year-old boy. Baby Jeanette wanted her attention but Mama was in terror of losing Arnold. I felt neglected and rejected and never forgave her. Feeling abandoned by Mama fits exactly the feeling I screamed out in my journal.

Arnold's near death was followed by the death of Dad's only brother, Alois. Mother felt abandoned by her husband when he decided to work for his mother, the woman she blamed for the deaths of Florian and Leroy. Emotionally abused in her youth, then emotionally abused by in-laws, Mother had to make her way alone. She had no compassionate ear into which she could pour her grievances, no adult helping her to work through them—the curse of many in her generation. Now I could forgive her for staying lodged in her own grief during the earliest years of my childhood.

Uncovering these events explains me to myself and assuages me. Now I have something other than immaturity to explain my disconsolate crying at the sight of my crib brought down for the next baby. I felt deprived of baby-time in the crib while being cherished by Mama. Her depression explains at least a little of my lifetime insecurity, fear of rejection, and irrational lack of self-respect. And it explains my distance from Mama, sure that she didn't know me. My newfound realization came too late to share with her but in time to grace my latter-years' reflections.

Mother's last communication with me came from beyond the grave. While Verna was still living under the loving care of Leroy, he let me bring her to my house. I wanted to relieve him of his caregiving duties for a few days. We visited Mom's grave in St. Martin.

As Verna and I stood there, dread spread through my body, unlike anything I have felt before or since. I was strangely sick. It frightened me, but I said nothing, afraid that my mother or another spiritual entity was reproaching me for some offense against her. The feeling diminished while we walked through the cemetery visiting other graves. It disappeared as we left the cemetery and drove on.

The next day I drove Verna home to St. Paul. On my way back, still in the suburbs, my car broke down. It could not have happened at a worse time, as I was going to leave for Denver the next day to visit Mollie. Immediately I connected the breakdown with the foreboding that shook me at Mom's grave. I believe she wanted to warn me of what was in store for me. Leroy rescued me—so much for me relieving him. The foreboding does not return when I visit Mom's grave now.

Jerry and Evie, the only siblings still home on the farm while I was at St. Ben's, tell me that Mom favored me over them. I don't like hearing this, but I can understand their feelings and appreciate having my old impressions of Mom reversed. One summer I was working at St. Ben's between college semesters and living in a house off campus. Mom and Dad stopped to visit on their way home from shopping in St. Cloud. I asked for a loaf of specialty bread she had bought for herself, not available in stores where they lived. She left the bread with me.

A person from the past once told me that my mother had a nice voice. *Huh?* In reply to my obvious confusion she repeated it—she remembered her attractive voice. She meant Mom's speaking voice. Another turn in my perception. Today, my glance into a mirror sometimes mixes my mother's face with mine. If I could have conversations with her now, I would bring up memories both sweet and fraught with guilt.

Al

Al presided over the funerals of our parents and over another family funeral in 2001—that of Adelbert, our oldest brother. He had managed our parents' estate during their last years of life and after they died.

In June of 2005, Al celebrated his fortieth anniversary of ordination. He decided to celebrate the fortieth year because, he told people, he didn't know if he would "make it" to his fiftieth. The celebrations took place in Michigan and in Paynesville, where he ministered to the parish while the pastor went on vacation. Both events featured the performance of music Al had composed.

A year later, in anticipation of his annual visit in Minnesota I urged him to visit Aunt Margaret and Uncle Pete, who were not expected to live long. Al and I planned to do it together. Because we knew Margaret was dying, I said we had to visit her immediately when he arrived. He did visit her immediately, but a bad cold kept me home.

The following Sunday was the one scheduled for extended family attending the Mass in St. Louis Church, followed by the usual Hilltop gathering. After this, he invited us siblings to the rectory. We visited there for a while, but when we prepared to leave he seemed disappointed. I remember being slightly surprised because we had stayed longer than other years after the Hilltop gathering.

On the day we planned to visit Uncle Pete, Al and I could not get there at the same time. I spent time with Pete and left to make a school visit. Al visited Pete sometime after I left and anointed him. We exchanged emails about that but not about the series of disappointments during this visit of his to Minnesota. It may be that the whole time he was home in February we never once had much of a talk or a hug.

A few weeks later, I was on the phone and got the signal that another caller was trying to come in. Because the call I was on pertained to a matter that made me tense, I did not shorten it as I usually would for an incoming call. The incoming caller was unusually persistent, but I continued dealing with the first call that was making me nervous. Whoever was on the other line would have to find a better time to call, I thought.

Days later, I learned that Al was in a hospital and on a ventilator, making it impossible for me to talk to him on the phone. My heart broke with regret, certain he had been that frustrated caller. Because I did not pick up that line, he had no communication with our family before being placed on a ventilator. By the time we found out, he was unable to speak.

Connie, a friend of Al's in Michigan, visited him and emailed me in distress. I denied the grave import of her email because Connie's alarm seemed unreal. We in Minnesota didn't know much about the state of his health or his prospects for recovery. I thought I should stay here to continue my supervising duties. Celia had retired from nursing. She and her husband offered to go and, as a nurse, she seemed to be a good representative of our family.

When Al and I had been in Europe, smokers had free rein to pollute any atmosphere. One enclosed place, a train car, was suffocating us. Saying his lungs couldn't take it, Al left me to watch over our things and went somewhere else. I was peeved because I also had reduced lung function. Radiation had depleted the lung capacity on my right side. Al told me he had COPD, but I didn't know what it was, then. Now I do—chronic obstructive pulmonary disease, making it hard to breathe.

Celia emailed medical information, which I forwarded to our siblings and, as the news spread, to extended family. Soon, dozens of cousins and Minnesota friends of Al were on my list of people getting updates on his condition. Our cousin Leona and her whole family were close to Al. He often stayed in Leona's house during Minnesota visits, and she had cut his hair when he was home in February.

Gradually Celia's emails told us more. Two blood clots had traveled to his lungs, one in each lung. One blood clot burst. The inexorable end came into view. We had to make the decision whether to continue life support. My spiritual journey left no doubt that life on the other side continues in revelation and beauty. I urged that the ventilator be turned off. Celia's medical training made her disinclined, but I persuaded her to avoid prolonging Al's dying. It was his time to pass to the other side.

On the Sunday we decided to disconnect the ventilator, I woke in the middle of the night, wracked by memories and regrets. I rose, marked the time—3:40—and wrote this message to Al:

> I want to tell you how distressed I am that I didn't have an opportunity to say goodbye to you. I want to tell you "Sorry" for all and any ways I hurt you. I want to thank you for all the ways you helped me and enriched my life, most especially by taking me to Germany.
>
> You helped our whole family heal by connecting us to our relatives and our community in ways that would not have happened without you.
>
> When you were here in February, I was sure you and I would visit Margaret and Pete together. One thing after another prevented that. I got a chance to have final visits with them but not with you. So my goodbye has to come this way. Goodbye and I love you.

I could not have said these words during daylight. Our family did not say such things to each other. At my urgent request, Celia read my message to Al's inert form in the hospital. A few days later, she watched life leaving his body as his ventilator was disconnected. Leona lit a candle for Al that morning, not knowing what was scheduled for that day. When she told me about the candle later, we realized it expired the moment Al expired. Leona did not need Jung to tell her it had spiritual significance.

Al drove himself mercilessly toward the end of his life. I believe a deeper part of him knew of his impending death and accepted it. The last time I prepared food for him, I was appalled to see that he avoided the healthy foods Leona and I were recommending. He splurged on diet-busting foods.

A few weeks after his February stay in Minnesota, he was on his way to performing a ministry in Detroit, when his body gave alarming signs and he drove himself to the hospital instead. Mark and Betty Squier tell the story.

> Along with Fr. Al, we were responsible for coordinating the local Retrouvaille programs [of Metro-Detroit] serving from 200–300 hurting marriages annually. We were scheduled to present a Retrouvaille weekend together beginning March 10, the day he drove himself to Garden City Hospital rather than to the Doubletree Hotel in Romulus.
>
> We were home from work eating a quick dinner, loading our luggage and weekend talks into the car when Fr. Al called my cell phone. He had left a voice mail on Mark's phone also.
>
> [Al decided] he had better go straight to the hospital because when he stopped for a Lenten Fish Dinner at one of the local churches, he had a very difficult time breathing as he walked from his car to the church. It was so bad that as soon as he got to the church, he decided to turn around and walk back to his car and drive to the hospital which was only a few miles away.

The Squiers found a replacement to give the priest's presentation that weekend, and after their program ended, visited Al.

> Fr. Al had removed his oxygen mask to talk to us, and the nurse came in and told him that he had to keep it on. So he put it back on and talked through it. When we hugged him goodbye, I said, "You have to get well now, you know, because we're not done with you yet." He smiled at us.

Retrouvaille of Metro-Detroit had the rights to his book. It turned out that the way they were not done with him was to keep selling his book.

Al knew he was dying, maybe even before he arrived at the hospital where, one of the hospital staff reported, he told them he was dying. On his advance care directive, he had specified that he wanted no long-term mechanical respiration. I suspect he consented to the ventilator because he knew others needed time to accept his death.

Al's Mariannhill community invited us siblings in Minnesota to stay in their large compound in Dearborn to attend the funeral and make decisions about Al's personal possessions. We siblings rented a van and drove to their large facility, which housed a chapel, educational facilities, and students, as well as the Mariannhill fathers. I was told Al had tried to call me from the hospital but couldn't get me. It magnified my anguish over refusing that call. Was I tense at the time because my intuitive self knew who was trying to get my attention?

At the visitation in Dearborn, I read the words I had written in the middle of night and again at the memorial we arranged for him in Paynesville. There, in front of family and relatives, tears distorted my voice and I was unable to finish. My cousin Norma came to my side and finished reading it. Days later, I received phone calls from siblings upbraiding me for crying during the memorial service.

Al did not push church doctrine. Stories he told during his visits home showed he was valued for his intuitive understanding of emotional needs. Some of his stories bordered on the paranormal. It was clear he helped people to understand how feelings drive human relations. I realized he was an extraordinary person who had an extraordinary impact on people.

As we went through Al's things in Michigan, I got a new appreciation for his artistry. Many paintings of his showed up and a wealth of classical records. One room in the Mariannhill complex seemed to be his music room. I still have some of his LP records and a high-quality phonograph. His confreres told us that Al's artistic contributions would be missed. One mourner close to them described the impact he made:

> I am sure the Fathers missed Al's Christmas decorating. He had decorations all over the place! The dining room was always festive as well as both chapels and little nooks and crannies besides his office. He really got into it and was proud to show it off. I had to follow him all over the place to admire his work. He transformed the place.

His words brought to mind a scene on the farm when I was one of "da kits." Arnold was rearranging decorations on the Christmas tree after Christmas Day. It shocked me—trying to improve on the work of *Christkindchen*! But he seemed so comfortable fussing over placement of lights and ornaments, like he'd done it before. And then I noticed that Mama motioned him to stop in the presence of us "kits."

Al had a will. As a chaplain for Marriage Encounter and Retrouvaille, and as an author, he had a bank account separate from that of his Mariannhill congregation. This was surprising news, and the contents of the will were more than surprising. Jerry was the one reading it to us, and he seemed to enjoy the surprise.

Al left all his money to me. It felt wrong. I was uncomfortable. I said I would turn it all over to Mariannhill, but Jerry advised me to keep most of it.

I tried to find a reason for Al's will. When he told me in the St. Martin cemetery that Albert Mandernach's death from appendicitis helped to save his own life, did I tell Al why the date was significant for me? I remember telling him of my earliest unhappy memories of Mama and wonder if he somehow felt responsible. While we siblings were combing through his effects in Michigan, I offered to take his personal writings. In one I read the words, "I feel like I fathered Jeanette."

Al's passing affected me more than the deaths of our parents, for whom the time of death seemed appropriate. I regretted my failure to overcome family conditioning and withholding the approval and affection that Al craved from his family. In Europe he revealed his need for compliments, but I grumpily withheld them. Now, I mourned in my journal that he and I could have been closer had I behaved differently.

Memories came. In one I am a pre-schooler after a great snowstorm. My big brothers have been outside shoveling. Evie and I are dressed warm and let out to play in the snow. Our brothers proudly show us a snug little room created by the storm as it curled snow around the smokehouse. At one edge are steps going up, neatly carved in the snow. I give them the admiration my brothers want, then ruin them by stupidly trying to step on them. Now I know who created those steps.

Only after he died did I fully realize Al's importance in my life. The spiritual journey he reveals in his memoir illuminates my own journey of release from fetters clamped on us by family and Catholic training. Years after Al's death, I was reviewing my drawer-full of notes made while studying at the SOT and came upon two photocopied sheets covered front and back. In the margin someone had written, "A few pages from Andrew Greeley's book, *The Catholic Myth*, I thought you'd be interested in."

The writing looked familiar, and then a wave of feeling passed through me. It was Al. He'd underlined parts of Greeley's writing about Catholic guilt, my favorite statement underlined: "If you enjoy something

it must be wrong." Al evidently shed this implicit Catholic teaching sooner than I did and guessed its significance for me. I discarded most of the
notes, but not these sheets.

Al's desire to share more of himself with his biological family would
be forever frustrated. Maybe travels compensated. He set foot on five
continents and every single one of the fifty states. The last became a goal
he completed close to the end of his life by serving as minister on cruises
to Alaska and Hawaii. The long, cramped plane trip to and from Hawaii
probably produced the two blood clots that traveled to his lungs and took
his life.

Jim

Jim maintained a good relationship with Pat and Mollie. In fact, he
seemed to cherish them more after the divorce and supported them at
least as much after as before. He wrote novels during the last years of
his life. Although lacking in literary merit, they reinforced my belief that
thwarted artistry accounts for many of his life problems.

His second marriage failed. Jim told a few people that he never
stopped loving me, but he never apologized to me. What did he come
to realize later in life? He developed colon cancer and started a several-
years-long decline. On the phone, I told him that Fr. Al was dying. "I'm
dying," said Jim. I didn't know what to say. Feeling guilty that Al's rapid
descent was disturbing me more, I could not think of a single thing to say.
I hope he read my silence as compassion. It was.

A few years after Al's death, I visited Jim in the hospital. When I
walked in, his face lit up with surprise and joy. His quick glance at other
visitors in the room said, "See this?" After they left, I summoned the
strength to resist my training in never expressing matters of the heart.
I said, "Thank you for parenting Pat and Mollie after we divorced. You
continued to be their dad." He accepted my compliment proudly. As he
drew closer to death, he named me first responder on his Lifeline Medical
Alert System.

A few weeks before he died, I developed a bowel obstruction that
would keep me in the hospital and acute care for an entire month. Jim
called me from his hospital bed and sounded glad that I was in the hospital, too. I do not think it was *Schadenfreude*. While we were married
it had seemed the right order for me to die first. After we divorced, I

continued having multiple ailments and frequent hospitalizations. Gradually my emotional and physical health had improved to make me conspicuously healthier than years earlier. So what were my guts telling me now? Did I have emotional baggage that needed cleaning up from the marriage? Nothing like that ever showed up. The emotional charge I get when thinking about Jim now is positive.

After his death, Jim's sisters along with Pat and Mollie organized a memorial. I have fond memories of it, although other persons who saw me there would expect the opposite. Brother-in-law Bill was sent to drive me from the sub-acute therapy center where I was recovering from surgery that had shortened my intestine by eight inches. When Bill saw the shape I was in, he didn't want to take me away from my bed. Soon he saw that he could not persuade me to miss the memorial.

Finding enough energy to walk to Bill's car and then from car into another building wore me out. Weakly I lay still with eyes closed. Hearing a circle of people around me, I recognized Pat's voice and asked, "Is Mollie here?" After a pause he said, "She's here." Later she told me she didn't trust her voice to answer.

Gradually I gained enough strength to catch glimpses of Pat and Mollie interacting with relatives. I had my eyes closed when all was quiet as a beautiful female voice, without accompaniment, began to sing a haunting Irish melody. After some seconds, it occurred to me that it might be Mollie. It was. Then a male voice joined her in harmony—Pat. Their voices blended beautifully to produce a heavenly sound I wish had been recorded. I will always cherish that moment.

Bill used his technical skill to create an appealing video of Jim's life. It pictured me but not his second wife. I am grateful to the Clancy family for keeping me enfolded in their extended family. They felt more like family than my biological family when siblings turned preachy and judgmental. But my siblings came to Jim's memorial, which pleases me immensely. Our upbringing said it's the responsible thing to do, but I also take it as support for me.

The Clancy family helped me transition from my German-culture farm to more typically American life. To Mother Clancy I owe kitchen know-how and utensils. I still rely on the pots, pans, and cookbook she gave me. After our divorce I continued my relationship with Jim's parents. I had cleaned for them before and went on cleaning. I visited them in nursing homes when that time came.

Several months after Jim's death, I wrote to him in my journal.

Jim, I got divorced to take care of myself, but in doing that I know I hurt you. I'm sorry it hurt you. I figured out that your alcoholism was at least partly the result of your artistic bent. You have a strong internal impulse toward artistic values, which to me means spiritual values.

It is no accident that alcoholic drinks are called spirits.

I continue finding benefits from having married Jim, gifts he and his family gave me, ways our relationship challenged me to grow in maturity. Perhaps Jim called me from his hospital bed to mine because he thought we might pass from this life together. But I had more work to do, more lessons to learn.

18

God Is Not Three Guys in the Sky

The Rule of Mars

My zealous work of consuming book after book in the Alcuin Library at St. John's and using the subversive information in writings of mine was not for nothing, although I had far too much content for a book. I still mine those writings for names of sources and bits of information. Besides relying on the library that supplies the School of Theology, I consumed a small library of Goddess literature accumulated by Sandy, the feminist in my writers' group.

Before *God Is Not Three Guys in the Sky* was published, I contributed to another book that subverted patriarchy. Cristina Biaggi, an artist and thinker whom Sandy and I met at the Women and Spirituality conferences in Mankato, invited us to submit chapters for an anthology she was planning. It became *The Rule of Mars: Readings on the Origins, History and Impact of Patriarchy*. Among contributors was Riane Eisler, who wrote what anthropologist Ashley Montagu called "the most important book since Darwin's *Origin of Species*." This ground-breaking feminist work is *The Chalice and the Blade*.

Eisler identifies domination and aggression (the blade of the Father) as patriarchy's model for ordering society. A countervailing model structured Europe, the Middle East, and some of Asia during the Paleolithic and early Neolithic ages—partnership and nurturing (the chalice of the

Mother). In sharp contrast to later art, writes Eisler, Neolithic art presents no

> imagery idealizing armed might, cruelty, and violence-based power . . . no images of "noble warriors" or scenes of battles. Nor are there any signs of "heroic conquerors" dragging captives around in chains or other evidences of slavery. (17)

Instead, archaeologists find symbols from nature such as "serpents and butterflies (symbols of metamorphosis)" and everywhere images of the divine Mother, often cradling her divine child.

Eisler cites evidence uncovered by archaeologist Marija Gimbutas showing that warrior tribes invaded and conquered mother-centered, peaceful, and egalitarian cultures during the fifth and fourth millennia BCE. The warrior tribes had male gods who overpowered goddesses. Societies turned militant and hierarchical. Power-over became the rule rather than power-with.

I spent my entire life in the dominator paradigm but didn't know it until I read about Neolithic art. Before I knew about Great Mother societies, I could not imagine a world where fighting enemies was not a main job of government. Prehistoric images prompted me to think our "Defense Department" is misnamed. It focuses on offense.

Today the dominator model is breaking down, writes Eisler, and I can see this. Despite the spate of strongmen ravaging nations today, their stereotypically masculine "strength" is less admired than stereotypically feminine values of cooperation, compassion, gentleness, and nurturing. I said "despite" but I could have said "because." Toughness amplified puts its cruelty in stark relief, which repulses people and energizes a reverse movement. Never before have women and people of color been so respected, never before so many men nurturing children and doing housework, never before so much alarm over unequal wealth and power.

Stereotypically feminine values are gaining power. This return to balance allays my fears as we ride out crises in the world. At the School of Theology I observed and wrote about the gradual shift in our God-image, from the god up there and over us to divinity within. When outer surroundings seem to say we are going backward, I am reassured by the long view that shows patriarchal forces losing out.

I felt honored to join the group of distinguished authors in *The Rule of Mars*. My chapter's title, "Taming Testosterone," borrowed a phrase from Ken Wilbur's *A Brief History of Everything*. To urge doing away with domination and competition, I cited examples of societies ancient and contemporary built on cooperation and partnership. I reasoned that "war may be conditioned behavior and violence may be learned, rather than the unavoidable result of the way we are."

Contributing to *The Rule of Mars* built up confidence in seeing myself as a serious author delving into large issues. With the help of prestigious thinkers, I was synthesizing information from voluminous readings, not always realizing how long the material had to marinate in me before I could make it digestible for others.

God Is Not Three Guys

A clamor of frustration was building inside. I felt compelled to publish the book I'd envisioned almost twenty years earlier. My only outlets were writings brought to writers' group, talking to a few friends who also deplored the power of the patriarchy, and presenting at the Women and Spirituality conference once a year. I itched to poke holes in common misconceptions. An inveterate educator, I wanted to share electrifying information coming to me. *These things should be known!*

Besides my inner push, outer signs appeared telling me it was time. At a peace rally, I fell into conversation with a fellow demonstrator who worked for St. John's Liturgical Press. She advised me to treat the manuscript like a kid: "Send it forth. Stop polishing and perfecting." Her "send it forth" propelled me to finish *God Is Not Three Guys in the Sky* and look for a way to get it published.

Knowing that only a tiny portion of my information could fit into one book, I pared down the content I'd written, reworked it, and submitted the manuscript to dozens of publishers. Typically, they said agreeable things but turned down the manuscript for publication. I got the sense they did not think its unconventional content would sell. Publishers need to make money. I did not submit it to Liturgical Press at St. John's because it had just killed a feminist book by first accepting it and then obeying orders from the Vatican to stop publication. I was afraid of losing rights to my manuscript and never getting it published.

Gradually I arrived at the decision that self-publishing was the way forward. Now, with Al's gift, I had the money. In 2007, self-publishing was leaving behind its earlier reputation of producing inferior products. A company in Edina, a Minneapolis suburb, offered self-publishing services for what its editors deemed manuscripts of merit. My respect for it rose when an acquaintance of mine submitted her manuscript but was turned down.

Beaver's Pond Press was expensive. Without Al's gift, I would not have considered it. In time I learned the expense was worth it, because the editor procured by Beaver's Pond insisted on detailed citations. I had avoided footnotes or endnotes as a way of appealing to nonacademics. My editor soon helped me to see the foolishness of that. My content demanded citations. Back to the library I went for page numbers. It meant substantially more work and delayed publication, but as a result I refined my presentation of source material and my own message.

The Rule of Mars came out the same year as *God Is Not Three Guys in the Sky: Cherishing Christianity without Its Exclusive Claims.* In my book I distinguish the mythic Jesus from the man in history and offer a symbolic reading of the myth. Summing up my critique of Christian belief, I state that Christians mistake our myth for history and our symbols for facts.

Producing *God Is Not Three Guys in the Sky* changed my life. In my world, Christian belief had reigned without challenge. Many years earlier I had confessed to a lesbian that I don't believe Jesus is God and added, "My secret is more dangerous than your secret." She agreed. Publishing my book was my coming out. It exposed my true beliefs.

After it circulated, explosions of relief came from Catholics and other Christians who also disbelieved unbelievable doctrines. I detected in readers the effect that Jung had on me—vindicating me, validating my interpretations, and leading me to deeper insights. By translating the thought of Jung and other experts, I could help others feel vindicated. In my book they were reading what they had vaguely intuited.

Exuberant responses from readers reached me. "She wrote the book just for me," said one. "I like Jesus a whole lot better since reading Jeanette's book!" said another. A Methodist reader observed that my book clarified the distinction between the Jesus of history and the Christ of faith. I was delighted when a Protestant minister approved my combining of Jungian depth-psychology with historical-critical research. I felt honored by the Franciscan who said I write about science and spirituality in a way she can understand. "Clancy's book," she wrote, "reminds me of a simpler version of Ilia Delio" (a theologian who expounds on the work of Teilhard de Chardin). The affirmations erased my fear of critiquing Christian belief. I was no longer alone.

Twenty years earlier, a monk at St. John's had responded to my idea for the title by saying, "You'll get rocks thrown at your house." Should I publish the book anonymously? Impossible. Too many people had heard me say, "God is not three guys in the sky." Would I be shot down by a fanatic? Pat and Mollie were very concerned, but all our concern turned out to be needless.

The reception given my book surprised me, then made sense. During its incubation period of twenty years, religious understanding had evolved, preparing Christians to rethink their childhood faith. Loud voices filling the airwaves were shouting dogmatic and even preachier old-time religion than was heard in the 1980s, but an astonishing number of people were ready to accept critiques of conventional religion.

I gave presentations and started blogging. In my blog I reflect on a wide gamut of faith matters, frequently criticizing sexist God-talk. Occasionally I write about politics. From book and blog developed relationships with people around the country. Whether or not they agree with my interpretations, they are moved to freely express their own. We are part of a widespread shift toward independence from religion.

One reader had survived a painful rupture in her life that put her at odds with Church authority. Consoled and supported by my book, she sees my mission as helping those who feel spiritually isolated, "if not alienated from God, Life, Spirit." I understand this. When I felt isolated from my religion, I found assurance in Unity and Twelve-Step that the inner realm exists free of religious dictates. I return to them and other beloved readings with regularity. When assailed by self-doubt, I have even sought solace from my own book and reader comments on my website.

Some readers confessed that my book profoundly disturbed them but they could not dispute its undeniable truth. A religious brother from St. Martin who expected to be critical of it told me that, as he continued reading, he could see its validity.

I got much less pushback than I expected. People who didn't like what I wrote didn't bother to tell me and didn't throw rocks. Someone said I wanted to start a new church. It amused me and helped to dissolve my fear. A nephew reported me to the Chancery of the St. Cloud Diocese, but nothing happened. I concluded I have too little influence to get serious attention from a Church official.

After *God Is Not Three Guys* had been out for a while, I thought it wise to tell Sister Bethany of its contents, expecting her to have qualms. I wanted her to hear it from me, not from others. Fearing her response, I think I shaded my book's message too darkly. Without adding context to explain it, I stressed my dissent from Christian doctrine. "What did I do wrong?" she moaned. I should have added that some deeply spiritual persons with shoes firmly planted in Catholicism, including members of her own religious community, resonate with *God Is Not Three Guys in the Sky*.

One was Sister Nancy Hynes. The Sister Nancy Hynes Institute for Women's Leadership at the College of St. Benedict was named in her honor. Nancy had felt the kind of pressure I felt. This is apparent in the words of a fellow Benedictine who has her own stories of trying to breach patriarchal power. Sister Ann Machtemes writes,

> When our Sister Nancy Hynes was asked to chair a committee to rewrite our psalms into inclusive language, she tried, but I noticed that she had done nothing with the Godhead. I asked her if she would continue to rewrite doxologies using "Father, he," etc. She responded that she could not fight that battle. It was hard enough to do what she did accomplish.
>
> Now there are other communities in our federation that have changed our liturgy to more inclusive language. Nancy did not live long enough to regain her energy for anything. Change is so dang hard for us.

I visited Nancy when she was close to dying. Enthusiastically she praised *God Is Not Three Guys in the Sky* and wanted many people to read it. "Barack Obama should read it," she said. At the time Obama was campaigning to be president.

In one group discussion, a man said he liked my book, but it wasn't what he wanted. What did he want? The book, and now me in person, telling him why he should stay in the Church. I declined. I stay because my religious connections nourish me. If that's not the case for others, I see no reason they should go to church. The questioner's statements suggested to me that he was being led to leave, but I didn't say this.

In *God Is Not Three Guys in the Sky* I wrote that, as the twenty-first century progresses, "a formal religious setting will become increasingly irrelevant to many spiritually aware people." The year my book came out, the phenomenon of the "nones" erupted and by 2017 it comprised more than 20 percent of the US population. They were identified in surveys of religious participation by the Pew Research Center.

"Nones" are nonaffiliated with any religion but believe in spiritual reality. Many were cradled in Christianity but reject the doctrines and authority of organized religion. The growth of "nones" indicates a massive shift in spiritual understanding underway today. I hope to contribute by provoking deeper and broader awareness of religions' role in mediating the realm of the sacred.

Al

Before his death, I had been sending Al chapters of my manuscript, but I don't know how much he got to read before his death. He happened to be in my house after I'd written the final chapter. I brought it up on my computer and left the room to let him read while I puttered with housework. Eager for his response, I wondered why it was taking so long to read that short chapter. Finally I asked if he was finished. He was but didn't comment. I took his thoughtful look as comment.

Milt Adams, founder of Beaver's Pond, assured me of my book's worth by telling me he read the last chapter three times. In answer to my look of disbelief, he said he had the book on a plane when it circled several times before landing. Turning to shelves behind him, Milt pulled down Beaver's Pond books he thought would interest me, titles like *The Science of the Soul*.

Al used to say, "You should get to know Connie. You think alike." Finally, I contacted this friend of his and we quickly became email friends. I sent her chapters of my manuscript as I was finishing them, until finally she had read the whole thing, the first to do it. Connie resonated with my spiritual views more closely than anyone else. No reader has surpassed her comprehension and resonance with my thinking.

After reading the last chapter, she wrote,

> What a book!! I sit here, speechless, having been touched by the profoundness of spirituality, psychology, our humanity, and the holiness of it all. This chapter is such a beautiful climax. Jesus has taken on even more meaning for me. Thank you.]

Connie gave me more than confidence to publish. Besides possessing a metaphysical perspective that Al did not possess, she has deep intuitive wisdom. I think her influence made it possible for him to accept my interpretation. Her maturity guided me during decisions I made for publishing and during the ordeal of Al's death. I have a reader comments page on my website, but Connie's, the most precious to me, are not on there.

Connie performed another service. When we were in the Mari-annhill complex after Al's death, going through his personal effects and deciding their destinations, I took all his personal writings. Apparently, he journaled during periods at Marriage Encounter and Retrouvaille when all participants are asked to write out their feelings. He was the ordained leader but participated with everyone else. I think he was able to minister so effectively because he was totally honest with himself.

The first journal I read had been written when Cardinal Ratzinger was elected pope—Ratzinger, the bully of gays. Al's words were so full of despair that I couldn't stand it. I burned that journal. After I absorbed that one, there was no avoiding the fact of Al's gayness frankly present in the body of his journals.

Disturbing me was not that Al was gay but that he apparently had not felt safe enough with me to confide in me. I'd suspected he was gay and, reflecting on past conversations, I suspect he came close to telling me. I felt better when I recalled times I had expressed dissent from Church teaching about gays. He must have known that confessing the truth to me would have been safe. Maybe it was fortunate he didn't, because it would have been hard for me to keep his secret from siblings. Did this occur to him?

Mulling over his secret, I became certain he had confided in someone. Who? My intuition said Connie. A phone call confirmed it. She had gotten Al's permission to tell her husband because she spent many hours with Al. I credit Connie, Al's staunchest supporter and comforter, for contributing to his skill in ministering.

I decided my siblings needed to be informed of Al's secret to confront their prejudice, but I wanted endorsement from Connie. She said it could be a way for Al to teach from beyond the grave. "Shock" is not a strong enough word to describe sibling reactions. One asked an indirect question about his affairs. "Professed religious take a vow of celibacy," I said, stating something she knew as well as I, but letting her know she had been trained in an unfair assumption. It was formed by John Paul II, who together with Cardinal Josef Ratzinger led the Church into blaming gays for the clergy sex scandal, contrary to all evidence.

Al's turmoil developed not from having violated his celibacy vow—he did not—but that he was defined by the Church he was serving as "intrinsically disordered." The pope's aggressive campaign against homosexuals gnawed at Al's insides. He had hoped for a change at the papal conclave in 2005. When Josef Ratzinger became Pope Benedict XVI, it felt like a personal affront, nearly tearing Al apart. The first journal I read contained his immediate reaction. He was deliberately expressing his feelings to purge them from his body, mind, and soul. Apparently he had the understanding I developed during my womb/tomb period, that healing happens when we feel out our feelings.

His conduct in the last years of his life indicate that he absorbed the blow and continued ministering to people. Had he lived much longer, I think Al would have come out, because his writings suggest that his secret was burdening him. On a deep level he made the decision to die rather than come out. I am glad because in 2006 gays had not yet won respect. I am destroying his personal journals, not proud of reading them first but think it fortunate I did, so that my brother can teach from beyond the grave.

19

In Chapel

Most Sunday mornings I leave my computer to dress up for Mass in Sacred Heart Chapel with the Sisters of St. Benedict in St. Joseph. I choose to stay connected with them. They positively impacted me from youth to the present, and they enhance the spiritual journeys of people in the community around them. Monastic women have the same personality tensions we all have, but they practice spiritual values more earnestly than most and they exude goodness. My liking and respect for them—also my history with them—draw me to their Eucharistic liturgy. In their chapel I feel the sacred presence, but patriarchal language in the Mass spoils this.

Vatican-imposed words make the liturgy a trial for me. The required Mass text and scripture readings command worship of two lords, Father and Son, as almighty kings, rulers, and judges. Every description of what is called "God" refers to a male lord, a he. Old Testament readings portray this lord-god punishing people when they worship other deities. Male dominance / female submission pervades the entire Eucharist.

Women theologians show how Bible passages chosen for readings at Mass contribute to this by deliberately omitting stories of women leaders in the Lectionary. Sister Ruth Fox, in a presentation on "Women of the Bible," directed attention to outstanding women never mentioned in Mass readings. She cited Esther, "a great heroine in a time of oppression," who receives no account anywhere in the Lectionary "of the bravery with which she saved her people." Phoebe, a Christian leader mentioned by Paul, is sliced out of the Lectionary by beginning Romans 16 with verse 3.

Verses 1 and 2 say, "I commend to you our sister Phoebe, who is a deacon of the church of Cenchrae." This is never read at Mass.

Phyllis Trible, in *God and the Rhetoric of Sexuality*, shows God in the Bible conceiving, being pregnant, giving birth, and nursing a baby, as in Deuteronomy 32:18b: "You forgot the God who writhed in labor pains with you" (Trible's translation). Patriarchal redactions of Bible passages mask the feminine attributes of what is called "God."

Wisdom literature features a feminine prototype of Christ—Sophia. So writes Raymond Brown, foremost scholar of the Fourth Gospel. I quote verses from Wisdom literature and the Fourth Gospel in a blog post, "Sophia & Jesus Mixed," to show their resemblance to each other. Scripture abounds in feminine God-images, but Mass texts and Church teachings omit them.

Jesus-piety cultivated at Mass encourages worship of a god-man who clashes with the earthy and revolutionary Jesus living and teaching two thousand years ago. He was made apparent to me by scholars whose historical-critical works prompted me to read the gospels with fresh eyes.

Now I can see Jesus behaving like a rebel. He violates Jewish customs by breaking the Sabbath, teaching women disciples, and touching "unclean" flesh. He rails at religious authorities for their hypocrisy: "They tie up heavy, cumbersome loads and put them on other people's shoulders, but they themselves are not willing to lift a finger to move them" (Matt 23:4). People call Jesus "a glutton and drunkard, a friend of tax-collectors and sinners" (Matt 11:19; Luke 7:34). His hometown folks think he is "out of his mind" (Mark 3:21).

In the Good Samaritan story, Jesus challenges the norms of his society as soundly as an American praising the goodness of Muslims or communists, because Samaritans were despised foreigners. If he were living today, Jesus would hang out in gay bars, with drug addicts, in homeless shelters, in fields with Hispanics harvesting vegetables, and on gang-controlled street corners. He would raise the hackles of family and neighbors as well as enemies.

It sickens me that the liturgy turns this provocative sage who denounced oppressive religion into a tool of oppressive religion as part of the male-supreme Father/Son myth. The Gloria of the Mass seats Jesus on a throne:

> You are seated at the right hand of the Father, have mercy on us. For you alone are the Holy One, you alone are the Lord, you alone are the Most High, Jesus Christ.

What a mismatch this god makes with the countercultural rebel who lived in Palestine! I understand the human impulse that elevated him to a god worshipped in church, but I am not appeased.

Some Sundays, the repetition of "Lord/Father/Son/He/Him/His" God-talk ignites unruly feelings in me. I pacify myself by making up alternative texts that translate sexist God-talk into universal spiritual images. It is tiresome, but the mental activity keeps me sane and makes possible my continued participation in the Sunday services. I don't want to stop attending. The Sisters and other congregants are dear friends. I know many of them do their own translating during Mass, although I'm sure no one in chapel veers from conventional devotion as radically as I.

To preserve my integrity, I make outward signs of my true beliefs. I don't recite the Creed. It contains only a few phrases I can honestly profess. I make the sign of the cross only if the words are gender inclusive. My right hand stays by my side when I hear the formula imposed by the Vatican—"In the name of the Father and of the Son and of the Holy Spirit." In liturgies with women priests—not in Sacred Heart Chapel because it wouldn't be allowed—I sign because they subvert male supremacy with inclusive texts like "We gather in the name of God, Source of Being, Eternal Word, and Holy Spirit." Or "In the name of God our creator, Jesus our brother, and Holy Spirit Sophia."

In Sacred Heart Chapel, Fr. Patrick McDarby used to intone, "In the name of the Creator, the Redeemer, and the Sustainer." Happily I signed. That was before the Vatican clampdown. For decades after Vatican II, international experts—theologians, linguists, poets, and musicians—had labored to produce elegant translations. All English-speaking bishop conferences accepted their work. But the Vatican under Benedict rejected it and imposed a translation widely criticized as awkward and inaccessible. St. John's monk and musician Anthony Ruff, who contributed to the rejected text, called the Vatican-imposed text "stilted, unnatural English . . . an incoherent mess."

I make substitutions to relieve male dominance: "Mother" for "Father," "God" for "Lord," "One who" for "He who," "Jesus" for "Christ," or "Christ" for "Jesus," depending on meaning in the sentence. "Jesus" refers to the man who wandered the paths of Palestine two thousand years ago and taught people about the invisible Reign of God. "Christ" is divinity within us and guiding us. It is feminine as much as masculine. Paul referred to it in Galatians 2:20—"Christ is living in me."

I relate to Christ as my Higher Power. The same concept imbues Eastern religions whose devotees bow and say, "Namaste," to honor divinity in each other. In Christians terms, they see the Christ in each other.

When I imbue language of the liturgy with my inclusive understanding of "Christ," much of it aligns with my beliefs. This interpretation relieves the liturgy's incessant worship of external gods, which denies the divinity residing in humans and all creation. Jesus taught that the Reign of God lives within us (Luke 17:21).

I dislike the penitential "Lord, have mercy" at the beginning of Mass. It feels like obsequious bowing and scraping before an overlord and reinforces male power. No one would say "Lord, have mercy" to a divine Lady. Today's climate makes "Lord, have mercy" painfully inappropriate. I think of a teenage sex slave begging for mercy from a male pimp or client after daring to refuse sex to a despicable buyer of sex.

Christians need to bear responsibility for the way our God-talk contributes to gender abuse. We see the consequences today of never praying to *Her* and always praying to *Him*. It surely lies at the bottom of clergy sex abuse and abuses uncovered by the #MeToo movement. Against this backdrop, appealing to tradition does not cut it anymore.

Nicholas Kristof and Sheryl WuDunn detail gender violence around the world in *Half the Sky: Turning Oppression into Opportunity for Women Worldwide*. They quote a victim who sincerely, not ironically, says, "If the wife is truly disobedient, then of course her husband has to beat her" (69).

Monks from St. John's preside at Masses in Sacred Heart Chapel because the Vatican prohibits women from presiding, another insult. Occasionally a monk softens the penitential tone of "Lord-have-mercy" with helpful reflections. This part of the Mass could spur meaningful substitutions if the Vatican allowed them.

At woman-priest Masses, we used to recite words composed by Diarmuid O'Murchu, an Irish Catholic priest. The presider named typical life situations and we responded, "Do not repay evil for evil or insult for insult. We repay only with blessing." With these words we took responsibility for our moral growth instead of begging forgiveness from a god ruling over us.

It embarrasses me to admit that I participate in singing some texts just because I like to sing. It's almost impossible to avoid sexist language while singing in church. Despite its paeans to male gods, I sing parts of the Gloria, changing a few words. If the music would allow it, I'd like to replace, "We praise you, we bless you . . . Lord God, heavenly King," with texts like, "We praise and bless you, Mother Bear, for teaching your cubs to catch salmon and eat berries." This would better express my spirituality.

Prayers of the Faithful often contain the most inspiring words of the liturgy because they are written by Sisters today instead of spouting stale theology. We pray

> for the alienated who do not find church a place to call home,
>
> for the least, the lost, the misunderstood, and the desolate,
>
> for people in nations torn apart by war and brutality,
>
> for peaceful solutions to unrest in [global hotspots].

The only jarring note in them is the answering refrain, "Lord, hear our prayer." That darn lord sticking his face in it again.

When I wrote the Prayers for woman-priest Masses, I aimed to expand spiritual understanding. We prayed,

> for religions to transcend doctrinal definitions,
>
> for religious people to seek truth larger than they can imagine,
>
> for political leaders to accept guidance from unexpected avenues,
>
> for us to let divine order unfold in our lives.

The congregation responded, "Gracious God, hear our prayer."

In the "Mystery of faith," the prescribed text strikes me as ludicrously incongruent with contemporary belief. The congregation sings or recites,

> Save us, save us, Savior of the world,
>
> for by your Cross and Resurrection
>
> you have set us free.

Another version states,

> When we eat this bread and drink this cup,
>
> we proclaim your death, Lord Jesus, until you come again.

How many people believe that Jesus' death saves people from going to hell? Certainly not all who dutifully recite the words. I imagine billions of people standing before the gate to heaven, waiting for Jesus to be born. Or St. Peter standing at the gate and keeping out unbelievers.

As the chapel obediently sings the prescribed text, I sing,

> When we eat this bread and drink this cup,
>
> we proclaim the life of Christ alive in all of us.

Or I compose a text fitting the music that ends,

> by our Cross and Resurrection
> we set ourselves free.

Jung taught me to see that *we* have crosses and resurrections in *our* lives, little deaths followed by resurrections, upturns or renewals. I believe people resonate with the myth because *we* are Christ experiencing Death and Resurrection. *We are the Incarnation.* I died and rose during my midlife meltdown and subsequent healing. Before the Vatican imposed the literal Latin translation, we sang, "Christ has died, Christ has risen, Christ will come again." With my understanding of "Christ," this sums up my theology.

I take communion. Human beings have eaten god-food together since our species began; it's a common feature of religions. With this history as a backdrop, I receive bread and wine, joining in communion with the congregation around me and multitudes before us. Typically, the communion service in churches has neighbors accommodating each other in a cooperative way, fostering relationships, the real Holy Communion. In Sacred Heart Chapel, Benedictine hospitality shines through the service.

One Sunday, the first Bible reading was from Joshua 24, where the Lord demands that the Israelites worship himself and not "the gods your ancestors served." Here the Lord is a tribal god in jealous competition with other tribal gods—a common theme in the Hebrew Scriptures (Old Testament). Among deities inciting the Lord's jealousy would be Asherah, the subject of Raphael Patai's *The Hebrew Goddess*. Asherah is the most common image for the Goddess in the Bible, a figure beloved by the Hebrews. Patai's meticulous research reveals that Her statue stood in Solomon's temple for 370 years, worshipped by king, court, and Hebrew priests.

But in Joshua 24:16, the Israelites answer, "Far be it from us that we should forsake the Lord to serve other gods." As I see it, this violates the First Commandment, which states:

> You shall have no other gods before me. You shall not make idols
> for yourselves . . . you shall not bow down and worship them.

I was taught that this commandment condemns pagan deities, but *any* image becomes an idol when its dominant presence replaces what is called "God," the ineffable mystery beyond human conception. The ineffable presence is conveyed in Exodus 3:14—I AM WHO I AM—and in 1 Kings 19:11–12, where God is not in wind, earthquake, or fire, but a tiny whispering sound. These passages contrast starkly with the militaristic tribal god in Joshua.

The reading from Joshua begs for a homily that addresses God-images. Does the homilist acknowledge the jealous god in this reading and distinguish it from ineffable transcendence? I hear nothing so enlightening. This congregation is capable of discriminating insights, but the homilist, although a respected professor of theology, blandly encourages us to love God and Jesus. His Jesus is God, with no distinction. To me this makes Jesus an idol along with the Lord.

Before the reading is finished, I have another thought. The book of Joshua contains some of the Bible's most shocking examples of genocide. Will the homilist acknowledge the Lord commanding genocide earlier in the book of Joshua? He avoids it entirely. After Mass I look it up in my Bible. The Lord orders the Israelites to conquer the people of Palestine and slaughter them, leaving no survivors. He directs them to take "all the spoil and livestock of these cities as their booty" and exterminate the people. They do as told and "there was no one left who breathed" (Josh 11:14).

As the Mass progresses, I keep thinking. *That lord commanding the Israelites to conquer Palestine has no claim on me. I love this church and this monastery, but I pray to no lord.* I would admire a homilist who would refer respectfully to Asherah, *El Shaddai*, and other feminine God-images in the Bible. I would admire a homilist with the courage to admit that the Lord commands genocide.

My critique extends to scripture readings that women love. I like them for valuing motherhood, but I mind the patriarchal perspective embedded in them. Isaiah 49:15 consoles with a striking image:

> Can a mother forget the baby at her breast
> and have no compassion on the child she has borne?
> Though she may forget, I will not forget you!

It is lovely, except that the Lord is speaking, and no one imagines a female lord. Passages like this remind me of the Greek myth that Zeus gave birth to Athena. With such mythic details Zeus and the Lord rob women of power that in fact belongs exclusively to females.

"But I don't think of the Lord as a man." This is said in defense of references to God as "the Lord." Christian leaders explain that "Lord" does not have to connote cruelty and can stand for loving kindness. But we shouldn't have to try explaining away sexist God-talk. Let's clean it up instead.

"Lord" makes "Her" impossible. Always referring to God as He/Him/His cannot possibly leave the sexes equal. Slowly but thoroughly it indoctrinates by repetition, the drip drip drip of male pronouns stealing awareness of their implications. It conditions us to remain unconscious of sexist bias in our God-image. I have watched this happening in myself.

Another Bible verse subtly reinforces the male-dominant/female-submissive mind-set. Isaiah 62:1–5 states,

> The Lord makes your land his spouse. As a young man marries a virgin, your Builder shall marry you; and as a bridegroom rejoices in his bride so shall your God rejoice in you.

It seems a beautiful image. I used to wonder why I didn't like it. Delving deeper, I see its power dynamic: Male takes female. Male cherishes and rejoices in female. Male acts; female receives male action. Unconsciously, every churchgoer hearing this absorbs the lesson that God is male and male is dominant. As theologian Mary Daly observed, if God is male, male is God.

Male pronouns in phrases like "letting God mold us as He chooses" and "submitting to His purpose for us" suggests a strongman demanding obedience rather than quiet divinity guiding from within. "Teach us to prefer Your will to our own" calls to mind a lord more than a transcendent mystery. My guidance comes, not from an external judge, but from a whispering inner self. I accept "Christ" as one name for it because it can include the feminine. A Hindu might say her guidance comes from Shakti—same thing.

Sometimes I catch myself not paying attention and lazily joining the congregation in male-centered God-talk. I don't like it. I don't want to be desensitized to sexism. I am angry at the hierarchy for promoting male gods and angry at those who seem to stay willfully oblivious, until I remember the forces against waking up. All our lives long, lords have dominated the stage of the sacred, and ritual repetition numbs us. It provides seemingly-safe familiarity. It also robs the mind of critical thinking. That beautiful people are unconsciously harmed by God-images forced on them breaks my heart.

One homilist declared, "Loving kindness to others is not the highest thing; the highest value is loving Jesus Christ." It startled me. Dead wrong, in my view. Commitment to Jesus Christ may be a fine way to grow in goodness, but it is not essential. I don't call my Higher Power "Jesus." Almost any image of divinity will do, but kindness is a must.

Words of the prescribed liturgy rarely feed me spiritually, and often they offend me. So why do I return to chapel on Sundays? I often ask myself this. Multiple answers come. I love the monastery, its quiet repose, its history and traditions, my history with it, the Sisters working cooperatively together, and the campus combining their monastery with the college they founded. Many Sisters taught in the college and are informed of new interpretations in theology.

I appreciate their intelligent planning to make the liturgy an uplifting experience despite the patriarchal Mass text. Humans need ritual and the Sisters' liturgies satisfy this need. They manage to make the Eucharist a source of spiritual refreshment and depth despite the pernicious language. Their generous accommodation of guests, their reverence, the soaring dome and pillars, and the music, often sublime, create a ceremony worth experiencing.

I appreciate the community spirit created by the Sisters, which welcomes lay people joining them, whatever their religious views. I know that mine align with those of some Benedictines and other monastics. They may mind the monopoly of Father/Son imagery as much as I do, but I am more provocative because I want to wake people up. Having left, then returned, I'm less apt to forgive the patriarchal texts while the Sisters' paramount concern, it seems to me, is harmony in their community and with the institutional Church.

I appreciate religion at its best, when it truly mediates invisible reality. I can see why Carl Jung encouraged people to be religious. However imperfectly, religion directs people toward splendor and power greater than rational intellect can achieve. Churches empowered the Civil Rights Movement. Today, churches advocate for immigrants to America and give them sanctuary. In Africa, Catholic bishops persist in making peace amid violent warring.

I love and claim my Catholic heritage with its evocative rituals, its glorious art history, its contributions to social justice, and its resistance to fads in thought. I particularly love the growing body of Catholic thinkers who are moving past traditional belief to a deeper, less reified, more mystical understanding of ancient dogma.

Regular doses of Catholic living with the Benedictines inform my thinking about religions and spirituality. They help me to clarify my beliefs about transcendence and the role of religions. In church, lofty thoughts come, insights and intuitions emerge, sometimes *because* the readings and liturgical language disturb me. They point to the difference between clean Christian faith and institutional pronouncements.

Male presiders in Sacred Heart Chapel capitulate to He/Him/His God-talk prescribed for the Mass text, but in homilies they usually share worthwhile thoughts, perhaps expounding on wisdom they find in the readings. Many do contain wisdom. The variety of presiders appeals to me, as does their more intellectual approach than that of pastors in parishes. Some homilies excite me, spur reflection, and seed ideas for writing. And there is the moment when the chapel erupted in applause at the end of Abbot John's rousing endorsement of women's ordination.

At the SOT, Godfrey once confessed that he wondered if there were more persons in God than three. He seemed to be moving away from literal belief and asked us not to report him. In recent years, I hear less worship of three gods in homilies and more on Trinity's symbolism.

To me, Trinity symbolizes healthy relationships, the foundation of morality. I'm not nourished by the patriarchal liturgy but by warm relationships in chapel, the heart of spiritual life. Relationships govern all. Scientists and spiritual sages alike tell us that every individual thing connects with every other thing. The threeness of Trinity symbolizes this.

Monastic women and men lead progressive thinking in the Church, along with theologians who are penalized for challenging official teaching. They suffered under the oppressive, thirty-five-year-long rule of John Paul II and Benedict XVI, the former Cardinal Ratzinger. Even then, religious understanding evolved, and it speeds up under Pope Francis. He models basic goodness and urges the hierarchy to focus on teachings of Jesus rather than regulating worship and judging sins.

The Catholic brand is changing. Lords are losing ground. Today, Jesus comes off less a god to adore and more a spiritual master whose presence transported people to the inner realm.

Torn between rejecting Christian beliefs and wanting to preserve my tie with beloved companions, I keep one foot in the Christian tradition and one foot out. This tension becomes acute during Mass when sexist God-talk assails me. I shared my dilemma with Karen Tate, who hosts "Voices of the Sacred Feminine." She got an image of a person trying to balance on two boats moving forward "with one foot in one boat and the other foot in another boat, desperately trying to stay balanced." This comes close to nailing it. But I go on.

Occasions like funerals bring me to parish churches, where few examine religious beliefs, in conspicuous contrast to atheists. As one Benedictine said, "Atheists can think." My conversations with most Christians cannot go as deep. If beliefs of ordinary Christians seem uninformed to me, I attribute it to Lord/Father/Son/He/Him/His dominating every reference to the holy that enters their ears. It fosters misunderstanding of what God is. If some prayers were addressed to "Mother" or "Her," people would painlessly come to understand that "Father" is an imagined figure and not a fact.

Some years ago, I gave a presentation to Unitarian Universalists. Afterward, one of them asked, "Why do you call yourself a Catholic?" *Good question.* Others have asked the same.

"I'm a cultural Catholic," I answered. My beliefs match those of Unitarians more than Catholics because Unitarians don't profess belief in the Father/Son myth. But I was branded Catholic and have decided to stay and try to broaden understanding within my heritage-church. I urge Christians to stop worshipping male gods and embrace an inclusive concept of divinity. The potential for this already lies in our doctrines.

20

Mary Magdalene, First Apostle

When the fruit is ripe, it falls.

—RALPH WALDO EMERSON

FOR MORE THAN FIVE years I devoted energy and time to a Catholic woman-priest community—Mary Magdalene, First Apostle. I helped to plan its activities, wrote for it, wrote about it, talked about it, promoted it. Participating in MMFA focused my yen for research on women's ordination. While researching the issue, I learned more about patriarchal domination in the Catholic Church.

I used to think women were always barred from leading roles in the Church, that is, after the days of Paul. I had known that Paul names women leaders in Romans 16. Now I learned more amazing facts. Archaeological, artistic, and literary evidence indicates that Catholic women were ordained and ministering as priests until nearly 1000 CE. Women leaders were plentiful in New Testament times, but the patriarchy quashed their influence, notably that of Mary Magdalene. Evidently, she was the beloved disciple in the Fourth Gospel (John 1:6–7; 20:1–9; 21:20–24), but her name did not survive patriarchal redaction. Mary Magdalene authored this gospel in the sense that she led the tradition that produced it. I present the evidence in a blog post.

Disseminating information for Mary Magdalene, First Apostle, was fulfilling and satisfying because I think women priests present a highly effective challenge to Catholic gender injustice. For this reason and because MMFA enriched my life, I will continue to promote it and Roman Catholic Womenpriests (RCWP).

But "when the fruit is ripe, it falls." The time became right for me to leave the community as a planning member. While the decision was forming in me, I expected sadness to cloud my days afterward, although I felt no sadness at the time. Instead, relief and excitement bubbled up even before I left the meeting that clinched it. In the days following, joy surprised me. I marvel at how my inner self knew it was right for me before my outer self knew. Looking back now to the prior weeks and months, even years, I might have known what was coming.

The friction had started months, even years earlier. When I entered the Mary Magdalene community, nontraditional ideas were flourishing. I expected this to continue. It was said at a meeting that we would make liturgies an educational experience by explaining new practices and concepts. Our liturgy did not name Jesus our savior unless scriptural readings of the day required it. When we solicited views, an anonymous comment asked that the Jesus-savior concept be eliminated. I was all for this and felt supported in my aim of educating.

Apparently, pushback ensued that I didn't hear. I recall no discussion of needing to conform to traditional belief, but traditional worship of Jesus was entering our liturgies and planning meetings. Every time I tried introducing exhilarating information in meetings—say Hindu or pagan themes in Christian doctrines—someone would say, "Head over heart." I think she meant my thoughts were too intellectual, but this often did not fit the context. I began to interpret her "Head over heart" as "Shut up" and to resent it.

We all agreed on the injustice of denying ordination to women, but that was as far as some dissented from Church teaching. Always the educator, I like to introduce information that breaks new ground. As a progressive living in a traditional community, I was used to resistance and have no problem with it if new interpretations are heard. I wanted to move past literal understandings of Father and savior Son. Assuming that lack of vision comes from lack of information, I aimed to supply the information. But it was not allowed after . . . what? I don't know what caused the slide back to idolizing Jesus rather than relating to "Jesus our brother." Was it fear?

I chafed at the stultifying boundaries of conventional understanding. Spiritual talks in MMFA lost their zest, seemed insipid, lacked nourishment, as if we had not entered the twenty-first century. Whenever I tried to introduce ideas outside of the familiar box, I was silenced. One email in particular raised a ruckus. We had read "The Emmaus Moment," a reflection on Luke 24:13–35, which tells of Jesus's appearance after his crucifixion to disciples on the way to Emmaus.

The article reminded us that we all have moments when the inner realm suddenly breaks into ordinary life. Although written by a Catholic nun, it did not even mention Jesus. For this reason I found the article nourishing. We all did and wanted to share it with the wider MMFA community at a forum.

In preparation for this, we were emailed a "Guide for Group Leaders" to follow while leading discussions of the article. But the "Guide" ruined the message for me. Instead of discussing transcendent moments in a universal sense as the article did, we were to discuss times when Jesus appears in our lives—back to the exclusive Christian box. Intense disappointment and anger flashed through my body. I got up, left the computer, and paced. If I replied right away, I knew my hot words would offend. So I waited and paced. Then I wrote a reply, trying to be as clear and diplomatic as possible.

I had recently listened to Michael Morwood, whose impatience for change in the Church infected me. Members of MMFA knew about him and had wanted to attend his workshop in Fargo, although not many were able to spend the day there. Like Morwood, I was full of impatience to move away from worship of a Christian god and appreciate Jesus' authentic mission of teaching. In response to the "Guide" I replied that I was "sorry to throw cold water on this," but that I had difficulty with it.

> "The Emmaus Moment" works for me because it universalizes the lesson of the "Mysterious Presence" (Michael Morwood's phrase). The name "Jesus" does not occur in it. It can speak to those who have encounters with spiritual guides, with a Higher Power, with Divinity named in any other way.
>
> Jesus is not my god or God—he doesn't come to mind when I encounter and recognize divinity in daily life. I hope that is the case for others who come to our forums. While recognizing Jesus as the spiritual master of our religion, I hope we at MMFA have the ability to transcend the teaching, "only through Jesus."
>
> I hope we can lead our community to challenge the outmoded doctrine that turns Jesus into a god (influenced by Morwood again). Please forgive me if this hurts anyone.

I got a phone call from a person acting on the complaint of another. It seems I had disrupted the familiar landscape of that person's mind. I don't know if other traditional believers objected, but I sent an apologetic email to the group:

> I am comfortable living in a non-Christian framework and keep forgetting how hard that is for others, but I do know there's pain in having familiar religious terms and ideas be changed. I hope to keep in mind the difficulty others have of leaving the traditional Christian envelope.
>
> Challenging outmoded Christian claims and assumptions is not the mission of MMFA, but it is my personal mission, and I need to keep the two separate. I'm sorry if I offend by pushing non-traditional theology on others but do not regret suggesting alternative language because I am offended by language that seems to treat Jesus as God.

After this followed meetings with individuals and the whole planning group meant to promote harmony that I interpreted as letting me know my comments were not welcome. I think only a few disapproved of my objection to Jesus being worshipped as God. Emotionally, I took their opposition as a rejection of myself, so that what ensued devastated me.

Before a scheduled planning meeting, I was ambushed by a "spiritual" exercise. Everyone was invited to express their feelings. The author of the "Guide for Group Leaders" began by saying she was angry at me for my email. One by one, each person looked at me and said how she felt. It seemed to me that anyone who had approved of my email felt pressured to avoid saying this.

As persons around the table spoke what sounded like accusations to me, I felt like a defendant accused of a crime—judged and sentenced for the offense of not equating Jesus with God. Being a good actor, I swallowed my hurt and dismay. I accepted all of it, then dutifully took minutes, my job as secretary.

In the days following that circle of accusation, my insides rebelled. Throbbing distress set off by the "spiritual" exercise pounded me. It was so unfair! During the meeting I had pretended away my hurt. Now it was intensifying. I called principals in the group and defended myself, but the conversations didn't satisfy me. Expressing something was better than nothing, but I couldn't get relief because I couldn't say how much I hurt because I didn't know it. Until I described what happened during that meeting to a friend and she called it "abusive," I did not realize how much I hurt. Her affirmation released it, gave me permission to feel it.

Reflecting on earlier meetings, I saw as unrealistic my hope that MMFA could help to lead Catholics out of the parochial envelope to a grander vision. I keep forgetting how hard it is to escape religious indoctrination, keep forgetting the power of religion to dominate a mental landscape, keep forgetting that few people grapple with metaphysical questions. Impatient with ignorance, I forgot how long it took me to shed fear of defying religious authority.

The educator in me wanted to enliven talk of Jesus Christ/Father/Son/Holy Spirit with broadening insights. I would have liked to imbue discussions with the understanding that all humanity lives out the Incarnation, Passion, Resurrection, and Ascension. We are constantly embodying divinity, being crucified, dying, rising, and ascending.

Because I felt blocked to state what for me are soul-expanding ideas, MMFA reflections were dull. The port of entry to the spiritual realm for traditional believers—the story of Jesus Christ understood literally—is not mine, and mine is not theirs. Unconventional interpretations apparently frightened and irritated a few.

Being the maverick would have been comfortable had it not included silencing. Tension continued as did demands that I stop diverging from familiar paths. I do not think concepts I introduced always offended people, but I kept hearing, "Head over heart." Feeling muzzled, I was afraid to express myself. It infuriated me more than I admitted to myself.

In retrospect, I wish I had actively established a label for myself—one who challenges literal belief, who does not worship Jesus as God and savior of the world. I would have loved answering questions instead of having my unfamiliar ideas squelched. How I would have enjoyed opportunities to insert facts that invite questions! How I would have enjoyed members smiling and saying things like, "I suppose Jeanette would say something different. What would you say, Jeanette?" I love curiosity and willingness to explore new avenues of thought.

A series of meetings followed with individuals appointed to corral me. They claimed they only objected to the *way* I said things and the *times* I said things—"that's not what people came to hear." To those threatened by challenges to beliefs fixed in childhood, I think there never would be a good time. I would have loved inserting facts such as the Catholic Mass resembling pagan liturgies and paeans to Jesus in New Testament letters coming from paeans to pagan gods.

When I expressed my beliefs clearly as *my* beliefs, one person objected that I was demanding they change *their* beliefs. I was asked to stop using words like "transcend" and "beyond" the Christian story. At first, I accepted the rebuke—I should be humble! But then I decided there's nothing wrong with advocating an expanded horizon of awareness. I do not apologize for wanting to educate, but I readily accept the need to be gentle.

There is truth in the statement about the *way* I said things. Two persons appointed to curb my comments have a larger perspective, so I took the risk of explaining to them that I was feeling defensive, hoping they would help me to feel comfortable. But they were not sent to soothe me. They were responding to complaints of traditionalists, one of whom left because unorthodox ideas made her uncomfortable.

I felt stifled. The limited mindscape would have been tolerable had I been allowed to spice discussions with symbolic interpretations from Carl Jung, Meister Eckhart, Eastern religions, and others. I was suffocating, letting myself be thwarted, walking on eggs to avoid getting slapped down. I felt rebuffed by head-over-heart warnings even when voicing organizational suggestions. My fear of subtle harassment swelled.

One member tried to harmonize relationships, but to me pretty words about cooperation and harmony reminded me of the ambush-meeting and reinforced my growing paranoia. I felt blamed, devalued, and rejected. Facing upcoming meetings with dread, I could not speak naturally. My defensiveness turned into stridency.

As I write this, I observe my emotional state with chagrin. I'd forgotten how long it took me to shed fear of defying religious training, and now I still feared disapproval from others. How wildly unrealistic was my hope of enlarging the MMFA horizon! Those who understood the myth of Christ literally would keep thwarting a broader perspective. What felt elevating to me threatened others. I had known MMFA was no longer satisfying me spiritually but kept hoping to infuse more enriching fare. How clear it is now that I did not belong there anymore!

Finally, I had enough. At yet another meeting pressuring me to change, I said it might be good for me to leave (the possibility had come up before and been rejected). They did not want me to leave but wanted me to change. Giving in to that demand was impossible. To be true to myself, I could not pretend to go along with conventional interpretations and extinguish my drive to educate. Discovering in myself a surprising desire to leave, I wondered how I would feel after doing it. Would I have agonizing moments?

I made the firm decision to leave and we separated. Even before we parted, unaccountable happiness began whispering inside. I was asked, "How do you feel?"

"Relieved" was the word that leaped to mind. The questioner seemed to think this was unrealistic. I wondered the same and added, "I'll probably feel sad."

But a feeling of liberation reigned the rest of that day, a Friday. On my daily walk through the neighborhood, elation tripped through me. More than once, I stopped in surprise as delight rose up and through my body. No more would I have to dread meetings, no more be on the lookout for subtle put-downs and trying to placate the speaker. How could I have hung on so long?

During the night, I had a dream. The lasting image upon waking was of flushing poop down the toilet. Perceptive friends helped me to process the chain of happenings, but on Sunday I asked myself, "What else?" There was something I had yet to do, maybe something to discover. If I was being too self-serving, I should uncover it, be ruthlessly honest. My personality type, a Five on the Enneagram, can fall into paranoia, which I wanted to avoid. I had seen it in my journal entry a year or so earlier: "Here I am, working so hard for a group that rebukes me when I challenge traditional beliefs." On Monday morning, immediately upon waking, I realized that writing would help to clarify the relationship snags bringing on shame and guilt. This chapter is the result.

So why was it best for me to leave? How did I contribute? I had let myself be intimidated after I no longer felt safe in meetings of MMFA. Life experiences trained me to walk on eggs around a verbal abuser and ground this fear in me. Looking for rejection and sensitive to sidewise scolding, I found it. In the classic pattern outlined by psychologists, I was reliving my past in the present. Such introspective analyzing, I happily read somewhere, describes a habit of the Dalai Lama.

It was not over all at once. Weeks after leaving, I was playing old tapes of resentment against a few thought police in MMFA's planning group and berating myself for not getting over it. Good grief! Enough! But then I remembered that trying to squelch feelings only drives them deeper where they do more damage. So, when hurt and anger rose, I let myself feel them, then released them. In amazingly short time, the tapes stopped playing and the feelings dispersed. It helped that my friend had called "abusive" the painful meeting when I felt ambushed.

Gaining distance from Mary Magdalene, First Apostle, I am reminded of my tussle with Eleanor. Its lesson about forgiveness taught me not to minimize or deny my feelings. Honoring my hurt lets me see what drives those who hurt me. This releases compassion and seeing how I hurt them. It also stops my obsessing, which shows that I have forgiven. The words "I forgive" are not needed, but forgiveness can't happen without expressing feelings.

I'm sure I am not the only planning member of MMFA who took disagreement as personal affront, but others would write very different stories. Competing and wounded egos colored our communications. Power struggles played a larger role than beliefs. If I hadn't felt defensive but cheerfully acknowledged our differences in belief, there might have been less of a problem. Today I hope I would more calmly state my views and let them be accepted or not.

I also learned to stop beating myself up. A dream left me with the image of cleaning dust and dirt under a bed and an affirming feeling that I did nothing wrong. I am not fatally flawed. This really *is* cleaning house—dousing the perpetual flame of self-blame.

Unpleasant drama occupied only a small portion of my experience with MMFA. Feeling buffeted and muzzled intensified in the months leading up to my departure, but before that, I used to drive home from forums smiling over the uplifting events and gratified by interactions with people who attended our Mass. Planning meetings included love and caring. There were times of fun—favorites are times we got together to plan liturgy and spent almost as much time telling cat stories.

In the days after leaving, I laughed at my comical self—bouncing and dancing with excitement, relieved that I felt so good. Catching sight of myself in the bathroom mirror, I was surprised by how happy I looked, breaking out in smiles and chuckles, so relieved to be liberated. Now I can say that working for MMFA was good and leaving is good. Participants in MMFA are good and imperfect people who help to make the world a better place.

Understandably, my announcement that I was leaving surprised people because I had done so much. The volume of work had been weighing on me, but I have only myself to blame. At the first Masses I was asked to be the reader. When roles were chosen later, I offered to take the responsibility of finding readers and was told it meant writing the Prayers as well. This became my opportunity to expand spiritual horizons. Writing Prayers expanded into liturgy planning. And so it went. Falling into one job after another, I volunteered to write minutes of planning meetings, to keep the archive, to send MMFA announcements, to keep records, and to write the website, http://marymagdalenefirstapostle.com/. Its many pages developed from my writing habit—get me started on research and I don't quit.

For a social after Mass I brought deviled eggs. As it garnered compliments, I continued bringing them and congregants came to count on having them there. I loved their compliments for my "devilish eggs," as one appreciative man put it. After I stopped coming, they missed the eggs. Privately I thought, *I could feed you more substantial fare than deviled eggs.*

But I was wrong in thinking no one noticed or appreciated my contributions. At a meeting promoting harmony were garnered written messages we gave to each other. I hang on to mine: "You upset my applecart. It's been good for me." "You have broken the clay to let the light in." "Your contrariness forces us to redefine what we believe." "[Thanks] for hanging in there as challenger even though it is lonely and hard."

There were jobs for me to finish up because I didn't want to leave them in the lurch. I had secretarial documents and records to clean up and turn over, archival materials to complete and turn over. Jan suggested that I inquire of the Stearns History Museum whether the archivists there would like our archive. "God, yes!" came the reply.

Indirect apologies happened. We were all on the same side, after all. One beautiful move reconciled us completely. The planning group came to my house to celebrate my transition in a ritual, not my idea but theirs. That afternoon I received a great gift—a poem by John O'Donohue that describes the process in my heart's passage to freedom. The poem "For a New Beginning" in *To Bless the Space between Us* captures perfectly my fear of leaving what I had outgrown, then my delight when courage thrust me onto the ground of my life's purpose.

A veteran member of Catholic women priest groups reviewed this chapter and told me about her experience in a group with persons so radical they wanted to dismiss all cherished conventions. She saw both sides putting up the barrier of rigid intolerance. "Both sides," she said, "fear giving an inch because spiritual questions occupy the deepest part of our selves."

I left my former relationship with the community because it had become more frustrating than nourishing. I gave up wanting MMFA to be my forum for educating, but occasionally I still attend Masses of Mary Magdalene, First Apostle, because I value women priests whittling down the power of patriarchy.

21

Dialogue with an Atheist

Teilhard and Jung

WHEN I WAS TEACHING at Albany High School, a fellow English teacher said that one of her English professors in college used to direct them half-facetiously to look for "the inner deeper hidden secret meaning" in literature. All my life I have looked for it in everything. Two authors more than most fed my hunger for such meaning. The seminal thinkers Pierre Teilhard de Chardin and Carl Jung came to me early in life and inspired the rest of it.

Shortly after I graduated from college, Teilhard de Chardin fed my hunger for delving into large questions. He synthesized human knowledge by joining the domains of philosophy, religion, and the natural sciences in his *Le phénomène humain*, usually translated *The Phenomenon of Man* (in my opinion, it should be *The Phenomenon of Humanity*).

As both scientist and Catholic priest, Teilhard bridged religion and science by exploring the relationship between our inner, immaterial selves and the outer, material stuff we can see, hear, touch, and experiment on. In *Phenomenon*, he travels the length of the evolutionary ladder from the simplest stuff of matter—pre-life—to the most complicated and conscious entities—humans. At every stage of tangible things, from inanimate chemical structures to cells to creatures of ever greater complexity and consciousness, he unveils "the *within* of things."

His "*within* of things" thrilled me when I first read it and its thrill has not diminished with time because "the *without*" and "the *within*" express so well the difference between tangible and intangible. This dichotomy shows the relationship between science and religion. "The *within*" became for me another term for spiritual reality, what I call the inner realm and the Western world indiscriminately calls "God," as in "God told me."

Teilhard introduced the idea that thinking humans form a layer of consciousness he called the "noosphere," a concept that seems to have foretold the World Wide Web, also known as the global brain. His noosphere connected all human thought. In the context of today's divisiveness, how badly we need this unifying idea!

Carl Jung's thought is not easily intelligible in any one of his books or even in several—I had to read works by his disciples to absorb the subtle concepts. But from the first time I encountered Jung and Jungians, I was smitten. Jung kindles respect for religion without conforming to its dictates. He invites us to go deep, below the surface to unconscious impulses—inner, deeper, hidden, secret motivations. He unlocked awareness of my *within*, of transcendence in all things, of unconscious reasons for all human behavior—why Marilyn Monroe, JFK, and Elvis Presley have a mysterious hold on people.

Jung's writings supported my rejection of Jesus as a god and savior opening gates of heaven, but he also nudged me past seeing myths as stupid. He confirmed my rejection of literal belief in Christian myths but taught me to appreciate irrational myths. Mythic images comfort people. They express truth inexpressible in rational terms. They mysteriously convey meaning that generates profound emotions. Jung nudged me past judging them to seeing their value.

Together Jung and Teilhard de Chardin showed me how to join religion and science into one harmonious whole. Thanks to them, I have spent my adult life aware of the interplay between the *within* and the *without* of things. They started me on the path of living from the inside out.

Both thinkers decried dogma, whether religious or atheistic. They debunked atheistic belief that denies the existence of any spiritual reality. Materialists, writes Teilhard, see only half of reality, and religious people see the other half. He recommended "building a bridge between two banks of our existence—the physical and the moral—if we wish the material and spiritual sides of our activities to be mutually enlivened."

Carl Jung called atheism "a stupid error." He scorned scientific materialism by commenting, "I shall not commit the fashionable stupidity of regarding everything I cannot explain as a fraud." Responding to "God is dead," Nietzsche's famous saying, Jung declared that throughout Nietzsche's *Thus Spake Zarathustra*, "you get a feeling as if this god whom he calls dead were not absolutely dead." Jung discerned Nietzsche's vibrant spiritual impulse, his rejection of the Christian god but not God. Jung regarded Nietzsche "a better Christian and far more moral than the Christians before and after him."

When I met these thinkers I was trying to be an atheist and not succeeding. They knocked holes through atheist rationality and gave me reasons to return to my natural spiritual impulses. But atheist belief accompanies me daily. Paradoxically, it prompts exhilarating ideas in me about ultimate being, what is called "God." The atheists I know have rich interior lives and higher moral standards than many Christians. I once heard an atheist saying, "You can't be an atheist without caring about spiritual matters."

My Atheist Friend

A thoughtful atheist friend I'll call Ben visited me recently. We'd met about thirty years ago when he impressed me as a deep thinker. And he was kind. I noticed the way he helped an elderly woman navigate stairs. I don't know anyone more principled or with more integrity. I also like Ben because he and I agree on everything except the most profound questions of existence. We agree on politics and on much about religion.

Recently he returned to central Minnesota to visit family and friends. We hadn't seen each other since he moved to take a position far away, but we kept communicating. What draws the two of us together? We both are in thrall to metaphysical questions. I share Ben's disgust over the foolishness of literal religious belief, but I see value in religion and he does not.

Ben wonders why I keep going to church. He can't understand my friendship with Benedictines and other professed religious. I'd love to have him meet some of them. In conversation together, I think he and they would like each other. But that's not Ben's challenge. It troubles him that honorable people continue to support an institution responsible for so much offensive, even malicious, behavior.

After talks with Ben, my mind teems with points I want to make in debating him. The morning after our pleasant and scintillating talk, I woke up before 4:00 a.m. a little dizzy from a whoosh of thoughts coming in quick succession. Dozens of times I turned on the bedside lamp to write them down. Always I had to turn the light off for the next thought to surface. Interesting, that it took darkness for them to show themselves.

This fact is not irrelevant to the issue crowding my mind, the invisible sphere, which likes to show itself in unobtrusive, hidden ways. Parker Palmer says it's like looking for wild animals. You learn to wait quietly in the woods a while before they show themselves. Darkness and letting go allow more messages from the inner realm to show themselves.

Religion's doctrinal claims booted me out and into the lap of atheism. After I returned, I became aware of organized religions' hypocrisy, corruption, stupidity, and cruelty. It seems to me that many atheists consider them proof that God doesn't exist. Ben is not stuck there where many atheists stay stuck—railing against institutional religion—but long as I've known him he has been a scientific materialist. This is how we disagree. Scientific materialists reject belief in *any* spiritual reality. They think nothing exists except the stuff we can see, hear, smell, taste, and touch.

How do they account for thoughts? Ben used to be sure that the physical brain produces thoughts, that physical stuff creates nonphysical stuff. I believe the opposite; I believe our ideas manifest in physical form. While Ben and I were debating, I thought of a book by two physicists—*Quantum Enigma: Physics Encounters Consciousness*, by Bruce Rosenblum and Fred Kuttner. To me it asserts that consciousness or mind activity creates physical reality.

Experiments in quantum mechanics always, without fail, include an experimenter's observation creating the physical reality observed. The experimenter's consciousness has an effect on matter, making denial of spiritual reality's power impossible, as I see it. Ben accepts the fact of consciousness because quantum science gives evidence of it, but he does not interpret consciousness as spiritual. I do.

Consciousness includes all mind activity—thoughts, beliefs, feelings, attitudes, expectations, and intentions. All are nonphysical, therefore spiritual. To me, quantum physics demonstrates that, instead of brains creating thoughts, our thoughts create changes in the cells and molecules of our brains.

I found *Quantum Enigma* on my shelves and brought it out to Ben. He recognized it as a book an amateur-physicist friend of his recommended. I was led to it by a theologian friend. Ben has not read *Quantum Enigma* yet. He doesn't dare let himself get started with our mutual fascination because he knows it will consume him. Being younger than I am, he needs to keep his mind on his job. I'm eager to hear his thoughts after he reads the book.

Ben has a more scientific mind than I do. I expect him to be more patient with parts I skip. When I read science books, I race past torturous (to my nonscientific mind) explanations of how experiments are set up and carried out. "Get to the result!" I say, impatient to know what the result will imply about the nature of existence.

Admitting the existence of spiritual reality is a problem for scientific materialists. I think it's because "spiritual" used to be called "religious." I have never seen an exception in books written, say, before 1960. Carl Jung deplored literal religious belief, and his observations of spiritual phenomena clearly were not religious. But translators and commentators call them "religious." Jung's work, among others, led me to speak of "secular spirituality," meaning nonreligious spirituality. It is the kind of introspective life I associate with scientists who are not materialists and thoughtful "nones," the growing body of Americans nonaffiliated with any religion.

Quantum experiments bring physicists face to face with the mysterious nonphysical something that has power over physical stuff. It discomfits materialist physicists. Rosenblum and Kuttner, the authors of *Quantum Enigma*, write:

> For many physicists, this mystery, the quantum enigma, is best not talked about. It displays physics' encounter with consciousness. It's the skeleton in our closet.

One physicist criticized Rosenblum and Kuttner for presenting quantum theory to nonscientists:

> Though what you're saying is correct, presenting this material to nonscientists is the intellectual equivalent of allowing children to play with loaded guns.

I am one of those children playing with loaded guns. To me, the findings of quantum physics give undeniable evidence of our spiritual selves. How can scientists talk about consciousness in quantum experiments and deny that spiritual reality exists? I don't understand their logic.

Years ago, Ben used to scoff at the idea of an individual consciousness without a body. I believe in unembodied consciousnesses. I believe the invisible sphere is full of them and my brother Arnold received messages from it. And I did. When the cup from high on my hutch shot into my hands, when Serena, the Angel of Abundance, assured me, when I needed $200 and my pastor called to ask if I could use $200. And many other times, most of them indescribable. I believe unembodied consciousnesses told Joan of Arc to fight for France. Jung sought instruction from the inner realm full of unembodied consciousnesses and received messages in dreams.

When I'm working in the kitchen, I'm always listening to MPR/NPR. My attention waxes and wanes, depending on the fare. One day my focus sharpened when I detected the talk of a scientific materialist. Quickly I grabbed paper and pen and wrote down the words of the neuroscientist, "All of our behavior comes from our brain. It's a matter of chemistry, not character."

Ridiculous! I believe our brains merely register what's happening in our thoughts. When the patterns of our thoughts change, our brains change. In conversation with Ben I kept repeating, "Outer and inner reality are two sides of the same reality." I believe our inner reality—our thoughts, feelings and so on—are paramount. Cells and molecules don't make a child disruptive in school. His or her thoughts and feelings do.

When I read *Quantum Enigma*, when I so much as open the book and reread parts I highlighted, excitement surges through me. The book presents quirky facts that seem to challenge logic but only challenge old assumptions about reality. Rosenblum and Kuttner say the enigma in physics "challenges our classical worldview." Their book and talks like the ones I have with Ben bring me into encounter with the fundamental mysteries of being. By contrast, church talk seems stale and deadening.

What Is God?

A different speaker on MPR caught my attention one day when he said, "We can't say what God is any more than a horse can say what a human being is." So true. But bearing this in mind does not keep me from listing possible synonyms for the word "God." My list includes Energy, Source,

Transcendence, Divinity, Infinity, Vastness, Creator, Force, Mystery, and Consciousness. None of these alone completely satisfies me. Lao Tzu said, "The Tao that can be told is not the eternal Tao." I distinguish between ultimate Consciousness and individual consciousnesses flowing in it like waves in the ocean.

It would be interesting to try out some of my God-synonyms on people I know—believers and unbelievers. I'd like to think some would appeal to Ben. He and I used to think of "God" as the flawed humanlike individual conjured up by Church talk. Where does Ben's moral integrity come from? I think it comes from the nonphysical source called "God." Being an intellectual, Ben might find an abstract term like "Energy" or "Transcendence" more appealing than the word "God." So do many informed believers.

Two more substitutes for "God" live in me—Teilhard de Chardin's *within* and the Reign of God preached by Jesus of Nazareth. Jesus and Teilhard both wanted earthlings to know that beneath and behind the *without* we live out with our physical senses is a *within*.

Quantum Enigma's ability to transport me reminds me of another book—*The Little Book of Atheist Spirituality*. Its author, André Comte-Sponville, is a French atheist philosopher. How did this book, just the right book at the right time, find me? A mystery.

At the Mankato Women and Spirituality conference, I read a passage in Comte-Sponville's book for a presentation titled "Atheist Spirituality." It brought a meditative hush to the room. With rapt attention, my listeners participated in the atheist's mystical experience, his communion with luminous, unfathomable, and dazzling presence.

> Night had fallen. We were walking. Nothing remained but our friendship, our mutual trust and shared presence, the mildness of the night air and everything around us. . . . My mind empty of thought, I was simply registering the world around me. . . .
> And then, all of a sudden. . . . What? Nothing: everything! . . .
> A seemingly infinite happiness. A seemingly eternal sense of peace. Above me, the starry sky . . . , of which I was a part, . . .
> I contained only the dazzling presence of the All. Peace. Infinite peace! Simplicity, serenity, delight. (156)

These the words of an atheist! A mystic in this moment, Comte-Sponville freely acknowledges his communion with "Perfection. Plenitude. Bliss." His description rivals any I have seen from religious believers, and it is not the only one by nonbelievers that I have encountered. Clearly, no religion controls communication with the inner reign, but in their defense, religions try to mediate that invisible, indefinable something-more.

The Little Book of Atheist Spirituality exemplifies secular spirituality. It tells me that thoughtful people with rich interior lives cannot avoid relating to what is called "God," even Nietzsche, who declared God dead. Although I don't agree with everything Comte-Sponville says, he bolsters my respect for atheism and enriches my fascination with the human need for something more than physical reality.

"'Secular spirituality' sounds like an oxymoron," said an agnostic friend.

It is if we conflate spirituality with religion. They are not the same. Some of the "nones" identified in Pew Research polls demonstrate healthy interior life without religion. They derive inspiration from nature and relationships. Most pray and believe in spiritual reality—some call it "God"—but all abandon institutional religion. Pews are emptying because science refutes the gods in stale religious texts, propelling moves out of the Christian box. I identified with "nones" in a piece I wrote for *Minnesota Women's Press*.

The number of American "nones" is growing rapidly, although most don't know they fall into the category. When I described it to a college senior who hadn't heard of "nones," she recognized herself as a "none." When I described it to a septuagenarian, he recognized himself as a "none."

In Europe, magnificent cathedrals attract more tourists than worshippers. I don't take this as a sign that Europeans have grown less principled, high-minded, or spiritual. I take it as a sign that the Western world is growing independent of religion. When Patrick and Mollie stopped going to church, I welcomed it as evidence of their ability to think critically. They are not less spiritual for having left the Church. Their faith is secular, free of religious dictates.

Can traditional religions survive? I expect this question will occupy minds after my generation is gone. Does God exist? Wrong question. I prefer to ask, "What do you believe about God?" I agree with atheists who say, "There is no god." And I agree with believers who say, "God fills my life."

22

Dialogue with an Agnostic

"Interesting!" Allison, an agnostic, was reacting to my sentence, "Before Teilhard, I had not thought of thought as spiritual reality." I had asked her to read my manuscript critically. We communicated by email.

I'd told her I stopped calling myself agnostic because agnostics say we can't know anything for sure, but I know that the spiritual realm exists. I can't define or understand it, but I know it exists. I suspect other self-described agnostics also do not doubt its existence.

Allison didn't buy it. "You can't know spiritual reality exists. You can't prove it." She is more scientific than I am. For her job, Allison charts observations of behavior. She must record only things she hears and sees, not her own thoughts and impressions. To me it looks like she's trained to value external evidence more than intuition. I have grown more intuitive as I've grown older. When I denounce He/Him/His God-talk, I accuse it of damaging human relationships, taking an intuitive leap past external evidence.

To my statement that thought is spiritual, she responded. "Do you also think of thought as physical? I do."

"Its effects are physical." After this email dialogue occurred, I clarified my thinking. Thoughts, ideas, and feelings are not physical, but they manifest in physical ways. We read faces to discern happiness or sadness, worry or exuberance. I urged my student teachers to change activities when they saw boredom in student eyes. I learned of my own unconscious feeling when I exploded in "Pay attention to me."

"Do you believe energy is physical?" asked Allison. "I do. I believe, therefore, that thought is traceable and has form."

"Energy, thoughts, and ideas are not physical," I answered, "but we see their physical effects. We say it's windy because the energy of the wind moves physical things."

Allison disagreed. "Energy is what holds atoms together. It is very definitely real and detectable. Wind can be measured and quantified, very definitely real also. It is not immaterial. It contains air, which, although in the gaseous state, is matter."

"Yes, they're all real," I replied, "and gas is one state of matter. But energy and wind only *seem* to be material because we see their material effects. They leave traces that scientists can measure and quantify. Like many spiritual things, we know them by their manifestations in our physical world."

"This is where you and I diverge," replied Allison, "and it also brings the definition of agnosticism into play. I do not claim to know anything. I like to entertain possibilities but do not choose the one that I want to believe, just because I want to believe it."

"This is where the definition of 'know' comes into play." I remembered knowing that Jim would treat me better after divorce than during marriage. I knew him intuitively.

Allison wrote, "We think differently. Both viewpoints about spirituality are equally valid/invalid, because neither can be proven or disproven, which is why I say I do not know. Everyone can believe as they choose."

I agree that we think differently. Our email dialogue ended, I thought of William James, an eminent philosopher-psychologist. In *The Varieties of Religious Experience*, James observes that people who have been deeply affected by a spiritual presence say they *know* they experienced it. I found *Varieties of Religious Experience* on my shelf and looked for accounts that say this. Individuals quoted there sense an objective presence—"something there," said one, "the presence of Something I knew not what," said another.

One account came from a person identified by James as an "intimate friend" with a keen intellect. His friend felt the "consciousness of a presence" that impressed him as "indescribably stronger" and "more real" than ordinary, close companionship. This friend of William James did not wonder whether spiritual reality exists, because he experienced it. I have experienced it, usually in ways easy for unbelievers to dismiss.

I communicate with my Higher Power—it's called praying—and receive guidance from it. I know its worth but cannot prove it.

The Other Side

My belief in the nonmaterial realm invites the testimony of other believers, friends upright, intelligent, and normal. At my request, my classmate Carol wrote her story for me, and I adapted it in my blog.

> She and her father had always been close, sharing with each other thoughts not revealed to others. While she was visiting him as he lay dying in the nursing home, he pointed to things he saw floating around the room and asked, "Do you see those?" She didn't see anything. It saddened him that she could not see what he was seeing, and this went on for a good ten minutes. Finally, he had one on his knee. "It's right here," he said, and gently placed her hand on it.
>
> She felt only him but now it came to her. In a voice filled with wonder, she said, "Papa, I think those are the angels coming to escort you to where you need to be." Without another word, he dropped into a deep, peaceful sleep. It was not yet the end, but a harbinger of the end.
>
> They both loved Christmas, loved it. The December after he died, she was happily hanging Christmas decorations in her living room, two of them large jingle bells. As had happened before, she felt her father's presence. He had been with her often when she hiked the Arizona mountains or the trails in Death Valley. There, with ease she communed with her father.
>
> But this time he spoke. She had walked to the other side of the room, her back to the bells, when they clearly gave a short ring. No other person was there, no breeze, no physical explanation, and no fear in Carol. Instead, peace and comfort surged through her. "Papa, is that you?" she said, smiling.

I recounted similar stories to my hairdresser. It motivated her to tell me about visitations from her deceased mom. "I didn't know what to think," she said. "I don't talk about this." She seemed afraid others would not credit them. Heartened by my belief, she let me include her example in my blog.

Her mom had always been deathly afraid of hospitals. As she lay dying in one, Sandy worried aloud to the nurse that her mom was screaming inside without being able to say, "Help me!" As Sandy left the hospital, she looked up at an exceptionally bright moon. Suddenly she felt her mom saying, "I'm OK." Sandy still sees the moon as it looked that night when she thrilled to the feeling of her mother's presence. There were further assurances in dreams, her mom letting worried daughter know she was fine.

Cindy also defied pooh-poohing of the scientific community by writing this story for me:

> As Mom was dying of breast cancer I was fortunate to spend the final 10 days at her side. At one point we spoke about a story I'd heard of a young woman who had lost her father to cancer. He told her that after he passed he would somehow let her know he was fine.
>
> After the funeral she went back to her home, a very old house she was renovating. A light suddenly came on for a few minutes in her hallway. She was amazed because this light had never worked before. A few days later she had an electrician come in to check it out. There were no wires connecting the light and the electrician said it could not possibly have turned on. She then realized it must have been her father letting her know all is well.
>
> I told Mom that story and asked her to somehow let me know she was OK after she passed. She said she would. A few days later Mom died. I was sitting at her computer in the laundry room when the Cremation Society wheeled her body out the door. One of my sisters immediately stripped Mom's bed and put the sheets in her 6-month old front-loading wash machine—just about 5 feet from me. She turned on the washer and it started beeping and a light flashed with an error code. I found the washer user guide and read the error code that was flashing. It said, "Mother Board is out."
>
> This is the honest to God truth! I knew it was Mom talking to me. The rest of my family thought I was nuts. But I KNOW it was her. That couldn't have been a coincidence. We had been using that washing machine for the past week and had no problems with it at all.
>
> There was another time—perhaps a week or two later. As I sat at my kitchen table crying and missing her and talking to her, an angel that I had suctioned to the window popped off at me. I had to laugh. It was Mom again. She's still letting me know she's OK. I'm sure she is. It's just that I miss her so much—I still cry when I remember this.

I never tire of accounts like these and seem to attract them. Often they are shared at the death of a loved one. Death brings us to the threshold of the spiritual realm, to life beyond the grave.

My cousin Laura gave me permission to tell this next story. Her son Larry travels to other states to combine for farmers. His father used to accompany Larry on these trips before he died. One year, Larry called his mom from Oklahoma to say, "I don't know what to do. It's raining too much. My truck is sitting in water." Four days later he called again but was very quiet.

"What's up?" asked his mom.

"Did you try calling me?"

"No."

He waited. Then, "I just had a missed call from Dad." His dad had died close to three years earlier, but Larry hadn't deleted the number from his phone. He recognized the number marked "Dad" on his phone and tried calling it. He got no answer and no message.

"Even if someone else had gotten that number," says Laura, "why did he call Larry at this time? I get goose bumps telling the story." Others say the same when they hear it. My non-believing friends will scoff at stories like this and try to find physical explanations for them. But I see them as testaments to the nonphysical realm.

I asked a thoughtful and literary, but materialist, friend why he doubted his own experiences when they give evidence of the inner dimension. His delightful reply? The words of Scrooge when confronted by Marley's ghost in *A Christmas Carol*:

> "Why do you doubt your senses?"

> "Because," said Scrooge, "a little thing affects them. A slight disorder of the stomach makes them cheat. You may be an undigested bit of beef, a blot of mustard, a crumb of cheese, a fragment of an underdone potato. There's more of gravy than of grave about you, whatever you are!"

Clever. But William James points out that if you experience an immaterial power, "something in you absolutely knows that that result must be truer than any logic-chopping rationalistic talk, however clever, that may contradict it."

What my friend did not quote was Dickens' next lines.

> Scrooge was not much in the habit of cracking jokes, nor did he feel, in his heart, by any means waggish then. The truth is, that

> he tried to be smart, as a means of distracting his own attention,
> and keeping down his terror; for the spectre's voice disturbed
> the very marrow in his bones.

Uncanny encounters with the other side unsettle more people than Scrooge. William James points out that many who experience the invisible try to explain away their shuddering dread. Not I. I welcome the goose bumps they give me because they indicate a mysterious realm beyond the imaginings of religion or science.

In our hyper-scientific culture, I do not talk about such phenomena with just anybody, because I want to avoid scorn and incomprehension. People who deny the existence of spiritual reality say it must be comforting to believe, and they imply this is the reason for faith. Allison says, "You seem to want proof."

Do I believe only because I want to? It is true that I love hearing stories of people speaking from the other side—it's exhilarating, and they reinforce my faith when materialist belief threatens to smother me. But my faith also rests on rational appraisal of evidence. To me it seems that materialist science believes what it wants to and tries to explain away phenomena that don't fit its beliefs.

Brain scientist Jill Bolte Taylor addressed this in an article appearing in *Unity* magazine. She wrote, "True science has to accept all that is. It can't say, 'Those mysterious things we don't understand don't exist.'" She was echoing Carl Jung, who argued that science ought to stop ignoring data that challenges its belief system.

I find this viewpoint in writings by great thinkers through the ages, Einstein among them. He employed intuitive intelligence as well as analytical intelligence in thought experiments that produced his greatest discoveries. Einstein is credited with saying, "Science without religion [spirituality] is lame. Religion without science is blind."

I believe my spiritual self, my total mind, both conscious and unconscious, governs my body and things that happen to me. I see its power in my life. To climb out of my hole of poverty, I needed to stop believing in the saintliness of poverty. To heal relationships, I needed to stop expecting rejection. To improve my health, I needed to give up self-defeating beliefs. More mind-over-matter evidence in medicine comes from the placebo effect and the power of prayer.

Every seven to fifteen years, every cell in my entire body has been replaced, but I am still the same I. My knowledge, opinions, and patterns of thinking today differ from my mind activity in the past, but I am the same I. My essential self, my non-bodily, spiritual part endures. And it will survive when I die. Death has no power over me or any of us. In each of us resides the eternal. By using the power of my consciousness, I intend to go on improving my life, and I hope to help others by raising awareness of the mind's power.

23

Serenity

Unlearning

AFTER DIVORCE, MARRIAGE WAS a siren call that never pulled me all the way in. Single men the right age ignited imaginative yearnings, but my rational mind kept reminding me they were not real. And I didn't follow the example of acquaintances by actively looking for a mate. Successful second and third marriages looked attractive, but I let my Higher Power guide me toward whatever was best.

Gradually I realized that staying single suited me. I'd wanted attachment to a man for the wrong reason. Had I gotten married again, I might not have grown past insecurity into strength and independence. My mental and psychic energy would have gone into sustaining the relationship. It would have stolen energy from my writing and latter-years' purpose in life—inspiring awareness of spirituality independent of religions. I hope my life story has become a vehicle for this purpose.

As for emotional intimacy, I satisfy this need in relationships of all kinds. Besides love, they provide opportunities for emotional/spiritual growth. Friends, family, acquaintances, and daily living prod me to shed mental habits I want to unlearn.

My neighbor/friend Mireya and I went walking one day. Thunder and a gray sky told us our walk might be interrupted by rain. It was. We hurried back toward my house, but before we reached it, she saw a house with an overhang by the entrance. As we stood there waiting for the rain to stop, Greg across the street opened his car door, took out something, and came toward us offering a large umbrella. I smiled and said, "Thank you" but shook my head.

Mireya mumbled something behind me, and Greg's look said, "Why ever not?" But I kept smiling and shaking my head. He gave up, put the umbrella back into the vehicle he'd taken it from, and went back into his house.

As we stood, waiting for the rain to stop, Mireya decided she could tell me something. "You don't find it easy to take gifts from people."

I got it immediately. "Thank you! I've been working on changing that very habit and now I did it again!" The habit was ingrained by religion and upbringing. This time it denied a good to someone else. Mireya wanted to accept the umbrella.

"Something else," I added. "I still feel wrong wanting more than just enough. I feel like I should do without if possible and settle for only enough."

A few minutes later she decided to tell me something else. "When you give, you tell people you're paying them back for favors they did for you."

The truth of that also hit me immediately. A few weeks before, I had been about to leave for an event when Mireya arrived at my door, appealing for help. Her husband Jim needed to go to the ER and she couldn't get their car started. Quickly I made some phone calls to explain my absence to persons who had expected me, and we were on the road to the hospital.

"I'm paying you back for when you took me to the hospital," I said on the way. A jerk of unpleasantness invaded the car. It reminded me that strict accounting of giving and receiving was another habit I'd detected in myself and resolved to change. Mireya and I decided the rain had given us a good talk, arranged by divine appointment.

I am in my seventies and expect to keep growing in wisdom as long as I am lucid. Striving to unlearn my own harmful patterns of mind, I resolve to help others unlearn what I consider the most pernicious element of traditional religion—imposing belief in an exclusively male image of transcendence. Consequences follow. If we were asked to imagine giant geniuses in any field of knowledge, how many of us would name women? Immediately we would think of men and no women. More horrifying consequences are seen in #MeToo testimonials.

We need to unlearn the male bias. It cannot happen unless we shed belief in the Father/Son myth, the Western foundation upholding male domination. We Christians need to stop mistaking our myth for history and our symbols for facts.

Simple Beauties

While I was studying at the School of Theology, I decided to join other students in a retreat. I forget where we went, the theme of the retreat, and what we did or talked about. All I remember is deciding that weekend that my own home is my retreat. Here I ponder almost without ceasing—while reading or writing, puttering in house or yard, taking in radio or television, or visiting with friends.

I love where I live, and proximity to I-94 does not impede my feeling of living a luxury of stillness. As I write this, I face a window showing two pileated woodpeckers on trees overhanging my driveway, one on the oak, the other on the maple.

I have wash lines and use them to save the environment and my pocketbook. Nothing beats the pleasure of hanging clothes on the line while enjoying birdsong and the beauty of glorious green all around. At night I breathe in the fresh smell and feel privileged that my sheets are sun and breeze dried.

One summer I was upset that a small shrub I'd planted in front of my house was cut down the next spring. What had done this? I'd looked forward to seeing it grow, but it already was too large to attract squirrels or rabbits. To my question at a meeting, someone said, "Deer." *Hmm.* They would have had to cross the frozen lake in winter because I-94 precludes any other access. Mireya clinched it by saying she had seen a deer on this side of the lake. Having started out peeved, I am now pleased that deer visited my house while I was sleeping. Years ago, a small black bear appeared in a tree. We left it alone and it disappeared. This was before Highway 52 became Interstate 94 with a fence blocking access to animals.

I like country mixed with town. On winter evenings I enjoy looking at my backyard when a full moon lands on new-fallen snow. Amid an ethereal, whitish glow, long shadows of trees create the columns of my cathedral. Across the way, Christmas lights become vigil lights.

During the day, the sacred perfection is profaned by animal tracks, mostly squirrels. Snow-blowing completes the desecration, but I would not want to do without it or the animals. When I was young and read that we should find joy in simple, ordinary things like sunshine, birdsong, and green grass, I did not accept it. These simple things did not yet have the power to dispel desolation. But today I regularly give thanks for just such beauties in life.

Neighborliness blesses me. A typical walk can result in long conversations. Many a downhearted day has been lightened by exchanging a few words with a neighbor. Together we sing praises of the neighborhood, feeling fortunate. I say "Hi" to dogs that bark a greeting as I pass by. In spring we look forward to the first call of the loons and happily yield right-of-way to ducks crossing the road with their ducklings. Our refuge makes it easier to bear the miseries of the world.

My daily companion is Maxwell. I didn't want another cat after my sickly and expensive Katharine died. I called her "my thousand-dollar cat" and didn't want to care for another. But Evie and Steve lived in the country by a highway and people considered their home a convenient place to drop off unwanted pets. Most learned to fend for themselves. One cat hung around, refusing to leave. The previous year another had done this and the following spring they found its carcass. Steve and Evie knew that Katharine died and asked me to take the cat who wanted to be adopted. I complied. Months later I told Steve, "God told you to give me a cat to teach me patience."

Maxwell is teaching me a lot more, but it took a while before he charmed me into loving him. Before he was neutered, he sprayed in my house, producing one of the vilest odors I've ever smelled. No other cat of mine had done this. Annoying in the extreme, he yowled much of the day about nothing I could identify. Gradually he became better behaved after neutering, minutes of solitary confinement in closets, and squirts from a water bottle. The squirts plus love work best.

I named him "Mitzi," an affectionate German term for cats I like the sound of—fits cats. But Pat and Mollie scorned it as "too cutesy" and "a girl's name." I let Mollie name him Maxwell. At first I didn't like it, but I've warmed to it because it fits his personality. This guy has a strong will. I keep telling him I'm the boss but find I do things differently to accommodate him. We are training each other how to live with each other. The rare times he still annoys me, I remind him that I saved his life.

When he was still more irritant than companion, I noted that his affectionate nature might win me over. No matter how long he's been consigned to a closet, he emerges eager to be with me. After I've been away for half a day, he meets me at the door to meow greetings. He has an irresistible habit of putting his paw on me to say it's time to do something.

Although his idea of time comes way before time, he has saved me from forgetting my medicine.

At the beginning of bedtime, he crawls under the covers with me, but I lock him out of my room after nightly bathroom visits. First, I give him a hug, before setting him gently down in the hall and closing my door. He does not mind it when it bears no resemblance to being angrily dumped into a closet. In the morning he is so ready for a new day that he meows me awake before I'm ready to rise, but not if he's outside my room. Then he waits until I emerge.

He's a lot smarter than I thought cats could be. When I laugh at Maxwell, his face changes, responding to my love. When people laugh at his antics, he plays harder to impress them. He reads my mind telepathically. I have tested this. When I am about to open a can of tuna, he's in the kitchen before the sound of can, cupboard door, or any other physical signal. My intention to eat tuna interrupts his snooze and he comes for the promised drink of tuna water. He also likes to drink water from the bathtub, which motivates me to pour a little water for his drink while I'm getting ready for my bath. One time I changed my mind—decided against taking the bath I'd planned. Maxwell jumped into the empty tub, looking for the drink my prior thoughts had promised.

Animals do not depend on rational power to know. Their knowing comes more directly from the invisible domain. I think this partially explains their knowing a storm is coming before humans know. And they do telepathic communication better than humans. When I'm watching television and profoundly moved by a sad or inspiring story, Maxwell raises his head and looks searchingly at me. I was present when a friend of Mollie was startled by a death announcement. Mollie's cat, who normally signaled dislike of the man, nevertheless walked across the porch to him and swished her sympathy onto his neck and back.

The Woods

After a drive of five miles I can be in the woods of St. John's where I have often gone walking. One autumn day, Mireya and I walked a path different from the popular one alongside Lake Sagatagan to Stella Maris Chapel. Maples were displaying finery in a palette of colors before surrendering their leaves and closing down for the winter. Deep, steep hillsides ran down, down into inviting depth, where flourished moss-covered logs and ferns. The delicious, sweet smell of rotting wood and leaves perfumed the air.

We walked to the footbridge over I-94 where the roar of 18-wheelers tried but failed to spoil the spectacular view of forests adorning the sides of the freeway going northwest to Fargo and southeast to Minneapolis and Wisconsin. Gorgeous view each way. Walking back, we stopped and sat down to meditate at one spot, beholding the beauty of blackish tree trunks contrasting with bright orange, rose, and shades of green. Wind bullied the tops of trees, but below we sat quietly undisturbed. The scene spoke depth and transcendence. I basked in the benevolence.

Jeanette Blonigen Clancy

Siblings Adelbert, Jeanette, Victor, Arnold, Gerald, Evelyn, Alverna, Cecilia

Siblings Back: Gerald, Alverna, Arnold, Adelbert, Cecilia, Victor

Front: Jeanette, parents Herman and Lena, Evelyn

Herman Blonigen, Magdalena Fuchs Blonigen, Aloysius (Aloys) Blonigen,
Agnes Fuchs Lieser

Blonigen farm, St. Martin, Minnesota

Die Mädchen. Blonigen sisters Monica, Agnes, priest from India, Froni, Rose, Regina seated

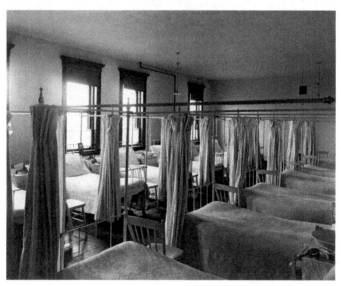

Curtains separate alcoves in convent dormitory
(archival photo, St.Benedict's Monastery).

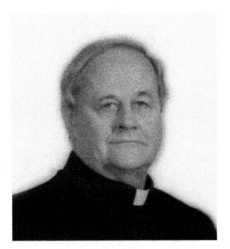

Aloysius (Al) Blonigen, CMM

Bibliography

Bauer, Walter. *Orthodoxy and Heresy in Earliest Christianity*. Philadelphia: Fortress, 1979.

Berger, Teresa. *Gender Differences and the Making of Liturgical History: Lifting a Veil on Liturgy's Past*. Surrey, UK: Ashgate, 1988.

Biaggi, Cristina, ed. *The Rule of Mars: Readings on the Origins, History and Impact of Patriarchy*. Manchester, CT: Knowledge, Ideas, and Trends, 2005.

Biale, David. "The God with Breasts: El Shaddai in the Bible." *History of Religions* 21 (1982) 240–56.

Blonigen, Al. *Discovering My Inner Child*. Dearborn Heights, MI: self-published, 1992.

Clancy, Jeanette Blonigen. "*Deutsch und Katholisch* in Stearns County." *Crossings* (Stearns History Museum, St. Cloud) 40 (2014). Reused with permission.

———. "Mid-Life." In *Womenpsalms*, compiled by Julia Ahlers et al., 28. Winona, MN: St. Mary's Press, Christian Brothers Publications, 1992. Reprinted with permission.

———. "Simple Beauties." *St. Cloud Times*, June 7, 2016. Reused with permission.

———. "Surrender." *Sacred Journey* 56 (2005) 25. www.fellowshipinprayer.org. Reprinted with permission.

———. "Why Not Leave?" In *Awaken the Feminine: Dismantling Domination to Restore Balance on Mother Earth*, curated by Karen Tate, 50–57. Boston: Create Space, 2018. Reused with permission.

Collins, Raymond. *Introduction to the New Testament*. New York: Doubleday, 1987.

Comte-Sponville, André. *The Little Book of Atheist Spirituality*. Translated by Nancy Huston. New York: Viking Penguin, 2007.

Eisler, Riane. *The Chalice and the Blade*. San Francisco: Harper & Row, 1987.

Fleischhacker, Roman. *The Fruit of Faith and Witness*. Onamia, MN: Crosier, 1970.

Fox, Ruth. "Women of the Bible." FutureChurch.org. https://www.futurechurch. org/women-in-church-leadership/women-and-word/women-in-bible-and-lectionary. Originally from the May/June issue of *Liturgy* 90 (1996).

Gimbutas, Marija. *The Goddesses and Gods of Old Europe: Myths and Cult Images*. Berkeley: University of California Press, 2007.

Havener, Ivan. *Q: The Sayings of Jesus*. Wilmington, DE: Glazier, 1987.

James, William. *Varieties of Religious Experience*. New York: Macmillan, 1961.

Jung, Carl Gustav. *Memories, Dreams, Reflections*. Edited by Aniela Jaffe. Translated by Richard and Clara Winston. New York: Vintage, 1989.

Marty, Martin. "Head North for the Magic Kingdom." St. John's University (Collegeville) Alumni Magazine 30 (Spring 1991). http://cdm.csbsju.edu/digital/collection/ SJUArchives/id/5523/.

Mylonas, George E. *Eleusis and the Eleusinian Mysteries.* Princeton: Princeton University Press, 1961.

Patai, Raphael. *The Hebrew Goddess.* Detroit: Wayne State University Press, 1990.

Reid, Lucy. *She Changes Everything: Seeking the Divine on a Feminist Path.* New York: T. & T. Clark International, 2005.

Roscoe, John, and Robert Roscoe. *Legacies of Faith: The Catholic Churches of Stearns County.* St. Cloud, MN: North Star, 2009.

Rosenblum, Bruce, and Fred Kuttner. *Quantum Enigma.* Oxford: Oxford University Press, 2006.

Rubenstein, Richard. *When Jesus Became God: The Epic Fight over Christ's Divinity in the Last Days of Rome.* New York: Harcourt Brace, 1999.

Saiving, Valerie. "The Human Situation: A Feminine View." *Journal of Religion* 40 (1960) 100–112.

Storr, Anthony, ed. *The Essential Jung.* Princeton: Princeton University Press, 1983.

Teilhard de Chardin, Pierre. *The Phenomenon of Man.* Translated by Bernard Wall. New York: Harper & Row, 1955.

Trible, Phyllis. *God and the Rhetoric of Sexuality.* Philadelphia: Fortress, 1973.

Venberg, Rodney. "The Problem of a Female Deity in Translation." *Bible Translator* 35 (1984) 415–17.

Wilber, Ken. *A Brief History of Everything.* Boston: Shambhala, 1996.

Woolger, Jennifer Barker, and Roger J Woolger. *The Goddess Within: A Guide to the Eternal Myths That Shape Women's Lives.* New York: Fawcett Columbine, 1987.

INDEX

CPSIA information can be obtained
at www.ICGtesting.com
Printed in the USA
FSHW011732110619

9 781532 672828